QUALIFIED

THE GUIDE TO BECOMING AN
APPROVED DRIVING INSTRUCTOR

QUALIFIED

THE GUIDE TO BECOMING AN APPROVED DRIVING INSTRUCTOR

PETER BRABIN

AMBERLEY

First published 2019

Amberley Publishing
The Hill, Stroud
Gloucestershire, GL5 4EP

www.amberley-books.com

Copyright © Peter Brabin, 2019

The right of Peter Brabin to be identified as
the Author of this work has been asserted in
accordance with the Copyrights, Designs and
Patents Act 1988.

ISBN 978 1 4456 9682 9 (paperback)
ISBN 978 1 4456 9683 6 (ebook)

British Library Cataloguing in Publication Data.
A catalogue record for this book is available
from the British Library.

Typesetting by Aura Technology and Software
Services, India. Printed in the UK.

CONTENTS

Contents

ABOUT THE AUTHOR

Peter Brabin has worked in the driving industry for over fifteen years; initially as a driving instructor and currently as Head of Training for a national driving school. He is a qualified ORDIT trainer (Official Register of Driving Instructor Training). A DVSA-registered Fleet Trainer, Peter runs Fleet courses, ORDIT Train the Trainers courses and is a qualified RoSPA Advanced Driver at Gold Standard and holds a Customised Award – Level 4 in Advanced Behavioural Driver Training (Diploma) at Distinction level. Additionally, he is a recognised Energy Saving Trust Eco-driving Master Trainer, guiding and training driving instructors to deliver eco-driving within the fleet industry. Peter is married and lives in North Yorkshire.

INTRODUCTION

The purpose of this book is to give a comprehensive guide to anybody who wants to train to become a driving instructor.

It will cover all the stages involved in the Driver and Vehicle Standards Agency (DVSA) procedures to become an Approved Driving Instructor (ADI). This will involve getting a Disclosure and Barring Service (DBS) check, to make sure that you're a fit and proper person to teach pupils, taking your part 1 theory exam, your part 2 practical driving test and your part 3 ability to teach exam.

The book also covers teaching pupils on a trainee licence, the learner driver test and the ADI Standards Check.

Furthermore, the book will look at coaching skills in a client-centred environment. Coaching is naturally client-centred and quite correctly focuses far more on the pupil than the instructor. In recent years the DVSA have focused heavily on a client-centred approach to teaching learners and on 7th April 2014 introduced the ADI Standards Check to replace the Check Test, which was based far more around the instructor rather than the pupil.

On 23rd December 2017 the DVSA then replaced the fault-based part 3 preset test assessment with the client-centred Part 3 test in line with the ADI Standards Check. This change was long overdue and welcome.

There are existing publications on the market that cover guides to client-centred learning and books that cover technical aspects of teaching learners to drive, but this book covers both from the perspective of a career move into becoming a driving instructor. The book will also be a useful source of reference for existing ADIs when it comes to taking their Standards Check and also for newly qualified ADIs wishing to use the book for reference.

The book provides a comprehensive guide to all the steps required to become a driving instructor. The role of the modern driving instructor now is far more complex than it used to be, yet subtle at the same time – placing the client at the centre of the learning process.

Today's driving instructors require sound technical knowledge in order to coach and teach. As always safety is of paramount importance and all lessons must be conducted in a safe manner. Parents seeing their children embark on learning to drive will always be wanting to see their child progress, especially as it's the parents who will probably be paying for the lessons. But most importantly of all, they will always want to see their children return home safely after each lesson.

There is quite a degree of psychology involved in teaching pupils. Driving instructors not only need to be good at teaching. They also need to be good at business and be good at sales. Combined, this is quite a challenge for anybody coming into the industry.

Chapter 1 looks of the processes involved in the preparation for becoming an approved driving instructor. It's about the application process, the Disclosure Barring Service checks, looking into any potential criminal history. Timescales are discussed alongside costs and the structure of the various tests alongside information about the trainee licence for those wanting to practice with real learners prior to the Part 3 test – the test of instructional ability.

Chapter 2 looks in detail at the ADI part 1 theory and hazard perception test. A theory mock test is also included along with answers provided in the appendices section on page 284.

In Chapter 3 we look at the ADI part 2 test of practical driving ability and all the preparation that is needed for this demanding test. This will also include the vehicle safety questions often known as show me, tell me questions. On the Part 2 test there will be 3 tell me and 2 show me questions, with the show me questions being carried out whilst the vehicle is on the move.

In preparation for the ADI part 3 test of instructional ability, Chapter 6 looks at the trainee licence scheme, where potential driving instructors (PDIs) can gain valuable teaching experience with real learners for a period of up to 6 months. Linked into this chapter, Chapter 5 covers lesson plans and topics allowing the potential driving instructor to look at the practical requirements of teaching learner drivers.

Chapter 4 looks in detail at the ADI part 3 test of instructional ability and covers the syllabus for the client-centred test that came into effect on 23rd December 2017.

WHY WRITE THIS BOOK?

Initially we need to look at the number of people who are killed or seriously injured on British roads each year.

Collisions can be caused by many factors. Driving too fast; driving too close to other vehicles; drivers not aware of their surroundings; inexperience; driver errors in general; poor time planning and therefore in a rush; poor observation skills; errors in judgement; over confidence; poor weather conditions; red mist/road rage; insurance scams (deliberate collisions); loss of control of the vehicle; pedestrian problems; sudden braking; a sense of invincibility; showing off; stress; and genuine 'accidents'.

In the year 2000, 3,409 people were killed on British roads. By 2012 this had fallen steadily to 1,754 and has remained reasonably steady since, with the figure in 2013 being 1,713 deaths; 2014 – 1,775 deaths; 2015 – 1,732 deaths; 2016 – 1,792 deaths; and 2017 – 1,793. This death rate average is just under 5 people each day.

In this final year of figures 2017, 24,831 people were seriously injured and 1,793 fatally injured. These figures were from a total of 181,384 accident casualties recorded on Britain's roads. Breaking these figures down further, of all the fatal accidents in the year 2016, 46% of these were car occupants, 24% were pedestrians, 24% were motorcyclists and the remaining 6% were cyclists.

Since records on accident casualties on British road started in 1926, a peak of 398,000 was reached in the year 1965. Fortunately this has fallen steadily to today's relatively low figure.

When you look at the global picture, more than 1.25 million people die each year as a result of road traffic crashes. This figure represents almost 3,500 people dead every day.

By comparison, the figures for deaths on British roads is relatively low and on a global scale only Sweden, Malta and Norway have a lower death rate.

So is being the 4th best country in the world a good place to be? Many people would argue that yes, this is a good place to be.

But is it for the 1,793 people who actually died in 2017, the 24,831 who were seriously injured, or the 170,993 who were accident casualties? Are these good figures for the family's relatives and friends of these victims and the dedicated emergency services teams that have to attend these accidents?

Of course not. 5 deaths a day is not good. But because of the comparatively low number compared to worldwide figures, deaths on British roads rarely make the news.

However, if we were talking about 5 doctors, 5 footballers, 5 news readers, 5 nurses, 5 school teachers, 5 pop stars or 5 of any other industry you can think of dying every day, day after day, year after year, do you think that would make the news? And furthermore, how much concern would there be to get this figure reduced instantly?

For those of you reading this book and considering going into the industry of becoming a driving instructor, we are the people who can make a difference to these figures. What a fantastic career to go into.

Statistically 17 to 24 year olds, particularly male drivers, are the most likely group to be involved in fatal accidents on the roads. As driving instructors, the influence we can have over these people is significant.

Traditionally driving instruction tended to involve telling pupils what to do and how to pass their test. The results of this was the learning curve tended to drop away significantly once the pupil had passed their driving test and the new drivers on the road were less capable of dealing with situations now that their driving instructor was no longer in the car with them.

Client-centred learning has gone a long way towards rectifying this problem by putting the pupil at the centre of the learning process and allowing them to analyse their own problems, come up with solutions and take responsibility for their driving and risk management. The results of which is a far more aware pupil who is able to cope better with road situations independently.

You can see from this that if you're coming into the industry, being a driving instructor is more of a vocation than a job. There needs to be the passion to make a difference. If you think about it, the people wanting to learn to drive initially know very little. Their brains haven't been wired up for driving yet. The connections have not yet been made and you have the ability and the task to do this with them.

One can now see how vital it is to get this task correct first time. It is about getting the teaching and the coaching correct first time, because if it is done incorrectly, an element of that will stay with the driver forever.

This career is about teaching learners safe driving for life – not passing driving tests.

That's why I'm writing this book.

Chapter 1

THE PROCESS OF BECOMING AN ADI

If you are thinking about becoming a driving instructor there are a few initial questions you may want to ask yourself. These would include:

1. How do I find out more about becoming a driving instructor?
2. What method of training am I going to use? What establishment would I train with and how do I find out more information about them?
3. What is the qualification process?
4. What are the pre-entry requirements to train as a driving instructor?
5. How long will the process take?
6. Can I fit the training in around my existing family commitments and work commitments?
7. Do I have the finances in place to cope with this?

To find out more about becoming a driving instructor, first of all visit the government website: www.safedrivingforlife.info.

This site will give you information about what the job involves and the people skills required.

It will give you information about the type of hours that are required for driving instructors and it will also give you links on how to apply for the criminal records check and the next steps you will need to take. There are also useful resources on the site that you will need when preparing for your part 1 part 2 and part 3 tests. There's also plenty of information on finding ADI training course from the many organisations in the marketplace dealing with this.

2

If you're wanting to teach for reward, then by law you must have a licence to teach. These are issued by the Driver and Vehicle Standards Agency (DVSA).

This requirement is part of the Road Traffic Act.

Therefore the initial part of the process is to get a DBS (Disclosure and Barring Service) background check which is an enhanced criminal record check.

If you already have a DBS check from another industry you will still require a separate one for the DVSA.

Other than a £6 processing fee at the post office the rest of the check is free of charge.

You will need to register at the following website:
www.onlinedisclosures.co.uk.

Complete your personal details. Select identity documents for verification. Print off the barcode ID verification form. Take this form to the post office.

Organisation pin	105205
Organisation name	DVSA PDI(PO)
Secret word	axis

Once your application has been processed and approved you will be sent a disclosure report and you can apply for your PRN number with the DVSA.

Please be aware that this process may take a number of weeks.

Also note you will not be able to book a test until the check is complete.

In order to get a PRN (personal reference number) with the DVSA, you can apply online at the following website
www.gov.uk/apply-to-become-a-driving-instructor.

The DVSA will issue you with a PRN and the DVSA will write to you to confirm when your number has been activated.

In order to qualify for entry to become a driving instructor you must fulfil the following conditions:

- You have to be 21 years or older to supervise a learner driver. You can usually apply to start the qualifying process 6 months before your 21st birthday. This is because it would take at least 6 months to qualify as an ADI.
- You must have held a full UK or European Union driving licence for at least 3 years to supervise a learner driver. You can usually apply to start the qualifying process 6 months before the

3rd anniversary of getting your full licence. Again this is because it will take at least 6 months to qualify as an ADI.
- You must have a successful DBS check, specifically for the DVSA.
- You must also be what is termed a 'fit and proper' person to be accepted on to the register.
- You cannot have been disqualified from driving at any time of the last 4 years prior to applying to being accepted onto the register.

The decision to allow you on to the register lies with the Registrar and the 'fit and proper' person check will take into account any motoring offences and non-motoring offences. These offences are not just current ones but will also include any previous convictions.

Having a criminal record will not necessarily bar you from being accepted as a Potential or Approved Driving Instructor.

Before reaching a decision on whether or not a person is fit and proper, the DVSA will assess the risk they are likely to pose to their pupils by considering factors such as:

- Whether the offence is relevant.
- The seriousness of the offence.
- The length of time since the offence occurred.
- Whether there is a pattern of offending behaviour.
- Whether their circumstances have changed since the offending behaviour.
- The circumstances surrounding the offence and any explanation.

Anybody convicted of serious violent, sexual, financial or drugs offences are unlikely to be successful regardless of when the offences were committed.

Once you have a PRN number from the DVSA, you can start your training towards the three ADI tests. These are:

- Part 1 theory test.
- Part 2 the practical driving test.
- Part 3 the test of instructional ability.

Once you've passed your part 1 theory test you then have a period of 2 years to pass your part 2 and part 3 tests.

You're allowed as many attempts as you require to pass the part 1 theory test, but then you only have 3 attempts maximum for each other part 2 and part 3 tests.

If you fail either of these tests 3 times, then you'll have to wait until 2 years after passing your theory test before you can apply again.

(ADI) part 1 – the multiple choice theory and the hazard perception tests

When you attend for your test you must bring your driving licence with you. If you have an old-style paper licence then you must bring a valid passport with you as visual identity. It should be noted but no other form of photo identification is acceptable.

This test is conducted in either English or Welsh and consists of two parts.

The test takes around an hour and 45 minutes and includes multiple choice questions. You will be asked 100 questions in total. 25 questions in each of the following four categories:

- Road procedures.
- Traffic signs and signals, car control, pedestrians and mechanical knowledge.
- Driving test disabilities and the law.
- Publications and instructional techniques.

The questions have several possible answers and will appear on a computer screen. Some questions need more than one answer. You can move between questions and flag questions that you want to come back to later. You're allowed up to 90 minutes for this part of the test.

How multiple choice scores work

To pass the multiple choice part you must get both:

- An overall score of at least 85 out of 100.
- At least 20 out of 25 in each category.

Hazard perception

Initially, you will be shown video clips of how the hazard perception test works. You will then be shown 14 clips that feature everyday road scenes using CGI (computer generated imagery).

There will be one developing hazard in 13 of the clips (worth a maximum of 5 points) and two developing hazards in one of the clips (worth a maximum of 10 points).

A developing hazard is something that may cause you to take some form of action such as changing speed or direction.

If you identify the developing hazard early enough you will be awarded 5 points. The longer it takes you to identify the developing hazard, then the lower the score you will be awarded down to a minimum score of 0.

Be careful not to click too frequently as this may be misinterpreted as cheating and will score of 0.

An example of a developing hazard would be as follows:

Initially on the video clip you notice an empty side road partially obscured by a hedge. Here you can click once to note that you have identified a potential hazard. If nothing changes in the side road then don't click again. However you now notice the front of a car emerging from behind the hedge to the junction in the side road. Click again to identify this developing hazard. If the car does not emerge, don't click again. You now notice the car starting to emerge so therefore click again for the developing hazard. Clicking early for the developing hazard will score 5 points.

In order to pass the hazard perception test you need to get a minimum score of 57 out of 75.

Once you have completed both parts of the part one test then you'll be given your results shortly.

If you pass you will be given a pass certificate and will also be given information about applying for your Part 2 test.

Preparing for the part 1 test

For the part 1 test you need to show knowledge of the Highway Code, the rules of the road and instructional techniques.

There are many good publications available on the market as well as apps for phones. The DVSA recommended reading for this one is the official DVSA Theory Test Kit for car drivers, which covers theory questions and hazard perception.

It is recommended that once you are consistently passing mock tests you should be ready to take your part 1 exam.

(ADI) part 2 – the test of driving ability

The ADI part 2 test is a test of your driving ability. This is the second of the three tests you have to pass to qualify to become an ADI.

You're allowed three attempts at this test.

The part 2 tests last around 1 hour and includes:

- An eyesight test.
- Vehicle safety questions.
- A test of your driving ability.

During the test you may be accompanied by your trainer if you wish and occasionally the examiner's supervisor may come along as well.

They will be watching the examiner's performance and won't have a say in how you're tested or in your final result.

You must bring with you your pass certificate from your ADI 1 part 1 test, your valid Great Britain and Northern Ireland photocard driving licence, or a paper licence with a valid passport, and you must also bring a suitable car. Details of a suitable car are covered in more detail on the ADI part 2 chapter later on in the book on page 50.

Eyesight test
For the eyesight test you'll have to read a number plate from a distance of

- 26.5 m for vehicles with a new-style number plate.
- 27.5 m for a vehicle with an old-style number plate.

You must use glasses or contact lenses during the whole test if you need them to read the number plate.

Note, you will fail the test if you don't pass the eyesight test. This will count as one of your three attempts allowed at the ADI part 2 test.

Vehicle safety questions
You'll be asked 5 vehicle safety questions. These are also known as show me or tell me questions. The examiner will ask you two show me questions where you have to show them how you would carry out vehicle checks whilst driving and 3 tell me questions where you have to explain how you would carry out the vehicle checks at the start of the test before you start driving.

A full list of show me, tell me questions is shown later in the book on pages 51–54.

You will get a driving fault for each incorrect answer. You will get a serious fault and fail the test if you get all 5 questions wrong.

During the practical driving test on the road you will have to show the examiner all of the following:

- Expert handling of the controls.
- Use of the correct road procedures.
- Anticipation of the actions of road users and taking appropriate actions.
- Sound judgement of distance speed and timing.
- Consideration for the convenience and safety of other road users.
- Driving in an environmentally friendly manner.

You will be driving a variety of roads and traffic conditions, including motorways or dual carriageways where possible.

Manoeuvres
You must be able to carry out the following manoeuvres:

- Move away straight ahead or at an angle.
- Overtake meet or cross the path of other vehicles.
- Turn left-hand and right-hand corners.
- Stop the vehicle as if you're in an emergency situation.
- Parallel park at the side of the road.
- Reverse into a parking bay and drive out.
- Drive into a parking bay and reverse out.
- Pull up on the right-hand side of the road, reverse approximately 2 car lengths and rejoin the traffic.

During the test you'll be asked to carry out two of the reversing manoeuvres.

Independent driving
You'll have to drive without turn-by-turn instructions from your examiner for 20 minutes. You'll have to follow either:

- Traffic signs.
- Directions from sat nav.

The examiner will provide the sat nav. You cannot follow directions from your own sat nav and this should be turned off where possible.

Your test results
The examiner will be assessing your drive during the hour and marking down any relevant faults. Once the test drive is complete you will be given your result and a verbal debriefing. There are three type of faults that can be marked:

- A dangerous fault. This involves actual danger to you, the examiner, the public, or any property.
- Serious fault. This is a fault that could potentially be dangerous.
- A driving fault. These faults not potentially dangerous, but if you make the same fault throughout the test it could become a serious fault.

Pass mark

You will pass the test if you make:

- No more than 6 driving faults.
- No serious or dangerous faults.

If you pass, you can book your ADI part 3 test.

Failing the test at the first or second attempt will mean that you can take the test again.

Failing the test at the third attempt will mean that you'll have to retake and pass the ADI part 1 test.

You must wait two years from when you originally passed the ADI part 1 test before you can take the ADI part 1 test again.

(ADI) part 3 – the test of instructional ability

The ADI part 3 test is a test of your ability to instruct pupils and is the last of the three tests you have to pass to qualify.

You must have passed your ADI part 2 test before you can book your ADI part 3 test. As part of the part 3 marking sheet includes a section entitled 'Were the practice areas suitable', naturally you can take the Part 3 test at a test centre of your choice.

You need to send your application to the DVSA and your appointment will be confirmed by them prior to your test. When you attend for test you need to take the confirmation of your appointment along with your driving licence (this must be a photocard driving licence or if an old-style paper licence, then this must be supported with a valid passport).

You must also bring to test with you a suitable car (this is covered in more detail in Chapter 3 on page 84).

The Part 3 test last about 1 hour and includes an assessment of the following:

- Core competencies.
- Lesson planning.
- Risk management.
- Teaching and learning strategies.

The examiner will observe you whilst you teach a pupil. Your pupil can either be a learner or a full licence holder.

Once you have passed you can apply for your first ADI badge and join the register.

How the test works

You will be conducting a one-hour lesson with a pupil on a topic of your choice. The examiner will sit in the back of the car and mark you on the three higher competencies of:

- Lesson planning.
- Risk management.
- Teaching and learning strategies.

These high-level competencies are then further broken down into 17 lower level competencies show later on in this book. You also choose the route and your pupil. Your pupil can be anyone except an ADI or PDI.

How the test will be marked

Marks will be awarded for the 17 lower level competencies as follows:

- 0 no evidence of competence.
- 1 a few elements of competence demonstrated.
- 2 competence demonstrated in most areas.
- 3 competence demonstrated in all areas.

ADI grades

- 0–30: unsatisfactory performance fail.
- 31–42: sufficient competence demonstrated to permit or retain entry on the register of approved driving instructors grade B.
- 43–51: high overall standard of instruction demonstrated grade A.

Note: if you score 7 or lower in the risk management section of the Standards Check this will be deemed substandard and a fail. Also, if the examiner believes that your behaviour is placing you, the pupil or any third party in immediate danger they may stop the lesson and record an immediate fail.

Types of students and lesson themes

Students can either be a beginner, partly trained learner, a trained learner, a full licence holder new or a full licence holder experienced.

Lesson themes can include

Junctions, town and city driving, interaction with other road users, dual carriageways and fast-moving roads, defensive driving, effective use of mirrors, independent driving, rural roads, motorways, eco-safe driving, recapping a manoeuvre, commentary driving recapping an emergency stop or another topic.

Please note that there is no role played by the examiner and teaching new manoeuvres with briefings is not permitted.

At the end of the test
Once the test is complete and you've got back to the test centre, there will be a delay of a few minutes whilst the examiner assesses the overall performance of your lesson. Once they have completed this, you will be given the result and debriefing together with the relevant paperwork.

If you pass
You can apply for your first ADI badge at the following site:
www.gov.uk/apply-first-approved-driving-instructor-adi-badge.

You must apply within 12 months of passing, or you will have to pass all 3 parts of the qualifying process again.

If you don't pass
You can take the test again if you fail the first or second attempt. You must book your next attempt within two years of passing your ADI part 1 theory test.

Failing the third attempt
You have to retake and pass the ADI part 1 and part 2 test again if you fail the ADI part 3 test at your third attempt and then retake and pass your Part 3 test.

You must wait 2 years from when you pass the ADI part 1 test before you can take it again.

If you wish to appeal your ADI part 3 test this is covered later in the book on page 87.

Chapter 2

ADI PART 1 EXAM

Booking the test

Once your application to start the ADI qualifying process has been accepted, you can book your approved driving instructor (ADI) part 1 test.

Although the test is split into 2 parts (multiple choice and hazard perception) you must book both parts as a single test.

To book online: www.gov.uk/book-your-instructor-theory-test
Telephone DVSA Customer Support: 0300 200 1122

When booking online you will need the following:

- UK driving licence number.
- Personal reference number (PRN) form the DVSA.
- Email address (book by phone if you do not have an email address).
- Debit or credit card.

Cost

The ADI part 1 test costs £81.00 (correct as of September 2018). For up-to-date costs you can check via this web address:
    www.gov.uk/approved-driving-instructor-adi-fees.

If you have reading difficulties

If you have reading difficulties you should state this when you book your test. You can ask for an English voiceover. This facility will allow you to listen to instructions and questions through headphones, and you can hear the questions and possible answers as many times as you like.

You may also ask for more time to answer the multiple choice questions.

In order to have these concessions you will be required to send proof of your reading difficulty to the DVSA for verification. This proof can be an email or letter from a teacher or other educational professional, a doctor, or medical professional. The contact details for this proof to be sent to are:

DVSA theory test enquiries: customercare@pearson.com

Postal address: DVSA theory test enquiries
                    P.O. Box 1286
                    Warrington
                    WA1 9GN

The part 1 exam is the first of the three exams that you will need to pass to become an Approved Driving Instructor (ADI). This exam is in 2 parts, the first of which is a multiple choice exam consisting of 100 questions. The second part of the exam is a hazard perception test using computer generated imagery (CGI).

When you attend your test you must bring with you your driving licence; if you have an 'old-style' licence without a photograph then your licence will have to be supported by a valid passport for visual identity. Licences from Northern Ireland will require the photocard and paper counterpart licence.

NB: Your test WILL be cancelled and you WILL NOT get a refund if you fail to bring the correct things with you.

You are not allowed to take personal items into the test room with you. This will include:

- Bags.
- Earphones.
- Mobile phones.
- Watches.

These items can be stored in a locker provided by the test centre.

Multiple choice test

The multiple choice test consists of 100 questions. You have 1 hour and 30 minutes to answer these. Before the test begins instructions are given, and an opportunity for you to practise some questions on the screen.

The 100 questions are broken down into 4 bands each consisting of 25 questions under the following categories:

- Road procedures.
- Traffic signs and signals, car control, pedestrians and mechanical knowledge.
- Driving test, disabilities, law.
- Publications, instructional techniques.

The questions do NOT follow the band sequence above and will appear randomly. Each question will have several possible answers on the screen and you will have to select the correct one.

Leaving a question

If you feel that you are struggling with a particular question, then the best advice is to 'flag' that question and return to it once you have completed all your other questions. Once you have done that, return to any 'flagged' questions; re-read the question, eliminate any answer that is clearly wrong and this will narrow down the possible answers.

Changing an answer

You may return to a question and change an answer at any point of the test.

When you have answered all the questions to your satisfaction (not forgetting any 'flagged' ones) you may end the test. You do not have to use all of the 1 hour and 30 minutes.

The pass mark is a minimum overall score of 85% (85/100) and a minimum of 80% (20/25) in each of the 4 bands.

You are allowed a break of up to 3 minutes before starting the hazard perception test.

Hazard perception test

Before commencing the hazard perception test you will be shown a video about how this test works. This video can be viewed at: www.gov.uk/adi-part-1-test/hazard-perception-test.

There will be a total of 14 video clips to watch. These clips feature everyday road scenes using CGI and each clip will contain at least one 'developing hazard'. However, one of the clips will feature 2 developing hazards.

A developing hazard is something that would cause you to take action, such as a change of speed or direction. When you observe a developing hazard you will need to click the mouse on the computer. As this hazard develops, you will need to click the mouse again. When the scoring window opens, the maximum score you can achieve is 5 for each developing hazard, therefore the clip featuring 2 developing hazards will have a maximum available score of 10 if you pick up both of the developing hazards early enough. To achieve the maximum score click the mouse as soon as you see the hazard starting to develop.

If you click and miss the hazard you will not lose any points, but you WILL be penalised with a score of zero if you click continuously or in a pattern.

Unlike the multiple choice test, you can NOT review or change your responses so, just like normal driving, the clips occur in real time since they are designed to test hazard perception skills as if you are actually driving.

The pass mark for the hazard perception test is 57 out of a possible 75 marks.

Example of a developing hazard
Ahead of you, on a narrow road, is a set of roadworks. This is a potential hazard. If there is no traffic coming toward you and nothing else happens, then this is NOT a developing hazard. As you approach further, you notice a car approaching from the opposite direction. You need to slow down. This is now a developing hazard.

Test result
Once you have completed the test (multiple choice and hazard perception) you will be given the result at the test centre.

When you pass, you will receive a pass certificate. This will show you the marks achieved for each part of the test. The multiple choice section is broken down into the bands.

You will require the pass certificate number when you apply for the part 2 test. Successful candidates have 2 years from this pass date in which to pass parts 2 and 3 of their ADI exam.

Should you fail, you will receive a breakdown of the scores but not by individual question. You will need to book the full test again. You MUST pass both parts of the part 1 test on that single test date in order to progress. There is no limit to the number of times that you can take the theory test. If you do fail, then you can apply again straight away. (In Northern Ireland, the theory test is limited to 3 attempts within a 2 year window.)

Revising for the part 1 test

As with most things in life, the amount of preparation and work you put in is related to the result that you get! The part 1 test is no different. As an experienced driver your theory knowledge should be reasonably good. However, serious study will still be essential in order to achieve a good solid pass at parts 1, 2 and 3.

Materials

The questions in the theory test are based on the following publications:

- *The Highway Code*
- *Know Your Traffic Signs*
- *Driving – The Essential Skills*
- *The Official Theory Test for Approved Driving Instructor Pack*
- *The Driving Instructors Handbook*

There are also many good mobile apps available that will help you revise and practise for your test. If you are doing your training through a driving school they will often provide you with the materials you will need. The DVSA also produce a publication – *The Official Guide to Hazard Perception* – to aid candidates for the hazard perception test.

Other recommended materials would include:

- *The Complete THEORY TEST* – Focus Essential
- *Driving Test Success Anytime* – Focus Multimedia

On the day of the test you should be confident if you have put in the hard work. Make sure that you arrive in good time for the test and that you have the right documents etc. with you. REMEMBER: if you are late or have forgotten your UK photocard driving licence (or 'old-style' paper licence plus your valid passport for visual identity) your test WILL be cancelled, and you will NOT get a refund of your test costs.

You will have around 1 hour and 45 minutes to complete the 2 tests. The multiple choice test allows you 1 hour and 30 minutes maximum for completion; this should allow you plenty of time to answer all the questions. Make sure that you double-check your work, that you have answered ALL the questions and that, as discussed earlier, you 'flag' questions where you are unsure of the answer – remember to return to these questions before finishing the test, eliminating obvious wrong answers before making your final selection.

Good practice prior to the test is the key to the hazard perception test. Be careful not to over-click the mouse, as this will almost certainly result in a score of zero. If you are clicking a second time for a developing hazard, *pause* between clicks.

Understanding vs Remembering

Throughout your journey, from registering with the DVSA to passing all three tests, to becoming a fully qualified ADI, there is a considerable amount of study required by the candidates, starting with theory and hazard perception study followed by the development work to raise your practical driving skills to the high standards demanded by the DVSA, all of which require a concerted and consistent study effort.

Once you have passed parts 1 and 2 you will then have to be able to transfer this knowledge to pupils in a client-centred learning style (CCL). Throughout the process it is important that you understand your subject and not simply learn by rote and try to remember it all.

In order to pass your theory test you will require a thorough understanding of the rules and regulations associated with driving. This will include a solid working knowledge of:

- Road procedures – how to drive safely and correctly in all circumstances.
- Traffic signs and signals.
- Car control – correct techniques.
- Mechanical knowledge – a sound, basic knowledge.
- Driving test – how it is conducted.
- Disabilities – a working knowledge of various disabilities.
- Pedestrians – dealing safely with other road users.
- Instructional techniques – a good working knowledge of the theory and practice of coaching, learning, teaching and assessing.

It would be quite normal to be practising for part 2 at the same time as you are studying for your part 1 theory test. As we have already discussed, it is crucial that you understand your subject matter, so if you are practising part 1 and part 2 side by side you will be able to see all the theory study put into practice on the road.

When you have started teaching and coaching learners either as a qualified ADI or as a PDI on a trainee licence, remember how you studied for your tests, i.e. from the part 3 marking sheet there is a low level of competence "were opportunities and examples used to clarify learning outcomes". This is under the higher level of competence 'Teaching & Learning Strategies'. This is an area where the clarity and understanding will take place – actually seeing the theory in practice. In order to pass your theory test you will need to dedicate time for practise. Become disciplined in your practise as this will help to develop the skills you need moving forward to become a driving instructor; after all, a good driving instructor is a coach, a teacher, a sales person and a business person! You need to be strong in ALL these disciplines.

When will I be ready to take my theory test?

A good question. If you have studied thoroughly and consolidated this with good on-road practise then your hazard perception will naturally develop as will your ability to respond correctly to the multiple choice questions. The study materials you have will allow you to carry out 'mock tests'; these tests (PC DVD-ROM or online) will enable you to see how close you are to the passmark of 57/75 for the hazard perception part, and an overall score of 85 or higher in the multiple choice part, with at least 20/25 in each of the 4 bands of questions.

Make sure when you practise that you are studying for the Trainee Driving Instructor test and NOT the test for Learner Drivers (this is an easy trap to fall into!) as they are both on the same disc! However, the Learner Drivers test has fewer questions on the test and the questions are not as comprehensive as those for the Trainee Driving Instructor test.

Should you have to retake your theory test, remember that there is no limit to the number of times you can take the test (with the exception of Northern Ireland, where you are limited to 3 attempts within a timeframe). However, with the theory test costing £81.00 per attempt (as at September 2018), thorough practise and a good first time pass is strongly recommended.

Theory questions for the part 1 test

MOCK TEST: 100 QUESTIONS

The pass mark is an overall score of at least 85/100 and a minimum of 80% (or 20 out of 25) in each of the following 4 bands:

BAND 1
- Road procedures.

BAND 2
- Traffic signs and signals.
- Pedestrians.
- Mechanical knowledge.
- Car control.

BAND 3
- Law.
- Driving tests.
- Disabilities.

BAND 4
- Instructional techniques.
- Publications.

Theory mock test

1. You are on a motorway. There are red lights flashing above every lane. You MUST:
   a) Pull up on the hard shoulder.
   b) Slow down and watch for further signs.
   c) Leave at the next exit.
   d) Stop and wait.

2. You must not drive if your breath alcohol level is greater than:
   a) 20 mg/100 ml.
   b) 25 mg/100 ml.
   c) 30 mg/100 ml.
   d) 35 mg/100 ml.

3. People with disabilities are:
   a) Not allowed to drive on motorways.
   b) Permitted to drive adapted cars only.
   c) Restricted to driving cars with automatic transmission.
   d) Permitted to drive any type of car depending on their disability.

4. Diamond-shaped signs give instructions to:
   a) Taxi drivers.
   b) Bus drivers.
   c) Tram drivers
   d) Lorry drivers

5. On approaching a roundabout you should:
   a) Stop at the Give Way line.
   b) Keep moving if the road is clear.
   c) Give way to all traffic.
   d) Always change down to 2nd gear.

6. If you are involved in an accident and do not have your insurance certificate with you, you must produce it at a police station within:
   a) 24 hours.
   b) 1 month.
   c) 7 days.
   d) 48 hours.

7. Reflective studs along the left edge of the road are:
   a) Red.
   b) White.
   c) Amber.
   d) Fluorescent.

8. You are entering a roundabout. A cyclist in front of you is signaling to turn right. What should you do?
   a) Overtake on the right.
   b) Sound your horn.
   c) Overtake on the left.
   d) Allow plenty of room.

9. Your vehicle is parked on the road at night. When must you use your sidelights?
   a) Where the speed limit exceeds 30 mph.
   b) Outside a school.
   c) When you are facing oncoming traffic.
   d) Where there are continuous white lines in the middle of the road.

10. Using the gears to slow down should:
    a) Save wear and tear on tyres.
    b) Help other road users to know that you are slowing down.
    c) Not normally be done.
    d) Improve fuel economy.

11. The Highway Code says that well before you turn right you should:
    a) Pull up at the side of the road to plan your route.
    b) Position your car to the left.
    c) Check that your horn is working.
    d) Use your mirrors to make sure that you know the position and movement of the traffic behind you.

12. When attending a theory test, candidates must produce:
    a) A student railcard.
    b) A birth certificate.
    c) A current valid provisional driving licence.
    d) Their instructor's name.

13. You are driving a goods vehicle not exceeding 7.5 tonnes maximum laden weight. What is the maximum speed limit on a single carriageway?
    a) 50 mph.
    b) 60 mph.
    c) 40 mph.
    d) 70 mph.

14. A long, heavily laden lorry is taking a long time to overtake you. What should you do?
    a) Speed up.
    b) Slow down.
    c) Maintain your speed.
    d) Change direction.

15. 'Red Routes' tell you that:
    a) They are for buses only.
    b) These are toll roads.
    c) Part-time traffic lights operate.
    d) Special waiting restrictions apply.

16. Defensive driving does NOT involve:
    a) Awareness and anticipation.
    b) Competitive driving.
    c) Consideration and courtesy.
    d) Forward planning.

17. What is the most common cause of skidding?
    a) Worn tyres.
    b) Driver error.
    c) Other vehicles.
    d) Pedestrians.

18. A convex mirror fitted to a car makes vehicle following appear to be:
    a) At the correct distance.
    b) Closer than it really is.

c) Further away than it really is.

d) Larger than it really is.

19. In choosing a method of instruction, a trainer should:
    a) Use or two distinct approaches to standardise training.
    b) Use the same lesson plan with all trainees.
    c) Persist with the same approach until the trainee understands the principles.
    d) Be prepared to vary the technique to suit the individual trainee.

20. At night you see a pedestrian wearing reflective clothing and carrying a bright red light. What does this mean?
    a) You are approaching roadworks.
    b) You are approaching an organised walk.
    c) You are approaching a slow vehicle.
    d) You are approaching an accident.

21. You are driving on a motorway in very wet weather. Your tyres begin to lose contact with the road. This is called:
    a) Aquaplaning.
    b) Coasting.
    c) Slipstreaming.
    d) Skidding.

22. A trainer's expectations of a trainee's ability can sometimes be too high. This can:
    a) Allow trainees to progress at their own rate.
    b) Provide reinforcement of what they have learned.
    c) Have a negative effect on the trainee's progress.
    d) Help trainees to reach their full potential.

23. The main purpose of a trainer giving feedback is to:
    a) Concentrate fully on teaching new skills.
    b) Make the trainee aware of how they are progressing.
    c) Make sure that the trainer has completed their paperwork.
    d) Advise the trainee about the remainder of the training schedule.

24. Circular road signs:
    a) Warn.
    b) Inform.
    c) Give orders.
    d) Always have red rings around them.

25. What is the overall stopping distance on a dry road at 70 mph?
    a) 53 m (175 ft).
    b) 60 m (197 ft).
    c) 73 m (240 ft).
    d) 96 m (315 ft).

26. Your vehicle collides with a bridge. You must report it to:
    a) The local authority.
    b) The police.
    c) The fire brigade.
    d) Your MOT garage.

27. A full driving licence is valid until the driver's:
    a) 80th birthday.
    b) 70th birthday.
    c) 60th birthday.
    d) Until they no longer want to drive.

28. You have a collision whilst your car is moving. What is the first thing you should do?
    a) Stop only if people are injured.
    b) Call the emergency services.
    c) Stop at the scene of the accident.
    d) Call your insurance company.

29. You must not drive if your blood alcohol level is greater than:
    a) 50 mg/100 ml.
    b) 80 mg/100 ml.
    c) 70 mg/100 ml.
    d) 60 mg/100 ml.

30. What is 'client-centred learning'?
    a) Always asking the pupil questions.
    b) Learning based on the abilities, needs and learning style of the pupil.
    c) Getting the pupil to write down answers.
    d) Always allowing the pupil to choose what to do.

31. On a learner driving test a pupil will be required to carry out:
    a) All reversing manoeuvres.
    b) Two reversing manoeuvres.
    c) A reversing manoeuvre only if the test includes a controlled stop.
    d) One reversing manoeuvre.

32. Pupils should apply for their theory test:
    a) After 10 hours of driving.
    b) 6 months after receiving their provisional licence.
    c) When they have studied and their driving instructor advises them.
    d) As soon as they receive their provisional licence.

33. 'Red Routes' in major cities have been introduced to:
    a) Raise the speed limits.
    b) Help traffic flow.
    c) Provide better parking.
    d) Allow lorries to load more freely.

34. You will use more fuel if your tyres are:
    a) Under-inflated.
    b) Of different makes.
    c) Over-inflated.
    d) New and hardly used.

35. In a diesel engine, which of the following fuels would most improve vehicle emissions?
    a) High sulphur diesel.
    b) Cheap diesel.
    c) low sulphur diesel.
    d) Red diesel.

36. You may cancel your driving test without losing your fee so long as you give:
    a) 5 days notice.
    b) 5 complete working days notice.
    c) 3 complete working days notice.
    d) One week's notice.

37. A pedestrian wanting to cross at a zebra crossing should:
    a) Stand well back from the crossing.
    b) Wait by the beacon.
    c) Hold one hand out.
    d) Put one foot on the crossing.

38. When coaching a pupil, the pupil should:
    a) Be encouraged to analyse problems and take responsibility for learning.
    b) Be allowed to deal with problems themselves.

c) Leave problem-solving to their coach/instructor.
d) Watch the instructor drive.

39. During a driving session an instructor observes a driving fault by the trainee. This should be:
   a) Used as a training opportunity.
   b) Used to warn the trainee.
   c) Discussed at the end of the session.
   d) Ignored, and the session continued.

40. A deaf person can drive:
   a) Only at night.
   b) Any Category B motor vehicle.
   c) No motor vehicle.
   d) Only specially adapted motor vehicles.

41. Eco-safe driving includes:
   a) Using unleaded petrol.
   b) Braking harshly.
   c) Planning ahead.
   d) Using peak revs in each gear.

42. Initial assessment would normally be carried out in order to determine:
   a) The trainee's expectations.
   b) The level at which training should begin.
   c) The level of the trainee's interest.
   d) The cost of the course.

43. What should you do if you have to use the dual controls?
   a) Say nothing and carry on.
   b) Inform the pupil you have used them and ask if they understand why you used them.
   c) End the lesson at that point.
   d) Explain why you used them when the lesson has ended.

44. Your vehicle has power-assisted steering. It's main purpose is to:
   a) Reduce tyre wear.
   b) Assist with braking.
   c) Reduce driver effort.
   d) Assist road holding.

45. In 'question and answer' technique, an open question:
    a) Highlights the pupil's level of understanding.
    b) Has only one answer.
    c) Requires a written answer.
    d) Provides little help for the coach.

46. Before crossing a one-way street, pedestrians should look:
    a) Both ways.
    b) All round.
    c) To the left.
    d) To the right.

47. When booking a theory test, if you have a reading difficulty:
    a) You can ask someone else to take the test for you.
    b) You can ask to hear the test through headphones.
    c) Headphones are not allowed on a theory test.
    d) You can ask a fellow candidate for help.

48. When travelling at 70 mph how many metres do you travel in one
    second:
    a) 27.0 m (89 ft).
    b) 45.0 m (148 ft).
    c) 22.5 m (74 ft).
    d) 31.5 m (104 ft).

49. Unless a moving vehicle creates a danger, do not sound your horn
    in a built-up area between:
    a) 11pm and 7.30am.
    b) On Sundays.
    c) 11.30pm and 7am.
    d) Midnight and 7am.

50. You have broken down on a two-way road. What is the shortest
    distance from your vehicle you should place a warning triangle?
    a) 5 metres (16 ft).
    b) 25 metres (82 ft).
    c) 45 metres (147 ft).
    d) 100 metres (328 ft).

51. The ADI regulations are part of:
    a) *The Driving Instructors Handbook*
    b) *Know Your Traffic Signs*

c) *The Road Traffic Act*
d) *Learning to Drive – The Official Guide*

52. On the driving test, if the examiner uses the dual controls this is marked as:
    a) A foot fault.
    b) A driving fault.
    c) A dangerous fault.
    d) A serious fault.

53. A police officer asks to see your documents. You do not have them with you. You may produce them at a police station within:
    a) 1 day.
    b) 3 days.
    c) 7 days.
    d) 14 days.

54. According to *The Official DVSA Guide to Driving*, what percentage of pedestrians survive a collision with a car at 40 mph?
    a) 5%.
    b) 20%.
    c) 40%.
    d) 60%.

55. On a training course, progressive learning should be measured by:
    a) Having an ongoing assessment.
    b) Having a final report.
    c) Only highlighting strengths.
    d) Only highlighting weaknesses.

56. Driving test routes are designed to:
    a) Be identical.
    b) Have at least 4 roundabouts on them.
    c) Always include rural driving.
    d) Cover a wide variety of road and traffic situations.

57. If a candidate fails the eyesight check at the start of the driving test (20 m/66 ft or 20.5 m/67 ft older style plates):
    a) It is marked as a driver fault.
    b) It is marked as a serious fault.
    c) It is marked as a dangerous fault.
    d) The test can continue if the candidate forgot their glasses.

58. The Highway Code states that where there is an advanced stop line for cyclists:
    a) Taxi drivers may use the second stop line.
    b) Motorists must stop at the first white line reached if the lights are amber or red.
    c) Cyclists must stop at the first white line reached.
    d) If the lights turn red you must continue if you cannot stop at the first stop line reached.

59. When should you assess a learner driver's progress?
    a) At the end of each month.
    b) Continuously, using dialogue and feedback.
    c) Whenever improvement takes place.
    d) Just before the test.

60. The 'learning plateau' sometimes occurs during instructional programmes. This refers to:
    a) A temporary halt in the learning process.
    b) A common fault experienced with hand and feet co-ordination.
    c) A slowing down in the pace of instruction.
    d) An increase in the pace of instruction.

61. From 4th June 2018 learner drivers can take motorway lessons when accompanied by:
    a) A full licence holder.
    b) A PDI with a car fitted with dual controls.
    c) An ADI.
    d) An ADI with a car fitted with dual controls.

62. According to Roadcraft the system of car control follows 4 phases:
    a) Acceleration, speed, gear, position.
    b) Position, gear, speed, acceleration.
    c) Position, speed, gear, acceleration.
    d) Speed, gear, position, acceleration.

63. A driving test pass certificate is valid for:
    a) 1 year.
    b) 2 years.
    c) 5 years.
    d) 6 months.

64. What is the thinking distance at 70 mph?
    a) 18 m (59 ft).
    b) 75 m (246 ft).
    c) 96 m (315 ft).
    d) 21 m (69 ft).

65. The 'halo effect' is where a trainer:
    a) Tends to subconsciously ignore minor faults committed by a favoured pupil.
    b) Treats the pupil as more likely to commit a fault.
    c) Instils greater confidence in a trainee, resulting in a better training session.
    d) Chooses a more demanding route for a good pupil.

66. According to Roadcraft you plan your driving in 3 key stages. In what order should these be applied?
    a) Order of importance, anticipate, decide on action.
    b) Decide on action, order of importance, anticipate.
    c) Anticipate, order of importance, decide on action.
    d) Anticipate, decide on action, order of importance.

67. The anti-lock braking system (ABS) allows the driver to:
    a) Prevent skidding in all road conditions.
    b) Pump the footbrake.
    c) Steer without using the brakes in an emergency.
    d) Continue to steer whilst braking firmly.

68. If you are receiving Higher Rate Disability Living Allowance you:
    a) Are not allowed to drive a motor vehicle.
    b) Can start driving at the age of 16.
    c) Must wait until you are 21 to start driving.
    d) Can start driving at the age of 17.

69. When coaching, the GROW model (Goal/Reality/Options/Way forward) is used:
    a) To allow the coach to goal set and problem solve.
    b) To allow the trainee to goal set and problem solve.
    c) To make the coaching process bigger.
    d) To follow a rigid teaching style.

70. The Highway Code states that you must not reverse more than:
    a) The distance that is necessary.
    b) The distance you can see to be clear.

    c) 10 metres.

    d) 100 metres.

71. A candidate who makes a serious fault on a driving test:
    a) Will pass if they do not make another serious fault.
    b) Must end the driving test where the fault happened.
    c) Will fail their driving test.
    d) Will be able to take another test the following day.

72. Before emerging at a junction a pupil should:
    a) Look right, left, right.
    b) Look left, right, left.
    c) Look effectively in all directions.
    d) Always check their mirrors.

73. The overall stopping distance at 50 mph is:
    a) 38 m (125 ft).
    b) 73 m (240 ft).
    c) 53 m (175 ft).
    d) 15 m (49 ft).

74. In 'question and answer technique' a closed question is one which:
    a) Has several answers.
    b) Has only one correct answer.
    c) Does not call for an immediate answer.
    d) Highlights the pupil's level of understanding.

75. On a driving test a potentially dangerous incident will be recorded as:
    a) A serious fault.
    b) A dangerous fault.
    c) A driving fault.
    d) Not recorded if nothing actually happened.

76. A zebra crossing with a central island is:
    a) 2 separate crossing during rush hour.
    b) 2 separate crossings.
    c) Used and operated by a school crossing patrol.
    d) Is a single crossing.

77. What is the braking distance at 70 mph?
    a) 75 m (246 ft).
    b) 23 m (75 ft).

c) 55 m (180 ft).
d) 38 m (125 ft).

78. During a structured session of training you should NOT:
   a) Have clear aims.
   b) Rigidly keep to a fixed lesson plan.
   c) Have a planned approach.
   d) Give praise to the trainee.

79. According to *Driving: the Essentials Skills*, you should be prepared to make allowances for someone else's mistakes. You should NOT:
   a) Keep calm.
   b) Show restraint.
   c) Drive in a spirit of retaliation or competition.
   d) Use sound judgement.

80. When turning into a minor road you should:
   a) Sound your horn if pedestrians are crossing the minor road.
   b) Stop on the major road and wave pedestrians across.
   c) Always use gear 1.
   d) Give way to pedestrians already crossing when you turn, as they have priority.

81. When parking downhill you should:
   a) Turn the steering wheel to the left and leave the vehicle in 1st gear.
   b) Turn the steering wheel to the right and leave the vehicle in 1st gear.
   c) Turn the steering wheel to the left and leave the vehicle in reverse gear.
   d) Turn the steering wheel to the right and leave the vehicle in reverse gear.

82. Which of the following is most likely to cause a burst tyre when driving?
   a) Frequent gear changes.
   b) Mixing tyres with different tread depths.
   c) Constant stopping and starting.
   d) Running at constant high speed.

83. In a skid what should you do if the back end of your vehicle skids to the right?
    a) Brake firmly and do not steer.
    b) Steer carefully to the left.
    c) Steer carefully to the right.
    d) Brake firmly and steer left.

84. Anyone supervising a learner driver must:
    a) Have passed their driving test in the last 2 years.
    b) Be at least 21 and have held a licence for that type of vehicle for at least 3 years.
    c) Must have dual controls fitted.
    d) Must be a driving instructor.

85. When following traffic in dry conditions you should leave a gap of at least:
    a) 2 seconds.
    b) 4 seconds.
    c) 6 seconds.
    d) 10 seconds.

86. When turning right at a box junction and you have to wait for oncoming vehicles, you should:
    a) Wait at the stop line.
    b) Find another turn where there is no oncoming vehicle.
    c) Wait in the yellow box if your exit is clear.
    d) Wait in the yellow box if your exit is blocked.

87. On motorways the earliest information sign of a junction is usually located:
    a) Half a mile in advance.
    b) At the slip road.
    c) One mile in advance.
    d) At the 300 yard marker.

88. At a puffin crossing what colour follows the green signal?
    a) Steady amber.
    b) Flashing amber.
    c) Flashing green.
    d) Red.

89. A white stick with a red band is used by:
    a) Someone with partial hearing.
    b) Someone who is deaf and blind.
    c) A blind person without a guide dog.
    d) Someone at the end of an organised walk.

90. For an instructor to accompany a pupil during the test:
    a) The instructor is not allowed on the car.
    b) The instructor can just get in the car.
    c) The instructor must ask the examiner.
    d) The candidate must ask the examiner.

91. As a professional driver you should:
    a) Keep to maximum speeds for shorter journeys.
    b) Plan routes to avoid busy times and congestion.
    c) Avoid route planning because it takes too long.
    d) Drive at faster speeds through hazardous areas.

92. You service your own vehicles. How should you dispose of old engine oil?
    a) Take it to a local authority site.
    b) Pour it down the drain.
    c) Put it in the dustbin.
    d) Tip it into a hole in the ground.

93. Before turning left you should have a final look into which mirror?
    a) Left-hand mirror.
    b) Interior mirror.
    c) Right-hand mirror.
    d) Overtaking mirror.

94. To help a trainee attain a good standard of driving the amount of verbal instruction should be:
    a) Monitored at the same level regardless of competence.
    b) Increased as the end of the session approaches.
    c) Reduced as their competence increases.
    d) Increased as their ability improves.

95. Anti-lock brakes reduce the chance of a skid occurring, particularly when:
    a) Braking in an emergency.
    b) Braking during normal driving.

c) Driving on good road surfaces.
d) Driving down steep hills.

96. At a pelican crossing what does the flashing green man mean for pedestrians?
    a) Cross the road quickly.
    b) Do not start to cross.
    c) Drivers have priority.
    d) You can start to cross.

97. According to the law the minimum tread on tyres should be:
    a) 2.0 mm.
    b) 2.6 mm.
    c) 1.2 mm.
    d) 1.6 mm.

98. The main cause of brake fade is:
    a) The brakes overheating.
    b) Air in the brake fluid.
    c) Oil on the brakes.
    d) The brakes are out of adjustment.

99. Freezing conditions will affect the distance it takes to come to a stop. You should expect stopping distances to increase by up to:
    a) 3 times.
    b) 2 times.
    c) 10 times.
    d) 5 times.

100. A theory pass certificate is valid for:
    a) 12 months.
    b) 6 months.
    c) 24 months.
    d) 18 months.

ADI part 1 summary

Total time allowed	1 hr 45 mins
Multiple choice	1 hr 30 mins
Cost	£81.00 per attempt (as of September 2018)
Multiple choice questions	100

Pass mark	85/100 min 20/25 in each band (multiple choice)
Pass mark	57/75 (hazard perception)
Overall pass	Multiple choice and hazard perception on the same test
About Part 1	www.gov.uk/adi-part-1-test

Contacts

To book theory test	www.gov.uk/book-your-instructor-theory-test
DVSA customer support	0300 200 1122 (Mon–Fri 8am–4pm)
Up-to-date fees	www.gov.uk/approved-driving-instructor-adi-fees
Special requirements (e.g. reading difficulties)	
DVSA theory test enquiries	customercare@pearson.com
Postal address	DVSA Theory Test Enquiries
	P.O. Box 1286
	Warrington
	WA1 9GN

Chapter 3

ADI PART 2 EXAM – THE TEST OF DRIVING ABILITY

The ADI part 2 test

When you pass your theory test (part 1 of the ADI process), you will be able to book your Part 2 test. This exam tests your practical driving ability. The duration of the test is approximately 1 hour, during which you will be tested on the following areas:

- Eyesight check.
- 'Show me, tell me' vehicle safety questions.
- General driving ability.
- Manoeuvres.
- Independent driving.

Booking the test

The application form for booking the Part 2 test will be given to you upon successful completion of the part 1 theory test.

You may book online at www.gov.uk/book-driving-test or telephone DVSA Customer Support at 0300 200 1122.

When you book online you will need select 'other' when choosing the type of test, and then 'ADI, Instructor and Trainer tests – ADI part 2.'

£111 is the cost of the ADI part 2 test (as of September 2018). For up-to-date costs you can check online at www.gov.uk/approved-driving-instructor-adi-fees.

When you attend the test you will need to bring with you following:

- Your UK driving licence.
- Your ADI part 1 pass certificate.
- A suitable car.

If you do not bring the correct items to the test then it WILL be cancelled and you will NOT be given a refund.

Suitable car

To be considered suitable, the car you bring must be:

- Taxed.
- Insured for a driving test – you will need to check with your insurance company.
- If over 3 years old it must have a current MOT.
- A saloon, hatchback or estate car in good working order **NB** *convertibles are not allowed.*
- There must not be any warning lights showing, e.g. airbag warning light.
- All tyres must be legal – no tyre damage, a legal tread depth, no space saver tyre fitted.
- The vehicle must be smoke free. If you smoke, this must be done away from the car.
- A speedometer must be fitted and capable of reaching at least 62 mph.
- 4 wheels with a maximum authorised mas (mam*) of no more than 3500 kg.
- *MAM – this information is contained in the vehicle handbook. It is how much the vehicle can weigh when it is loaded.*

NOTE If your car does not meet these requirements your test WILL be cancelled and you will NOT receive a refund. It is advisable that if you are uncertain you contact the DVSA before you book your test (customerservices@dvsa.gov.uk or call 0300 200 1122).

You should also ensure that your car is fitted with a rear-view mirror. If you forget to bring one, the examiner may be able to provide one. The car should also have passenger seatbelts. These would be for the examiner and in case a member of the DVSA sits in the back of the car during the test, as can occasionally occur in order for them to ensure the uniformity of the test. The car must also have correct passenger head restraints fitted.

Dashcams

These are permitted on the Part 2 test so long as the camera faces outside, the audio is switched off, and there is no filming inside the car.

Automatic cars

If you only have an automatic licence then you must take the test in an automatic car. Once you qualify, you will only be able to teach in automatic cars. Manual licence holder can take the test in either type of car and are able to teach in both types of car once they have qualified.

Hire cars

These are allowed on test so long as they conform to all the rules and are fitted with dual controls.

Eyesight

Understandably, the eyesight test for potential driving instructors (PDIs) is more stringent than for a learner test since it is important that, when supervising learner drivers, the instructors have the ability to plan well ahead. The requirement for the test is that you must be able to read a number plate at the distance of:

- 26.5 metres for vehicles with a new-style plate.
- 27.5 metres for vehicles with an old-style plate.

Should you need to wear contact lenses or glasses to drive then these MUST be worn during the test. If you fail the eyesight test this will be marked on the examiner's marking sheet (DL25) as a 'serious fault'. *You will not be allowed to take the test.*

Vehicle safety questions

Vehicle safety questions are also referred to as 'show me, tell me' questions. At the start of the test, before you actually drive, the examiner will ask you 3 'tell me' questions. Whilst on the move, i.e. during the 1 hour test, the examiner will ask 2 'show me' questions whereby you will be required to carry out a safety task on the move.

'Tell me' questions

Q1. Tell me how you'd check that the brakes are working before starting a journey.

A. Brakes should not feel spongey or slack. Brakes should be tested as you set off. Vehicle should not pull to one side.

Q2. Tell me where you would find the information for the recommended tyre pressures for this car and how tyre pressures should be checked.

A. Manufacturers guide, use a reliable pressure gauge, check and adjust pressures when tyres are cold. Don't forget the spare tyre, remember to refit valve caps.

Q3. Tell me how you would make sure that the head restraint is correctly adjusted so that it provides the best protection in the event of a crash.

A. The head restraint should be adjusted so that the rigid part of the restraint is at least as high as the eye or top of the ears, and as close to the back of the head as is comfortable. NOTE: some restraints may not be adjustable.

Q4. Tell me how you would check the tyres to ensure that they have sufficient tread depth and that their general condition is safe to use on the roads.

A. No cuts or bulges, 1.6 mm of tread depth across the centre three quarters of the breadth of the tyre, and around the entire outer circumference of the tyre.

Q5. Tell me how you would check that the headlights and tail-lights are working. You don't need to exit the vehicle.

A. Explain that you would operate the switch (turn on ignition if necessary), then would walk around the vehicle to check. (As this is a 'tell me', you don't need to physically check the lights).

Q6. Tell me how you would know if there was a problem with your anti-lock braking system.

A. Warning light should illuminate if there is a fault with the anti-lock braking system.

Q7. Tell me how you would check the directional indicators are working. You do not need to exit the vehicle.

A. Explain that you would operate the switch (turn on ignition if necessary) and then walk around the vehicle to check. (As this is a 'tell me' question you don't need to physically check the lights).

Q8. Tell me how you would check the brake lights are working on this car.

A. Explain that you would operate the brake pedal, make use of reflections in windows or doors, or ask someone to help.

Q9. Tell me how you would check the power-assisted steering is working before starting a journey.

A. If the steering becomes heavy the system might not be working correctly. Before starting a journey 2 simple steps can be taken:

1. Gentle pressure on the steering wheel, maintain slight but noticeable movement as the system begins to operate.
   Alternatively:
2. Turning the steering wheel just after moving off will give an immediate indication that the power assistance is functioning.

Q10. Tell me how you would switch on the rear fog light(s) and explain when you'd use them. You don't need to exit the vehicle.

A. Operate the switch (turn on the ignition and dipped headlights if necessary). Check the warning light is on. Explain the use.

Q11. Tell me how you switch your headlights from dipped to main beam and explain how you'd know the main beam is on.

A. Operate the switch (with ignition or engine on if necessary). Check with main beam warning light.

Q12. Open the bonnet and tell me how you would check the engine has sufficient oil.

A. Identify the dipstick or oil level indicator, describe how you would check the oil level against the minimum and maximum markers.

Q13. Open the bonnet and tell me how you'd check that the engine has sufficient engine coolant.

A. Identify high and low level markings on the header tank (where fitted) or radiator filler cap, and describe how to top up to the correct level.

Q14. Open the bonnet and tell me how you would check that you have a safe level of hydraulic brake fluid.

A. Identify the reservoir, check the levels against high and low markings.

'Show me' questions

1. When it is safe to do so, show me how you wash and clean the rear windscreen.
2. When it is safe to do so, show me how you wash and clean the front windscreen.

3. When it is safe to do so, show me how you'd switch on dipped headlights.
4. When it is safe to do so, show me how you'd set the rear demister.
5. When it is safe to do so, show me how you'd operate the horn.
6. When it is safe to do so, show me how you'd demist the front windscreen.
7. When it is safe to do so, show me how you'd open and close the side window.
8. When it is safe to do so, show me how you'd operate the cruise control.

The driving test

In order to pass the driving test the examiner will explain in a pre-brief that 'a high standard of competence is expected.' During the test you will be expected to demonstrate all of the following:

- Expert handling of the controls.
- The use of correct road procedures.
- Anticipation of the actions of other road users and then taking the appropriate action.
- Sound judgement of distance, speed and timing.
- Consideration for the convenience and safety of other road users.
- Driving in an environmentally friendly manner.

You will be driving in varied traffic conditions that may include motorways or dual carriageways where possible, urban roads and rural roads.

Reversing your vehicle
During the test you will be carrying out 2 reversing manoeuvres from the following list:

- Parallel park your vehicle at the side of the road.

OR

- Reverse park your vehicle into a parking bay and drive out (this will be carried out at the test centre).
- Drive forward into a parking bay and reverse out.
- Pull up at the right-hand side of the road, reverse for around 2 car lengths, and rejoin the traffic.

Independent driving
During the drive you will be required to drive for around 20 minutes by following either:

- Directions from a sat nav.
- Traffic signs.

The examiner will tell you which one you have to do and when.

The sat nav will be provided by the examiner who will set it up for you. The model used for the test is a TomTom Start52. This model has been chosen by the DVSA as it is the most adaptable to changing colour, contrast and volume to suit everyone's needs. You will not be allowed to follow directions from your own sat nav during the test.

Should you go 'off route' during the independent driving, then this will NOT affect the test result unless you make a fault whilst doing so. If you are following traffic signs and can't see the sign, then the examiner will give you directions until you pick up the next sign.

Pass mark and faults
The pass mark for the Part 2 test is no more than 6 driver faults and no serious or dangerous faults.
There are 3 different types of faults:

- A dangerous fault is where there is actual danger to you, the examiner, the public or property. If the examiner takes verbal or physical control, then this is a dangerous fault.
- A serious fault is one that is potentially dangerous.
- A driving fault is one that isn't potentially dangerous, but if you keep making the same fault, then it could become a serious one.

You could make a fault during your driving which may not affect the result of the test so long as it is not a serious or dangerous one. It is good advice to ignore the examiner's marking sheet until the test is finished as it is very easy to become distracted and may well lead to further faults being made as a result. The examiner will only stop the test if they believe that your driving is a danger to other road users.

Test result
When you pass your test, the examiner will tell you which faults you made, if any, and will issue your pass certificate.

Should you be unsuccessful on the test, the examiner will tell you which faults you made. If this test was your first or second attempt then you can rebook your test as long as the new test date is at least 10 working days away. NOTE: there may be a short delay for the examiner to register your test result.

Failing for a 3rd time

If you fail your Part 2 test a third time, then you will have to start the test process again by taking your Part 1 theory test again. You must wait 2 years from the date you passed your part 1 test before you can take it again.

There is a right to appeal the test result if you feel that the examiner didn't follow the regulations when carrying out the Part 2 test. The result of the test will not be changed, but you may get a free re-test if your appeal is successful. Appeals in England and Wales will be to a Magistrates Court within 6 months of the test. Appeals in Scotland are to the Sheriffs Court within 21 days of the test.

Appeals can be made using the following link: www.gov.uk/find-court-tribunal.

Cancelled tests

If your test is cancelled for any reason, including bad weather (icy roads, fog, high winds, flooding), then the DVSA will:

- Automatically book you the next available date for your test.
- Send you details within 3 working days.

You can change the date of the test if the date given is not suitable. If the DVSA cancel your test at short notice you can apply for out-of-pocket expenses.

Revising for the part 2 test

In order to be eligible to supervise a learner, a driver must have a minimum of 3 years' driving experience. However, as training to be an instructor will often take around 6 months, it is acceptable to apply to start the relevant training 2.5 years after becoming a qualified driver. During those 2.5 years you will already have experience as a driver. This can be a positive or a negative! The experience gained, in particular dealing with other road users, is invaluable. However, over the years it is very easy to develop bad habits, and these will be an issue as you prepare for your DVSA ADI part 2 test.

Some driving instructors will be capable of providing suitable tuition to enable you to prepare for the test. However, this does not apply to all driving instructors. So, what should you do? Certainly do look for assistance with preparation for this test as the standard required to pass Part 2 is at a high level and going into the test ill-prepared will most likely result in a failed test. The following table shows the pass rates for the Part 2 exam, and demonstrates that this is a test requiring a high level of competence to achieve a pass.

Year	Tests conducted	Test passes	Pass rate %
2007/8	16181	7734	47.8
2008/9	14573	7313	50.2
2009/10	14958	7697	51.5
2010/11	10916	5287	48.4
2011/12	7336	3873	52.8
2012/13	4834	2576	53.3
2013/14	4202	2293	54.6
2014/15	3927	2136	54.4
2015/16	4658	2649	56.9
2016/17	5740	3140	54.7
2017/18 ytd	5122	2801	54.7

Source: DVSA/DfT 8.3.18

With an average pass rate of 51.3% over the last 10 years, you can see that professional help will be required if you want to pass this test.

The DVSA holds a register under the ORDIT scheme (Official Register of Driving Instructor Trainers). Instructors on this register have been assessed by the DVSA and understand the standards required. ORDIT registered trainers are therefore in a good position to provide the assistance you will need. The following link will help you to find your nearest ORDIT trainer: www.gov.uk/find-driving-instructor-training.

An experienced trainer will be able to help you develop your driving skills to test standard; how long this will take depends on your current level of ability, your ability and willingness to learn, and the amount of time you have made available to practice. In between lessons, use your normal daily driving as practice sessions.

Roads

The types of roads used for the Part 2 test are intended to test the skills of candidates; these will include urban driving, rural driving, motorways (not always possible at some test centres), and dual carriageways.

Standard of driving required

During the test you will be assessed on:

- Expert handling of controls.
- Use of correct road procedure.
- Anticipation of the actions of other road users and then taking appropriate action.
- Sound judgement of distance, speed and timing.
- Consideration for the convenience and safety of other road users.
- Driving in an environmentally friendly manner.

Driving test report and your driving skills

A high level of driving skill is required to pass the Part 2 test, and you will therefore be driving on roads that will challenge those skills. The marking sheet used for the test is the examiners DL25 form, a copy of which follows for you to study.

There are 3 types of fault:

- Dangerous. These are faults that involve actual danger to you, the examiner, the public or property. An example would be causing other road users to take avoiding action when changing lane.
- Serious. These are faults that are potentially dangerous rather than causing actual danger. An example would be when turning right at a roundabout you fail to observe and check for vehicles on the nearside of your vehicle when exiting.
- Driving. These are faults that are not potentially dangerous but are worthy of note. If a driver fault is recorded then this is because the standard of driving has fallen below what is expected on the Part 2 test. *If a driver fault is repeated then it could become a serious fault.* An example would be driving too close to parked cars.

Driving Test Report

DL25A
0408 T

I declare that:

- the use of the test vehicle for the purposes of the test is fully covered by a valid policy of insurance which satisfies the requirements of the relevant legislation.

- I normally live/have lived in the UK for at least 185 days in the last 12 months (except taxi/private hire). See note 30.

X _____

Candidate

S   D/C

Application Ref.

Date D D M M Y Y   Time H H M M   Dr./No.

DTC Code / Authority

Reg. No.

Examiner:

Staff / Ref. No.

Auto   Ext

Cat. Type

1   2   3   4   5   6   7   8   9   0   V

Instructor Reg

Instructor Cert   Sup   ADI   Int   Other   C

	Total	S	D
1a Eyesight			
1b H/Code / Safety			
2 Controlled Stop			
3 Reverse / Left Reverse with trailer control			
observation			
4 Reverse/ Right control			
observation			
5 Reverse Park control			
R C obs.			
6 Turn in road control			
observation			
7 Vehicle checks			
8 Forward park / control			
Taxi manoeuvre observation			
9 Taxi wheelchair			
10 Uncouple / recouple			
11 Precautions			
12 Control accelerator			
clutch			
gears			
footbrake			
parking brake / MC front brake			
steering			
balance M/C			
PCV door exercise			

	Total	S	D
13 Move off safety			
control			
14 Use of mirrors- M/C rear obs signalling			
change direction			
change speed			
15 Signals necessary			
correctly			
timed			
16 Clearance / obstructions			
17 Response to signs / signals traffic signs			
road markings			
traffic lights			
traffic controllers			
other road users			
18 Use of speed			
19 Following distance			
20 Progress appropriate speed			
undue hesitation			
21 Junctions approach speed			
observation			
turning right			
turning left			
cutting corners			
22 Judgement overtaking			
meeting			
crossing			

	Total	S	D
23 Positioning normal driving			
lane discipline			
24 Pedestrian crossings			
25 Position / normal stops			
26 Awareness / planning			
27 Ancillary controls			
28 Spare 1			
29 Spare 2			
30 Spare 3			
31 Spare 4			
32 Spare 5			

33 Wheelchair   Pass   Fail

Pass   Fail   None   Total Faults   Route No.

ETA   V   P   D255

Survey   A   B   C   D   E   F   G   H

Eco Safe driving   Control   Planning

Debrief   Activity Code

I acknowledge receipt of Pass Certificate Number: Licence rec'd   Yes X

Wheelchair Cert. No: COA X

No X

There has been no change to my health: see note 29 overleaf.

X _____

© Crown Copyright 12/2017

DVSA – An executive agency of the Department for Transport

Form Ref. DL25 D0018000-00

Driving Test Report — DL25B

0113 T

I declare that:

- the use of the test vehicle for the purposes of the test is fully covered by a valid policy of insurance which satisfies the requirements of the relevant legislation.
- I normally live/have lived in the UK for at least 185 days in the last 12 months (except taxi/private hire). See note 30.

X _____

Candidate

S D/C

Application Ref.

Date D D M M Y Y Time H H M M Dr./No.

DTC Code / Authority Reg. No.

Examiner:

Staff / Ref. No.

Auto Ext 1 2 3 4 5 6 7 8 9 0 V

Cat. Type

Instructor Reg Instructor Cert Sup ADI Int Other C

	Total	S	D
1a Eyesight			
1b H/Code / Safety			
2 Controlled Stop			
3 Reverse / Left Reverse with trailer — control / observation			
4 Reverse/Right — control / observation			
5 Reverse Park — control / R C obs.			
6 Turn in road — control / observation			
7 Vehicle checks			
8 Forward park / Taxi manoeuvre — control / observation			
9 Taxi wheelchair			
10 Uncouple / recouple			
11 Precautions			
12 Control — accelerator, clutch, gears, footbrake, parking brake / MC front brake, steering, balance M/C, PCV door exercise			

	Total	S	D
13 Move off — safety / control			
14 Use of mirrors- M/C rear obs — signalling / change direction / change speed			
15 Signals — necessary / correctly / timed			
16 Clearance / obstructions			
17 Response to signs / signals — traffic signs / road markings / traffic lights / traffic controllers / other road users			
18 Use of speed			
19 Following distance			
20 Progress — appropriate speed / undue hesitation			
21 Junctions — approach speed / observation / turning right / turning left / cutting corners			
22 Judgement — overtaking / meeting / crossing			

	Total	S	D
23 Positioning — normal driving / lane discipline			
24 Pedestrian crossings			
25 Position / normal stops			
26 Awareness / planning			
27 Ancillary controls			
28 Spare 1			
29 Spare 2			
30 Spare 3			
31 Spare 4			
32 Spare 5			

33 Wheelchair Pass Fail

Pass Fail None Total Faults Route No.

ETA V P D255

Survey A B C D E F G H

Eco Safe driving Control Planning

Debrief Activity Code

I acknowledge receipt of Pass Certificate Number: Licence rec'd Yes X

Wheelchair Cert. No: COA X

There has been no change to my health: see note 29 overleaf. No X

X _____

DVSA – An executive agency of the Department for Transport Form Ref. DL25 D0018000-00

Weather conditions *(please ✓ appropriate box[es])*

DL25B
0113T

1. Bright / dry roads ☐
2. Bright / wet roads ☐
3. Raining throughout test ☐
4. Showers ☐
5. Foggy / misty ☐

6. Dull / wet roads ☐
7. Dull / dry roads ☐
8. Snowing ☐
9. Icy ☐
10. Windy ☐

11. Other ☐
If you tick this box, provide an accurate description of the weather conditions.

Vehicle details

LGV ☐ Length ☐ Height ☐ Artic ☐ Rigid ☐
PCV ☐ Width ☐ MAM ☐ Draw bar ☐ Automatic ☐

Brief description of candidate

Id

Remarks

Oral explanation comments

Examiner's signature

Disability Tests

Description of any fitted adaptations

Driving Test Report

DL25C
0113T

S ◯ D/C ◯

I declare that:

- the use of the test vehicle for the purposes of the test is fully covered by a valid policy of insurance which satisfies the requirements of the relevant legislation.
- I normally live/have lived in the UK for at least 185 days in the last 12 months (except taxi/private hire). See note 30.

✗ _____

Candidate

Application Ref. ◯◯◯◯ ◯◯◯ ◯◯◯ ◯◯◯

Date D D M M Y Y   Time H H M M   Dr./No. ◯◯◯◯◯◯

DTC Code / Authority ◯◯◯◯◯   Reg. No. ◯◯◯◯◯◯

Examiner:

	Auto	Ext
Cat. Type ◯◯◯◯	◯	◯

1 ◻ 2 ◻ 3 ◻ 4 ◻ 5 ◻ 6 ◻ 7 ◻ 8 ◻ 9 ◻ 0 ◻

Instructor Reg ◯◯◯◯◯◯

Instructor Cert ◯◯◯◯◯◯ Sup ◯ ADI ◯ Int ◯ Other ◯

	Total	S	D
1a Eyesight			◻
1b H/Code / Safety		◻	◻
2 Controlled Stop		◻	◻
3 Reverse / Left Reverse with trailer — control		◻	◻
observation		◻	◻
4 Reverse/ Right — control		◻	◻
observation		◻	◻
5 Reverse Park — control		◻	◻
R ◻ C ◻ — obs.		◻	◻
6 Turn in road — control		◻	◻
observation		◻	◻
7 Vehicle checks		◻	◻
8 Forward park / — control		◻	◻
Taxi manoeuvre — observation		◻	◻
9 Taxi wheelchair			◻
10 Uncouple / recouple		◻	◻
11 Precautions		◻	◻
12 Control accelerator		◻	◻
clutch		◻	◻
gears		◻	◻
footbrake		◻	◻
parking brake / MC front brake		◻	◻
steering		◻	◻
balance M/C		◻	◻
PCV door exercise		◻	◻

		Total	S	D
13 Move off	safety		◻	◻
	control		◻	◻
14 Use of mirrors- M/C rear obs.	signalling		◻	◻
	change direction		◻	◻
	change speed		◻	◻
15 Signals	necessary		◻	◻
	correctly		◻	◻
	timed		◻	◻
16 Clearance / obstructions			◻	◻
17 Response to signs / signals	traffic signs		◻	◻
	road markings		◻	◻
	traffic lights		◻	◻
	traffic controllers		◻	◻
	other road users		◻	◻
18 Use of speed			◻	◻
19 Following distance			◻	◻
20 Progress	appropriate speed		◻	◻
	undue hesitation		◻	◻
21 Junctions	approach speed		◻	◻
	observation		◻	◻
	turning right		◻	◻
	turning left		◻	◻
	cutting corners		◻	◻
22 Judgement	overtaking		◻	◻
	meeting		◻	◻
	crossing		◻	◻

	Total	S	D
23 Positioning normal driving		◻	◻
lane discipline		◻	◻
24 Pedestrian crossings		◻	◻
25 Position / normal stops		◻	◻
26 Awareness / planning		◻	◻
27 Ancillary controls		◻	◻
28 Spare 1		◻	◻
29 Spare 2		◻	◻
30 Spare 3		◻	◻
31 Spare 4		◻	◻
32 Spare 5		◻	◻

33 Wheelchair Pass ◯ Fail ◯

Pass	Fail	None	Total Faults
◯	◯	◯	◻◻

ETA V ◯ P ◯   D255 ◯

Eco Safe driving Control ◯ Planning ◯

Debrief ◯

I acknowledge receipt of
Pass Certificate Number:
◯◯◯◯◯◯◯◯◯

Wheelchair Cert. No:
◯◯◯◯◯◯◯◯◯

Licence rec'd
Yes ☒
COA ☒
No ☒

There has been no change to my health: see note 29 overleaf.

✗ _____

Guidance Notes

DL25C
0113T

More detailed advice about the test requirements and the items marked for your attention overleaf are given in "The Driving Test Report Explained".

Further information may also be obtained from the relevant publication from the series of OFFICIAL driving books and other media products from DVSA for all drivers and motorcyclists, including drivers of goods vehicles, buses and coaches, tractors and specialist vehicles.

These publications can be purchased from all good book shops or by visiting www.tsoshop.co.uk/bookstore

Explanatory Markings

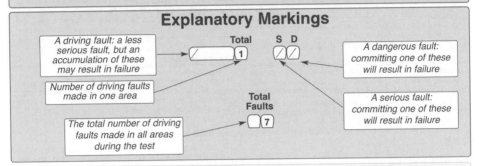

A driving fault: a less serious fault, but an accumulation of these may result in failure

Number of driving faults made in one area

The total number of driving faults made in all areas during the test

Total

S   D

A dangerous fault: committing one of these will result in failure

Total Faults

A serious fault: committing one of these will result in failure

The result of your test is marked overleaf. The following statement only applies if your result is marked as a fail.

Statement of Failure to Pass Practical Test – Test of Competence to Drive
Road Traffic Act 1988

This candidate named herein has been examined and has failed to pass the practical test / test of competence to drive prescribed under the Road Traffic Act 1988 (and for the purposes of Section 36 of the Road Traffic Offenders Act 1988 if an extended test).

Candidates are assessed against the items listed overleaf in deciding whether they are competent to drive. Items needing special attention are marked. You should study these along with the Guidance Notes above.

Unsuccessful candidates (dependent on category of test taken) may be required to wait a minimum period before taking a further test in a vehicle of the same category.

Appeals

If you consider that your test was not properly conducted in accordance with the relevant Regulations, you may apply to a Magistrate's Court acting for the Petty Sessions Area in which you reside (in Scotland to the Sheriff within whose jurisdiction you reside) which (who) has the power to determine this point. If you reside in England or Wales you have six months from the issue of this Statement of Failure in which to appeal or, if you reside in Scotland, 21 days. If the Court finds that the test was not properly conducted it may order a refund of the fee and authorise you to undergo a further test forthwith (see Road Traffic Act 1988 Section 90, for ADI qualifying tests see section 133).

You should note that your right to appeal to the Court under Section 90 or 133 is strictly limited to the question of whether the test was properly conducted in accordance with the relevant Regulations. **The examiner's decision and test result cannot be altered**.

Before you consider making any appeal you may wish to seek legal advice.

Data Protection Act 1998

The Driver & Vehicle Standards Agency (DVSA) directly manages all personal data it processes as an executive agency of the data controller, the Department for Transport. We use the personal information you provide to book and run the practical test. We also analyse the test details to assess how effective traffic patterns, safety initiatives and other transport issues are, to improve both customer service and road safety. We will not pass personal information to anyone else other than in line with the Data Protection Act 1998. This could include (but is not limited to) the police, HM Revenue and Customs and local authorities. For more information, please see our privacy notice on our website (www.gov.uk) or look for our 'Notification Documentation' on the Information Commissioner's website (www.ico.gov.uk). Our registration number is Z7122992.

The Driving Test Report Explained

DL25D
91/13 T

This explains the markings that were made on your test report. The report is labelled DL25D and DL25D Rev.

1(a) Eyesight Test

At the start of the test the examiner asked you to read a vehicle registration number. If you do not meet the eyesight standard then your test will not go ahead. If you need glasses or contact lenses to make sure you can read the number you must wear them whenever you drive or ride.

1(b) Highway Code / Safety

Highway Code: If you took a test for a tractor or specialist vehicle, at the end of the test you would have been asked questions on the Highway Code and to identify some road signs.

If you took an LGV or PCV test you were asked some Safety Questions. We asked you about some of the following: the location and operation of the safety components on your vehicle such as fire extinguishers, fuel cut-off switch and emergency exits.

2 Controlled stop

You may have been asked to show you were able to stop your vehicle in good time and under full control, as if in an emergency situation. Remember, when driving in wet or icy weather conditions, it will take you longer to stop safely.

3, 4, 5, 6 and 8 Reversing and turn in road exercises

Depending on the test you took, you may have been asked to complete one or more slow speed manoeuvring exercises. You needed to show you were able to keep control of your vehicle. This needed to be done whilst taking effective observations and acting correctly on what you saw.

7 Vehicle checks

It is important that the vehicle is in good working order and you can operate vehicle controls. The examiner asked you some 'show me / tell me' type safety questions. You needed to show a basic knowledge of the checks you should make on a regular basis. Depending on the test you took, you may have needed to safely demonstrate you can operate your vehicle's secondary controls whilst on the move.

8 Forward park (see above) / Taxi manoeuvre

You needed to show the examiner that you can safely turn the vehicle around to face in the opposite direction. How you did this was left to you, but you must not have used driveways or mounted the pavement. You were tested on your ability to select a safe place to carry out the manoeuvre whilst taking effective observation and acting correctly on what you saw.

9 Taxi wheelchair

You needed to show your ability to use wheelchair ramps competently. You needed to put the imaginary wheelchair user and his or her wheelchair into your vehicle. Then ensure the wheelchair and its user were securely installed ready for a journey. You were then asked to reverse this whole process.

10 Uncoupling and re-coupling (vehicle and trailer combinations)

You needed to show that you can uncouple and re-couple your trailer, using the correct procedure for your vehicle and trailer types. You were asked to uncouple the combination then drive forward and reverse alongside the trailer. To re-couple, you should have aligned and reconnected the towing vehicle and trailer. This should have been done accurately. You should then have checked they were secured and safe to go out on the road.

11 Precautions

These checks are simple but important. Before you started the engine, you needed to make sure that your seat was adjusted correctly to allow you to reach all your driving controls with ease. This is because an incorrect seat position can affect your ability to take observations and keep proper control of the vehicle.

12 Control

Throughout the test you needed to show you can use all the controls smoothly and at the correct time. This means less wear and tear on your vehicle and a smoother ride for your passengers.

13 Move off

You needed to show that you can move away on the level, on a slope and at an angle safely, under full control, taking effective observation. Move off only when it is safe to do so.

14 Use of mirrors – rear observation

You should have used the mirrors safely and effectively acting correctly upon what you saw. Where mirrors are not enough, for example to cover 'blind spots', then you must take effective rear observation. You must always check this carefully before signalling, changing direction or changing speed. You needed to demonstrate you can use the Mirror – Signal – Manoeuvre (MSM) routine effectively.

15 Signals

You should only use the signals shown in the Highway Code. On test you should have signalled clearly to let others know what you intend to do. This is particularly important if it would help other road users or pedestrians. You should have always signalled in good time and ensured that the signal had been switched off after the manoeuvre had been completed. You should not beckon to pedestrians to cross the road.

16 Clearance

You should have given parked vehicles and other obstructions enough space to pass safely. You needed to watch out for changing situations such as pedestrians walking out from between parked cars, doors opening and vehicles trying to move off. You should have been prepared to slow down or stop if needed.

DVSA – An executive agency of the Department for Transport

Form Ref. DL25 D0018000-00

The Driving Test Report Explained

DL25D
01 / 13 T

17 Response to signs and signals

You needed to show that you can react correctly to all traffic signs, road markings, traffic lights and pedestrian crossings. You should have obeyed signals given by police officers, traffic wardens, Highways Agency officers and school crossing patrols. You should watch out for signals given by other road users and carry on only when you are happy it is safe.

18 Use of speed

You should have made safe and reasonable progress along the road. You needed to keep in mind the road, traffic and weather conditions, road signs and speed limits. You needed to show confidence based on sound judgement. Remember, at all times you should have been able to stop within the distance you can see to be clear.

19 Following distance

You should have always kept a safe distance between you and the vehicle in front. You should be able to stop safely, well within the distance you can see to be clear. You should leave extra distance in wet or slippery conditions. Leave enough space when you are stopped in traffic queues.

20 Maintain progress

On test you needed to show that you can drive at a realistic speed appropriate to the road and traffic conditions. You needed to approach all hazards at a safe, controlled speed, without being over cautious or slowing or stopping other road users. You should always be ready to move away from junctions as soon as it is safe and correct to do so. Driving too slowly can frustrate other drivers which creates danger for yourself and others.

21 Junctions including roundabouts

The examiner would have looked for correct use of the Mirror – Signal – Manoeuvre MSM procedure. The examiner was also looking for correct positioning and approach speed at junctions and roundabouts. This is because these skills are essential for dealing with these hazards safely. Turning right across busy roads/dual carriageways is particularly dangerous. To drive safely and pass your test you must be confident that you can judge the speed and distance of oncoming traffic safely. You also need to look out for other road users emerging and turning at junctions and be ready to alter your course or stop. Be extra watchful in poor light or bad weather conditions for the more vulnerable road user, such as cyclists and motorcyclists.

22 Judgement

Your examiner will have assessed your judgment skills throughout the test. You will have needed to show sound judgment when overtaking, meeting or crossing the path of other road users. You should have only done this when it was safe and legal. You should have made your intentions clear and been sure that you understood the intentions of other road users.

23 Positioning

You should have positioned your car in a safe position; normally this would be keeping well to the left of the road. You needed to keep clear of parked vehicles and be positioned correctly for the direction that you intend to take. You needed to look for and be guided by road signs and markings. Other road users may judge your intentions by where you are positioned so be aware of where you are at all times.

24 Pedestrian crossings

You should have been able to identify the different types of pedestrian crossing and take the correct action. You needed to monitor your speed and time your approach to crossings so that you can stop safely if you need to do so. You should have paid particular attention where crossings were partly hidden by queuing or parked vehicles. You should also show consideration for elderly or infirm pedestrians who are trying to cross the road.

25 Position / normal stops

You should have chosen a safe, legal and convenient place to stop, close to the edge of the road, where you will not block the road and create a hazard. You should know how and where to stop without causing inconvenience or danger to other road users.

26 Awareness / Planning

You must be aware of other road users at all times. Your examiner is looking to see that you plan ahead to judge what other road users are going to do. This will allow you to predict how their actions will affect you and react in good time. You needed to anticipate road and traffic conditions, and act in good time, rather than reacting to them at the last moment. You should have taken particular care to consider the actions of the more vulnerable groups of road users such as pedestrians, cyclists, other motorcyclists and horse riders.

27 Ancillary controls

You needed to show that you can operate all of your vehicle's controls safely and effectively. The examiner was looking to see that whilst on the move you kept proper control of your vehicle whilst using secondary controls. These include demisters, heating controls, indicators and windscreen wipers.

Eco Safe Driving

You should drive in an 'eco friendly manner', considering your impact on the environment. Plan well ahead and choose appropriate gears, avoid heavy braking and over revving of the engine, particularly when stopped or moving off. If you have to stop for a long period such as at road works or railway crossings, consider stopping the engine to reduce pollution and save fuel. The examiner will assess this on your test; however this assessment will not affect the overall result of the test. If there are areas that need improvement you will receive appropriate feedback at the end of the test.

29 Health Declaration

You must declare any change to your health status since you last applied for a licence. It is a criminal offence for you (or anyone else) to make a false statement in order for you to obtain a driving licence, and can lead to prosecution.

30 Residence

Normal residence means the place where you normally live and have personal or occupational ties. However, if you have moved to the UK from another European Country or European Economic Area (EC/EEA), you should not take a driving test or obtain a first full licence unless you have lived here for 185 days in the last 12 months and are still living here at the time of your licence application. You may be asked to provide evidence of this.

Manage your booking online at www.gov.uk

Driver & Vehicle
Standards
Agency

Form Ref. DL25 D0018000-00

The examiner's marking sheet

Eyesight

At the start of the test you will have to read a number plate from a distance of:

- 26.5 metres for vehicles with a new-style plate.
- 27.5 metres for vehicles with an old-style plate.

If you fail the eyesight test you will fail your Part 2 test. This will count as 1 of your 3 attempts.

Controlled stop

During the test you may be asked to show that you are able to stop your vehicle in good time and under full control as if in an emergency situation. Remember that when driving in the wet or in icy conditions, it will take you longer to stop safely. You will have to react promptly, transferring from the accelerator to the brake. Brake firmly and progressively applying maximum brake force to stop the car safely in the shortest distance. Mirror work is not a priority as it delays reaction times. Ensure that the clutch is applied AFTER the brake. Keep both hands on the steering wheel to keep the car straight and to absorb your forward movement. The maximum brake force occurs just before the wheels lock. On cars fitted with ABS (anti-lock braking system) pressure should be maintained on the footbrake allowing the ABS to work; the system gives the driver increased direction control whilst braking in an emergency.

If a car is not fitted with ABS a manual system of braking will be required. Immediately before the wheels lock the footbrake should be briefly released and then reapplied quickly. This should be repeated until the vehicle stops. This method is referred to as 'cadence braking' and it prevents the wheels from locking.

The best way to deal with an emergency stop is not to have to perform one in the first place! Therefore, when you drive:

- Be spatially aware, creating a 'safety bubble' around the vehicle of at least 2 seconds front and back in dry conditions and 1 metre to both sides of the car.
- If the above gaps are not available, then adjust your speed to compensate.
- Drive at a speed that you know you can stop safely at.
- Use your anticipation skills to allow you to plan ahead and deal with hazards in a timely fashion.

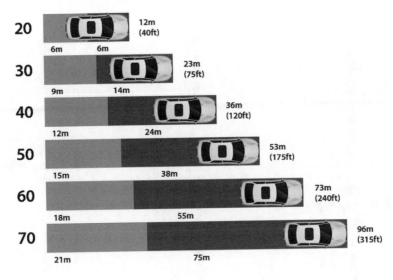

MPH	THINKING (FEET)	+	BRAKING (FEET)	=	OVERALL STOPPING DISTANCE (FEET)	=	MPH x ?
20	20	+	20	=	40	=	20 x 2
30	30	+	20	=	75	=	30 x 2½
40	40	+	80	=	120	=	40 x 3
50	50	+	125	=	175	=	50 x 3½
60	60	+	180	=	240	=	60 x 4
70	70	+	245	=	315	=	70 x 4½

- Good use of observation skills will allow you to know what is around you at all times.
- Drive in a style that is considerate to other road users, working in sympathy with the car, and driving in a manner that is always safe.
- Remember your stopping distances!

'Safety bubble' (figures are the minimum for dry conditions)

- Standard safety: 1 metre to both sides and a 2 second gap front and back.
- If the car behind is too close: 1 metre to both sides. Because the gap of the rear is reduced to 1 second, the gap in front is increased to 3 seconds.
- If the gap is reduced: The speed has to be reduced accordingly. This will depend on individual circumstances 'LESS SPACE – LESS SPEED'.

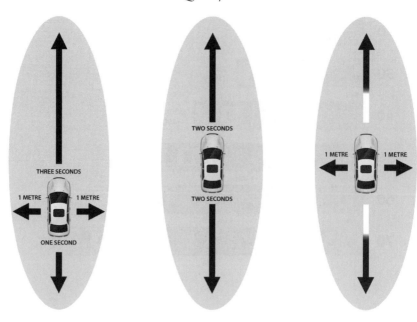

Manoeuvres

You will be required to perform 2 manoeuvres during the Part 2 test (on the marking sheet these are covered in boxes 4, 5, and 8). The 2 manoeuvres will be drawn from the following selection:

- Reverse park (into a bay at the test centre OR a parallel park in the road) (Box 5).
- Drive forward into a parking bay, reverse out to the left or right (Box 8).
- Pull up on the right and reverse back (Box 4).

Whilst carrying out the two manoeuvres you must show that your observation skills are excellent. This will entail your being fully aware of all other road users and taking action based on what you see; this would include giving priority where necessary. Your car control must also be excellent where you are able to control the vehicle at slow speed in all circumstances.

Accuracy must be demonstrated to a high standard on any manoeuvre that you are requested to perform and the following points are worthy of note in this regard:

- Reverse in a bay at the test centre at the start of the test. (This exercise only applies at test centres where parking bays are available).

You will be asked to drive out of the bay either to the left or right and then straighten your wheels to prevent your reversing back in on the same lock. You must finish inside the bay, although you are not normally penalised for crossing the lines when entering the bay.

- Parking on the road (parallel park).

This needs to be completed within about 2 car lengths of the stationary vehicle. You would be expected to complete the manoeuvre reasonably close to the kerb, and parallel to it.

- Driving forward into a parking bay.

This exercise is designed to check that the driver can manoeuvre the vehicle in a restricted space; car control, observation and accuracy must be at a very high level. You will be able to choose a convenient bay and are expected to park within it. You would not normally be penalised for crossing lines when entering the bay. When you have completed the manoeuvre, the examiner will consider whether the vehicle could reasonably be left in that position, and you will then be asked to reverse out of the bay, either to the left or right. A good point to make here is that having the windows down when reversing may help you to identify, by sound, other vehicles or pedestrians before you actually see them.

- Pulling up on the right.

On a suitable road you will be asked to pull up on the right at a safe place. You will then secure the car, at which point you will be requested to reverse for about 2 car lengths and then to drive off when you are ready. The purpose of this exercise is to assess your ability to move safely across the path of oncoming traffic, to reverse, and then move off again safely. Once again, car control, observation and accuracy are key and must be excellent.

Precautions (Box 11)
This section covers the cockpit drill – making sure that your car is secure, your seat is adjusted correctly allowing you to reach all the controls with ease. If the vehicle is not set up correctly then this will affect your ability to control the car accurately and to be able to take effective observation.

Controls (Box 12)

The test requirement for this discipline is that controls should be used smoothly and at the correct time. The best phrase to explain and describe this ability is 'vehicle sympathy'. You should always be in the correct gear, at the correct speed and in the correct road position for driving. You should also be safe at all times. Developing 'acceleration sense' will improve your drive. This is the ability to vary the speed of the vehicle according to changing and developing situations by precise use of the accelerator. When used correctly this method should result in less use of the brakes, thus reducing wear and tear on tyres and brakes and assisting in eco-driving.

The Part 2 test will require you to move off on a gradient under full control and also to use the controls precisely at slow speed for ALL your manoeuvres; acceleration and deceleration must be smooth and clutch and gears used smoothly so that gear changes are not noticeable. Remember, under most driving situations, to use the brakes to slow the vehicle, and not the gear box! The gear box may be used on downhill descents to allow engine braking to reduce the speed. You will need to make use of gradients, where present, to ensure smooth, safe and effective acceleration and deceleration.

A positive, business-like drive is required on the test and it must involve expert use of the controls.

As with other controls, the footbrake should be used smoothly; brake progressively in order to reduce speed. The use of the brakes and brake lights are important in controlling following vehicles, e.g. in a situation where you are being followed at a distance that is less than safe, then early, light and progressive use of footbrake, with brake lights showing, will allow you to deal safely with the situation. When using the footbrake you should be aware of the braking distances at various speeds (see Stopping Distances document under 'controlled stop' section). Typical stopping distances are also shown in the Highway Code rule 126. You will need to be aware of the overall typical stopping distances AND the component parts of thinking distance and braking distance. The figures are based on average reaction times and braking. Braking will vary from vehicle to vehicle and will be affected by:

- Weight of the vehicle (including passengers).
- Weather conditions (micro-climate).
- Road surface conditions.
- Maintenance of the vehicle's brakes.
- Tyres (tread depth, pressure, manufacturer).
- Driver's reaction times.

The following table shows how far a vehicle will travel in 1 second at various speeds:

MPH	Distance covered (metres)
1	0.447
5	2.23
10	4.47
20	8.94
30	13.41
40	17.88
50	22.35
60	26.82
70	31.39

1 hr = 3600 secs.
1 mile = 1609 metres.

The handbrake should be used:

- When a pause develops in to a wait.
- When parked.
- When the vehicle is stationary on a gradient.

When applying the handbrake in a queue of traffic, keep the brake lights on by use of the footbrake until the vehicle behind you has come to a stop; this will help reduce the risk of a rear impact.

Steering
Steering will be assessed on your ability to steer smoothly, safely and under control. Historically, the weight of the vehicle required the driver to adopt a push/pull method to steer, but over time technology has developed and power steering is now common on most vehicles used today, requiring much less effort being required of the driver. Drivers are therefore able to use their own style of steering where the emphasis is on control, rather than the method of steering. As a direct result of this, the examiner will look at your ability to control the vehicle and will not be looking at a certain method of steering. Therefore, it is not essential to hold the steering wheel at 'ten to two', although you should bear in mind that this position does have the following crucial advantages:

- It keeps the steering balanced.
- It allows you to turn the wheel immediately in either direction.

In order to steer to a good standard you should be in the correct seating position. A quick way to check that you are in the correct position is to extend your arms straight and your wrists should rest on the top of the steering wheel, thus when you have your hands at the 'ten to two' position on the steering wheel your elbows should be slightly bent. (If you want more information on steering, the book *Roadcraft: The Police Driver's Handbook* covers this in more detail. The detail here is intended to give you a general overview of requirements for the Part 2 exam. There is always lots more to learn!)

Move off (Box 13)

This section of the test will require you to demonstrate that you can move away smoothly and safely from rest. This will include, where possible, both uphill and downhill, and you will also be required to move off at an angle once you have pulled up behind a vehicle. The expectation is that you move away smoothly without rolling backward or forward. Your observation skills must be effective and all round and you should also consider the use of a signal.

Use of mirrors (Box 14)

During the test you will be marked on your effective use of mirrors. There is no set formula to how this is tested, but as a quality driver you should be aware at all times of what is happening around your vehicle. You will be marked down if you fail to make effective use of the mirrors before signalling, making a change of direction or before changing speed. You must act effectively and correctly on what you see, and where mirrors do not provide sufficient information you must take effective rear observation where appropriate – e.g. a blind spot when moving off or manoeuvering.

Signals (Box 15)

This subject covers how you communicate with other road users. In its basic form, it covers signal faults such as omitting a necessary signal, failing to cancel a signal, not signalling as per the Highway Code, and signalling too early or too late. Other signals would include the horn, flashing of headlights, brake lights, hazard warning lights, road position, arm signals and the speed of vehicles.

Flashing of headlights should only be used to let other road users know that you are there. Headlights should not be used to convey any other message (Highway Code rule 110). Similarly, the horn should only be used to warn other road users of your presence whilst your vehicle is moving, e.g. you may want to sound your horn or flash your headlights if another motorist is reversing out of a driveway and has not seen you, or you may wish to sound your horn to warn other motorists when approaching a tight, blind bend. Remember that the horn should not be used aggressively; nor should it be used whilst stationary on the road between 11.30pm and 07.00am unless another road user is posing a danger to you.

Signalling can come in more subtle forms too, where, for example, changes in speed and/or road position will have an effect on other road users. The progress of a car approaching a junction would clearly indicate to other road users waiting to emerge that the car is not turning if it does not slow down. However, a car that slows unnecessarily may give a false impression to a pedestrian waiting to cross, or to a driver waiting to emerge. Signals should be used to inform pedestrians of your intentions, and often eye contact with the pedestrian will confirm that you have seen them and ultimately reassure them. It is, however, important that you do NOT beckon pedestrians to cross the road since you do not know what the actions of other road users will be and therefore you may be putting the pedestrian in danger.

Clearance/Obstructions (Box 16)

When driving, candidates need to give enough space to pass parked vehicles and other obstructions with a safe gap. Anticipation and planning of the road ahead will allow your pupil to be able to deal with changing situations such as a car door opening or a pedestrian stepping out between parked cars. If the available gap reduces, your pupil should be prepared to slow down to accommodate the changing situation; this may include having to stop.

Response to signs and signals (Box 17)

This section of the marking sheet is where the examiner has looked at your ability to react correctly to all traffic signs, road markings, traffic lights and pedestrian crossings. Since you will already have passed your Part 1 exam your theory knowledge should be at a high level. A thorough understanding of the Highway Code and *Know Your Traffic Signs* is essential and assumed to be in place at this stage of the process.

During your test you will come across many signs, some of which may be time sensitive such as bus lanes. Make sure that you are aware of the time at which you encounter such signs and their relevance as you encounter them. Do not rely on other motorists as these signs are frequently misunderstood by many standard road users. Pay particular attention to box junctions and 'keep clear' markings when in heavy traffic conditions as these are often difficult to see when the roads are busy. Having said this, an understanding of box junctions and 'keep clear' markings should already be in place from your studies for Part 1 and thus should allow a good driver to anticipate them and therefore react appropriately to them.

At a 'stop' sign, STOP at the transverse line especially if the road is clear; wait at the 'stop' sign until it is possible to proceed safely without inconveniencing other road users. It is the law, and failing to do so will result in a serious fault.

You should also respond correctly to signals given by a police officer, traffic warden or other person(s) authorised to direct traffic. Remember that you should also be observant for signals given by other road users and must take appropriate action based on what you see.

Use of speed (Box 18)

The Part 2 test requires you to demonstrate that you can make safe and business-like progress. Your approach to this will be dependent upon traffic and weather conditions as well as road signs and speed limits. It is important to remember that, at all times, you should be able to stop within the distance you can see to be clear; and since a high standard of competence along with a business-like drive are expected, then your awareness of speed is vital, e.g. approaching a roundabout on a national speed limit dual carriageway will take skill in car control, excellent observation skills, planning and anticipation, as well as an awareness of the approach speed of your vehicle. You will need to adjust your speed based on many factors, and it will take practice to achieve the high standard required.

When travelling at higher speeds your observation will need to be further down the road in order for you to have sufficient time to plan. This will require scanning far distance, then middle distance and finally near distance and remember that as you scan further ahead you will naturally reduce your peripheral vision. However, once you start to focus more on the near distance due, for example, to a hazard, it would be necessary to reduce your speed. All this is to be done whilst still making good, safe progress and being aware of all other aspects of the road, road users, signs and road markings and not forgetting that the controls of the vehicle should be used smoothly and in sympathy with the car! Remember, also, that you should always be able to stop within the distance you can see to be clear, and this leads us neatly into the next section of the marking sheet...

Following distance (Box 19)

You will NOT pass the Part 2 test if you only demonstrate an ability to drive on normal roads at a low speed or in the low gears. You must drive in a business-like and safe manner. This includes keeping a safe distance to the vehicle in front of you and always being able to stop well within the distance you can see to be clear. Leave extra distance in wet or slippery conditions. A common fault on the Part 2 test is to drive at a pace that puts you too close to the vehicle in front, thereby increasing the risk by not having a safe gap in front of you. Should a vehicle be following you too close behind, you will need to adjust your driving to deal with the safety aspects of your driving and that of the car following you:

Issue: car behind is too close. You need to increase the distance to the vehicle in front of you to create a safe gap that allows you more time to deal with any hazards and allow the following driver more time to respond.

Solution:

- Check your mirrors and study the driver following.
- Slow down by gradually either coming off the accelerator or gently braking.
- Plan and deal early with any issues ahead of you.
- Brake gently when dealing with any hazards.

It is important that you manage the situation with the other driver rather than being managed by them. Managing other road users is an essential skill and one that only comes with practice.

'Following distance' will also include leaving enough distance to the vehicle in front when in a queue. Ensure that if there is an issue with the vehicles in front of you that you have a safe escape route. Instructors often use the phrase 'tyres and tarmac' when teaching as if this is an everyday phrase all drivers should know; by all means use this as a reference point to help transfer information, but please explain this rather than simply stating it!

Maintaining progress (Box 20)

During the test, and in general driving, you need to show that you can drive at a realistic speed that is appropriate to the road, traffic and weather conditions. This means that all hazards should be approached in a safe manner. Your approach speed needs to be controlled without being over-cautious; make sure that you do not slow or stop other motorists unnecessarily. When stopped, in order to avoid any undue hesitation you should always be ready to move off safely, and be prepared to move away from junctions as soon as it is safe and correct to do so.

In order to maintain progress in a safe and controlled manner you will need to plan well ahead, looking and scanning well ahead. Scan far distance, middle distance, near and rear distance so as to always put you in a situation where you can identify or anticipate hazards. Your speed should be carefully planned to deal with hazards in a safe manner without unnecessary slowing and you should always be aware of speed limits, be in the correct gear and at the correct speed. You should be aware of micro-climates, i.e. localised weather conditions, as well as study traffic conditions and the actions of other road users since, for example, you may have to give way at a meeting situation even where you have priority. Remember to be aware of what is behind you by effective use of your mirrors and taking appropriate action. Whilst you maintain a business-like drive, you will also need to drive in a courteous manner throughout keeping you, your car and its occupants and all other road users safe at all times. This may seem like a big ask, but it is precisely what is required of you to become an ADI and thus safely instruct future drivers to drive in the same manner!

Junctions including roundabouts (Box 21)
Junctions, by nature, are where roads meet. It is essential that you deal with these hazards safely as these are high risk areas, particularly where you have to cross the path of traffic. Make good use of the MSPSL routine (Mirrors-Signal-Position-Speed-Look) as you will need to be fully aware of what is around you, your approach speed and your road position. You will also need to demonstrate that you are able to safely judge the speed and distance of oncoming vehicles and have an awareness of the actions of other road users, remembering that it its often more difficult to identify cyclists and motorbikes.

Your approach speed at junctions and roundabouts must be correct in order for you to be able to deal with hazards safely, and this will include the correct and safe observation of other road users and the ability to move into/away from the junction without undue hesitation. Remember, your positioning of the vehicle MUST be correct at all junctions.

Judgement (Box 22)

You will be assessed on your judgement skills for the duration of the whole test. Judgement is therefore a continuous process. You will need to continually demonstrate sound judgement when overtaking, meeting or crossing the path of other road users; this should only be done when it is safe and legal, so ensure that you have made your intentions clear and that you understand what the intentions are of other road users. You will need to constantly assess hazards and make decisions on the action you need to take in order to deal with them effectively, making safe decisions by assessing the risk of each situation you encounter. The risk may change and develop as you approach a situation therefore risk assessment of each hazard is a continuous process requiring the skill to prioritise the risk and make sound decisions on the action(s) to be taken.

Positioning (Box 23)

The car will need to be positioned safely at all times dependent on a number of factors, such as the direction you intend to take, the road layout, road signs and markings and positioning correctly to keep clear of parked vehicles. You will need to make sure that if you change position, such as a lane change, that this is done in good time and gradually, making sure that your position allows sufficient space around the vehicle. A 'safety bubble' would allow at least a door's width to either side of the vehicle and, in dry conditions, a minimum of a 2 second gap front and rear; keeping this type of position will allow you to deal with any unplanned event. Should this method not be possible you should adjust your speed to suit the reduced gap. Your normal driving position would usually be well to the left of the road.

Pedestrian crossings (Box 24)

Pedestrian crossings come in various forms – zebra, puffin, toucan, pelican, equestrian and school formats. It is important that you are able to identify the different types and be able to take the correct action when dealing with them:

- Be fully aware of what is around you on approach, in particular the speed and position of any following vehicles.
- Monitor your own speed on approach so that you can stop safely if you need to.
- Show your intention early to other road users by use of brake lights if you need to stop. First pressure braking will illuminate

the brake lights without any significant reduction in your speed thus warning following traffic before you apply second pressure braking to reduce your speed.

- Pay particular attention where your view of a crossing is partly hidden by a queue or parked vehicles.
- Allow more time for elderly or infirm pedestrians as these people require more time to cross the road.

Position/normal stops (Box 25)

When asked by the examiner, you will be required to choose a safe, legal and convenient place to stop, close to the edge of the road. Do not block the road or create a hazard. If you realise you have stopped in an inconvenient place, then take a full, effective all-round observation and move the car to a more convenient location. You should know how and where to stop without causing inconvenience or danger to other road users.

Awareness and planning (Box 26)

This section is looking at how you observe other road users, your awareness of developing as well as potential situations. In order to give yourself time to judge and take action on what you see, you will need to be able to plan well ahead. You will also need to be aware of the actions of other road users so that you can predict how their actions will affect you and afford yourself a good reaction time. In order to reach and maintain the high standards required for this section you must constantly scan the whole driving scene. Take particular care to be aware of, and plan for, the actions of more vulnerable groups of road users such as pedestrians, cyclists, horse riders and motorcyclists. You can appreciate that once you have passed your Part 2 test, not only will awareness and planning skills be vital, but you will have the added task of studying the actions of your learner driver. Therefore, to be outstanding at awareness and planning could be said to be a basic requirement!

Ancillary controls (Box 27)

This section covers the safe use of the vehicle controls, e.g. demisters, heating controls, indicators, windscreen washers and wipers, cruise control, windows and any other relevant switches. You will be required to demonstrate that you can use these secondary controls safely whilst on the move (this is covered in more detail in the 'Show me' questions on page 51).

Eco-safe driving (Box 28)

You should drive in an 'eco-friendly' manner considering your impact on the environment, and although the assessment of eco-safe driving will not affect the overall result of the test, you will receive feedback at the end of it if there are areas that need to improve. The effect of eco-friendly driving multiplies as more people adopt this into their everyday driving so that this is a style of driving that should be encouraged with your learner drivers when you are teaching them.

Examples of good eco-safe driving would be:

- Using cruise control where fitted and where a fixed speed could be sustained for some distance.
- Identifying changes of speed early where you need to reduce your speed, and allowing the vehicle to slow under engine braking. This is referred to as 'trailing the throttle'. Ensure that you keep within speed limits.
- Choosing an appropriate gear to match the speed of the car.
- Anticipating gaps, for example approaching roundabouts so that you can flow rather than stopping and starting again.
- Changing through the gears at around 2000 rpm (revs per minute) for a diesel car and 2500 rpm for petrol. This avoids heavy demand on fuel during acceleration.
- Block changing gears rather than sequential gear changing.
- Using technology to allow the engine to switch off at red traffic lights and when in queues. Generally, the benefit comes in once the engine has been off for 6–10 seconds, therefore if the queue is about to move or you approach lights that have been red for some time, letting the engine to continue to run may save more fuel than a stop/start procedure.
- Tyres should be checked regularly and kept at their recommended pressure settings. Under-inflated tyres, where more of the tyre is in contact with the road will use more fuel.
- Removing roof boxes, roof bars or roof racks will help with fuel consumption as you are reducing wind resistance.
- Be careful in your use of air conditioning since use of this can seriously impact on fuel consumption.

Examples of faults on the part 2 marking sheet

- Failing the eyesight test.
- Controlled stop – inadequate braking, slow reaction to controls.
- Forward/reverse bay park – incorrect use of controls and/or inaccuracy.

- Lack of effective all-round observation during the reverse exercises.
- Pull up on the right – incorrect use of controls and/or inaccuracy. Not showing due regard for approaching traffic.
- Unable to answer or demonstrate correctly and safely a vehicle safety question.
- Failure to take proper precautions before starting the engine.
- Uncontrolled or harsh use of the accelerator.
- Uncontrolled use of the clutch.
- Failure to engage the gear appropriate to the road and traffic conditions or for junctions.
- Coasting in neutral or with the clutch pedal depressed.
- Not changing gear or selecting neutral when necessary.
- Late or harsh use of the footbrake.
- Not applying or releasing parking brake when necessary.
- Erratic steering, overshooting the correct turning point when turning right or left.
- Incorrect positioning of hands on the steering wheel or both hands off the steering wheel.
- Failure to make effective precautions before moving away.
- Inability to move off smoothly when moving straight ahead, at an angle or on a gradient.
- Failure to make effective use of mirrors before signalling, before changing direction or speed.
- Omitting a necessary signal.
- Signal not as per the Highway Code – failure to cancel directional indicator. Beckoning pedestrians to cross.
- Incorrect timing of signals – too early so as to confuse other road users or too late to be of value.
- Passing too close to stationary vehicles obstructions.
- Failure to comply with "STOP" signs including "STOP CHILDREN" sign carried by school crossing patrol.
- Failure to comply with directional signs or 'no entry' signs.
- Failure to comply with road markings, e.g. double white lines, box junctions.
- Failure to comply with signals given by a police officer, traffic warden or other persons authorised to direct traffic.
- Failure to take appropriate action on signals given by other road users.
- Driving too fast for the prevailing road and traffic conditions.
- Following too close to the vehicle in front.

- Not leaving a reasonable gap to the vehicle in front when stopping in lines of traffic.
- Driving too slow for the prevailing road and traffic conditions.
- Unduly hesitant.
- Approaching junctions either too fast or too slow.
- Not taking effective observations before emerging and/or emerging without due regard for approaching traffic at junctions.
- Incorrect positioning before turning right.
- Positioning too far from the kerb before turning left.
- Cutting right-hand corners.
- Overtaking or attempting to overtake other vehicles unsafely.
- Not showing due regard for approaching traffic.
- Crossing the path of traffic unsafely when turning right.
- Incorrect positioning of the vehicle during normal driving.
- Failure to exercise proper lane discipline.
- Failure to give precedence to pedestrians on a pedestrian crossing. Non-compliance with traffic lights at a pedestrian crossing.
- Normal stop not made in a safe position.
- Not anticipating what other road users intend to do, or reacting inappropriately. This includes pedestrians actually crossing a road.
- Failure to use ancillary controls when necessary.
- Failure to demonstrate an eco-safe standard of driving.

ADI part 2 summary

DURATION OF TEST	1 HR (approx.)
COST OF TEST	£111 PER ATTEMPT (as of Sept 2018)
NUMBER OF ATTEMPTS ALLOWED	3
PASS MARK	6 FAULTS MAX NO SERIOUS/ DANGEROUS FAULTS
ABOUT PART 2	www.gov.uk/adi-part-2-test
UP-TO-DATE FEES	www.gov.uk/approved-driving-instructor-adi-fees
DVSA CUSTOMER SUPPORT	0300 200 1122 (Mon–Fri 8am–4pm)
BOOK PART 2 TEST	www.gov.uk/booking-driving-test

Chapter 4

ADI PART 3 EXAM

Having passed your Part 2 test and practised, possibly by obtaining a trainee licence so as to practise with real pupils, the next stage of training is to take the ADI part 3 test; as per the Part 2 test, you are allowed 3 attempts at this test.

In this chapter we will look at the test itself, and the following section will comprise of an in-depth study of how to prepare for the Part 3 test by learning the skills of teaching and coaching pupils.

The part 3 exam is a test of your ability to teach pupils and you will need to demonstrate to a senior DVSA examiner your ability to teach and coach a pupil over a period of approximately 1 hour. The marking sheet covers 3 higher areas of competence that are in turn broken down into 17 lower levels of competency. The way in which candidates are assessed for this test changed on 23rd December 2017 to fall in line with the ADI Standards Check, which has been in place since April 2014. The following table shows the pass rates since 2007, and it is clearly demonstrated that this is NOT an easy exam to pass and requires solid practise and knowledge. The average pass rate is just 31%.

Historic part 3 pass rates

Year	Tests conducted	Test passes	Pass rate %
2007/8	11508	3166	27.1
2008/9	13427	4107	30.6
2009/10	12279	3634	29.6
2010/11	12128	3718	30.7
2011/12	8972	2730	30.4

Year	Tests conducted	Test passes	Pass rate %
2012/13	5882	1861	31.6
2013/14	4600	1486	32.3
2014/15	3807	1236	32.5
2015/16	3828	1316	34.4
2016/17	4866	1741	35.8
2017/18 ytd	3821	1404	36.7

Source: DVSA/DfT 8.3.18

Booking the part 3 test

You will be given details on how to book your Part 3 test when you have passed the Part 2 test. You will also be given the paperwork required for your trainee licence, should you wish to use this option.

Book your test online at: www.gov.uk/book-driving-test

If you require assistance with your booking you may contact the DVSA driving test booking support at customerservices@dvsa-gov.uk. Tel: 0300 200 1122 Mon–Fri 8am–4pm.

When you book your test you will need the following:

- UK driving licence number.
- Credit or debit card.
- Theory test pass certificate.

The current fee (as of September 2018) is £111.00.

Tests can be booked at any test centre. If you want a test at a test centre where times are not available then you can use the 'book to hold' facility that will come up at the bottom of the screen. You should hear within 2 weeks, although you may not have a confirmed date at this time.

If you need help preparing for your Part 3 test, the following link will help you find driving instructor training courses: www.gov.uk/find-driving-instructor-training

If you need to change the date of your Part 3 test, then use the following link: www.gov.uk/change-driving-test

If you need to check your driving test appointment details, then use the following link: www.gov.uk/check-driving-test

What you will need to bring to test

You must bring with you, the following:

- Your UK driving licence.
- A suitable car (see below).
- A pupil (examiner role play is no longer an option).

Suitable car

Rules for the car you take on test are as follows.

Your car MUST:

- Be taxed.
- Be insured for a driving test (you will need to check this with your insurance company).
- Be roadworthy and have a current M.O.T. (if the vehicle is older than 3 years).
- Be a saloon, hatchback or estate car in good working condition.
- Convertible cars are not allowed.
- Have full-size rear seats.
- Have no warning lights showing. For example, the airbag warning light.
- Have no tyre damage and have the legal tread depth on each tyre. You can not have a space-saver spare tyre fitted.
- Be smoke free – this means that you can't smoke in it just before test or during the test.
- Be able to reach at least 62 mph and have an mph speedometer.
- Have 4 wheels and a maximum authorised mass (MAM) of no more than 3, 500 kg.

MAM is the limit on how much the car can weigh when it is loaded. This information will be in the car's handbook.

Your test will be cancelled and you will lose your test fee if your car does not meet the rules.

Things that must be fitted

The car must have:

- L-Plates ('L' or 'D' in Wales) on the front and rear if the pupil is a learner.
- Working seat belts.

Dash cams

These can be used so long as:

- It faces outside of the car and doesn't film inside.
- Doesn't record audio from inside the car.

Hire cars

Hire cars are allowed on test so long as they have dual controls fitted and meet all the other rules.

Vehicle features

You can use a car with:

- An electronic parking brake.
- Hill-start assist.

Manual and automatic cars

If you have a manual licence, you can take the test in either a manual or automatic car. You will be able train people in both types of car when you are qualified.

If you have an automatic licence, then you must take the test in an automatic car. You will only be able to train people in an automatic car when you have qualified.

Cars with known safety faults

Check the list at: www.gov.uk/adi-part-3-test/car-rules

If your car is on the list of vehicles that has had a recall, you can not use the car on test unless you have proof that it is safe.

You must bring this proof with you when you attend for test.

ADI part 3 test structure

The Part 3 test is a competency-based assessment that is in line with the National Standard for Driver and Rider Training. The standard sets out skills, knowledge and understanding that you will need to be an effective instructor/trainer. The test is the same as the ADI Standards Check, which is used after you have qualified to ensure that you maintain the high standards that are required in order to remain on the register.

Your pupil can be a learner or a full licence holder, but they can not be an ADI (Approved Driving Instructor) or someone else who is preparing to take the Part 3 test (PDI).

During your part 3 assessment the examiner will sit in the back of the car and will observe you carrying out a lesson. They will be looking to see if your instruction helps someone to learn in an effective way; for this reason, you will need to present a normal lesson. The assessment is based on a client-centred approach and is intended to help emphasise the importance of risk management when teaching.

Before the start of the lesson, the part 3 examiner will have a short chat with you, where they will ask you about your pupil and will want to know what development areas the pupil is looking for.

At this stage you should show the examiner any training records you have for your pupil along with your own training records as a PDI. Once the examiner has the details of the driving history of the pupil and what the lesson will be about, they will ask you to be back at the test centre in one hour and won't take any further part in the lesson (unless they intervene as they consider the lesson to be dangerous).

Your lesson should follow a normal structure. This will involve introducing the pupil to the examiner and explaining that the examiner is present to assess you and not the pupil. You then need to recap the previous session you had with this pupil. There should be good use of question and answer (Q&A) to establish a starting point for the lesson. Try to get the pupil to do most of the work here! Aims and objectives then need to be set for the lesson which, again, should be led by the pupil. If your pupil is a beginner then you may well find that you will need to set the aims and objectives for them, but it is essential that, should you do this, you get the pupil's agreement. Either way, the pupil's needs should be clear. It would be useful here to use a 'scaling system' whereby the pupil can scale where they think they are between 1 and 10, and this can then be used again in the summary at the end of the lesson to see if progress has been made.

Risk management will need to be discussed, whereby an agreement of the level of help and instruction between yourself and the pupil must be agreed. Whilst you are out on the road you will need to use the 3 core competencies of fault identification, fault analysis and remedial action, to help the pupil achieve their aims and objectives. This may well include pulling up at the side of the road to assess how the lesson is progressing, what is going well and what needs to be improved. Pulling up at the roadside is a bit like a 'timeout' where the pupil can focus on issues without being on the move.

When the lesson ends summarise and recap on what has happened during the lesson. Look at what went well and, again, the pupil needs to be at the centre of the process whereby you encourage them to reflect on the lesson. The use of scaling (1–10) can be compared to the aims and objectives. Finally, have a talk with the pupil about what they wish to cover on the next lesson.

Test result

If you pass the Part 3 test you can apply for your first ADI badge at: www.gov.uk/apply-first-approved-driving-instructor-adi-badge

If you do not pass then you can take the test again if this is your first or second attempt. You must book the next (3rd) attempt within 2 years of passing your ADI part 1 test. A further five (5) hours additional training will be required if you fail your first or second attempt. This is so that you and your instructor can review the test(s) result and further develop your teaching and coaching skills to improve your chances of passing the next time. To rebook a Part 3 test go to: www.gov.uk/book-driving-test

Failing the 3rd attempt. If you fail your 3rd attempt then you will need to retake and pass the ADI part 1 and part 2 tests again before you can attempt the ADI part 3 test again. You must wait 2 years from the date you originally passed the ADI part 1 test before you can take it again.

Appealing your ADI part 3 test. There is a right to appeal your test result if you feel that the examiner didn't follow the regulations when carrying out the Part 3 test. The result of the test will NOT be changed, but you might get a free re-test if your appeal is successful. Appeals in England & Wales will be at a Magistrates Court within 6 months of the test. Appeals in Scotland are at the Sheriff's Court within 21 days of the test. Appeal a test at www.gov.uk/find-court-tribunal

Cancelled tests. If your test is cancelled for any reason, including bad weather (icy roads, fog, high winds, flooding), then the DVSA will:

- Automatically book you the next available date for your test.
- Send you the details within 3 working days.

You are allowed to change the date of the test given to you if it is not suitable at www.gov.uk/change-driving-test

Should the DVSA cancel your test at short notice, for example if an examiner is unwell, then you can claim for out of pocket expenses at www.gov.uk/government/publications/application-for-out-of-pocket-expenses

The examiner's marking sheet

The assessment form for the Part 3 test is based on 3 areas of competence:

- Lesson planning.
- Risk management.
- Teaching & learning strategies.

Putting these categories into everyday language:

- Was the lesson appropriate?
- Was it safe?
- Did it work/was it effective?

These 3 areas of competency are then further broken down into a further 17 lower level competencies.

Lesson planning

- Did the trainer identify the pupil's learning goals and needs?
- Was the agreed lesson structure appropriate for the pupil's experience and ability?
- Were the practice areas suitable?
- Was the lesson plan adapted, when appropriate, to help the pupil toward their learning goals?

Risk management

- Did the trainer ensure that the pupil fully understood how the responsibility for the risk would be shared?
- Were directions/instructions given to the pupil clear and given in good time?
- Was the trainer aware of the surroundings and pupil's actions?
- Was any verbal or physical intervention by the trainer timely and appropriate?
- Was sufficient feedback given to help the pupil understand any potential safety critical incidents?

Teaching & learning strategies

- Was the teaching style suited to the pupil's learning style and current ability?
- Was the pupil encouraged to analyse problems and take responsibility for their learning?

- Were opportunities and examples used to clarify learning outcomes?
- Was the technical information given comprehensive, appropriate and accurate?
- Was the pupil given appropriate and timely feedback during the session?
- Was the pupil encouraged to ask questions and were these queries followed up and answered?
- Did the trainer maintain appropriate and non-discriminatory manner throughout the session?
- At the end of the session, was the pupil encouraged to reflect on their own performance?

The following document is the examiner's ADI part 3 test report form:

The form is designed to identify the strengths in the PDI's instructional ability and to highlight any areas that need development. The examiner will also give you verbal feedback to help you understand your own instructional ability. Your overall performance will be based on the markings shown against the lower competencies. For each of those competencies a mark is given on a score of 0–3.

- Score 0 = no evidence of competence.
- Score 1 = competence demonstrated in a few elements.
- Score 2 = competence demonstrated in most elements.
- Score 3 = competence demonstrated in all elements.

In order to pass as a satisfactory assessment a minimum score of 31 must be achieved.

In addition, in the section of risk management a minimum score of 8 must be achieved. Pass marks are graded into 2 categories:

- 31–42   Grade B
- 43–51   Grade A

As well as by not achieving the required scores, you will also fail the test if the examiner believes that your behaviour is placing you, the pupil, or any third party in immediate danger. In these circumstances the examiner may well stop the test.

At the top of the examiner's marking sheet a number of recordings can be made. These are the PRN (personal reference number) of the PDI's trainer, whether the PDI's trainer is on the ORDIT register (Official Register of Driving Instructor Training), whether the PDI has presented a record of their training (log book) and also if the PDI is on a trainee licence.

Qualified

ADI Part 3 (SC)

INFORMATION

Driver & Vehicle Standards Agency

Candidate's name _____   **Location** _____   **Outcome**

PRN ☐ ☐ ☐ ☐ ☐   **Date** ☐☐ / ☐☐ / ☐☐

I declare that my use of the test vehicle for the purposes of the test is covered by a valid policy of insurance which satisfies the requirements of the relevant legislation.

Dual Controls
Yes ☐ No ☐   **Reg No** _____

Log book   **Trainer**
Yes ☐ No ☐   **PRN** ☐ ☐ ☐ ☐ ☐ ☐

Trainee Licence   **ORDIT**
Yes ☐ No ☐   Yes ☐ No ☐

Accompanied?   QA ☐   Trainer ☐   Other ☐

ASSESSMENT

Lesson

	Competence

Student: Beginner ☐ Partly trained ☐ Trained ☐ FLH New ☐ FLH Experienced ☐

	0	1	2	3

Lesson theme:

Junctions ☐ Town & city driving ☐ Interaction with other road users ☐
Dual carriageway / faster moving roads ☐ Defensive Driving ☐ Effective use of Mirrors ☐
Independent driving ☐ Rural roads ☐ Motorways ☐ Eco-safe driving ☐
Recap a manoeuvre ☐ Commentary ☐ Recap Emergency stop ☐ Other _____

	No evidence	Demonstrated in a few elements	Demonstrated in most elements	Demonstrated in all elements

Lesson Planning

Did the trainer identify the pupil's learning goals and needs?				
Was the agreed lesson structure appropriate for the pupil's experience and ability?				
Were the practice areas suitable?				
Was the lesson plan adapted, when appropriate, to help the pupil work towards their learning goals?				
Score for lesson planning				

Risk Management

Did the trainer ensure that the pupil fully understood how the responsibility for risk would be shared?				
Were directions and instructions given to the pupil clear and given in good time?				
Was the trainer aware of the surroundings and the pupil's actions?				
Was any verbal or physical intervention by the trainer timely and appropriate?				
Was sufficient feedback given to help the pupil understand any potential safety critical incidents?				
Score for risk management				

Teaching & learning strategies

Was the teaching style suited to the pupil's learning style and current ability?				
Was the pupil encouraged to analyse problems and take responsibility for their learning?				
Were opportunities and examples used to clarify learning outcomes?				
Was the technical information given comprehensive, appropriate and accurate?				
Was the pupil given appropriate and timely feedback during the session?				
Were the pupils queries followed up and answered?				
Did the trainer maintain an appropriate non-discriminatory manner throughout the session?				
At the end of the session – was the pupil encouraged to reflect on their own performance?				
Score for teaching and learning strategies				
Overall score				

REVIEW

	YES	NO
Did the candidate score 7 or less on Risk Management (A 'Yes' response to this question will result in an automatic Fail)		
At any point in the lesson, did the candidate behave in a way which put you, the pupil or any third party in immediate danger, so that you had to stop the lesson (A 'Yes' response to this question will result in an automatic Fail)		
Was advice given to seek further development?		

Feedback offered to Candidate _____

Examiner Name _____   **Signature** _____

??/2017

90

Assessment Notes
This form is designed to identify the strengths in your instructional ability and to highlight any areas which you may need to develop. The form is provided in conjunction with verbal feedback with the aim of helping you understand your instructional ability.

The examiner has assessed your overall performance based on the markings shown against the lower competencies.

Criteria for Scoring
Assessment is against three broad areas of competence:

- Lesson planning
- Risk management
- Teaching and learning strategies

A full description regarding the assessment can be found in the "National standard for driver and rider training" available on www.GOV.UK (Teaching people to drive).

Further information may also be obtained from the relevant publication from the series of OFFICIAL driving books and other media products from DVSA.

These publications can be purchased from all good book shops or by visiting www.tsoshop.co.uk/bookstore

If you are unsuccessful or if you require further development you should discuss the outcome of your test with your trainer or contact a DVSA accredited ORDIT trainer to assist you. A list of ORDIT trainers can be found at: https://www.gov.uk/find-driving-instructor-training

ADI Grades
Assessing the lower competencies will represent a 'profile' of Instructional Competence.

Score	Description	Grade
0 – 30	Unsatisfactory performance	FAIL
31 – 42	Sufficient competence demonstrated to permit entry to the Register of Approved Driving Instructors	GRADE B
43 – 51	A high overall standard of instruction demonstrated	GRADE A

Note: If you score 7 or less in the Risk Management section the instructional ability will be deemed substandard and a fail. Also, if the examiner believes your behaviour is placing you, the pupil or any third party in immediate danger they may stop the examination and record an immediate fail.

Appeals
You cannot appeal against the examiner's decision. You may appeal to a Magistrate's Court or, in Scotland, the Sheriff's office, if you consider that your test was not conducted properly. (See Road Traffic Act 1988, Section 133).

Before you consider making any appeal you may wish to seek legal advice.

??/2017

Assessment criteria
The breaking down of the 3 main areas of competence into 17 lower competencies has been mentioned a number of times, and the following section shows how this is done.

Lesson planning
The purpose of all driver training is to assess and develop the learner's skill, knowledge and understanding of the National Standard for Driver and Rider Training. Research by the DVSA has indicated that the best way to achieve this is by placing the client at the centre of the learning process.

Did the trainer identify the pupil's learning goals and needs?
This would normally take place at the start of a lesson. In most cases it is envisaged that the ADI/PDI and learner have worked together for some time and the basic structure of the pupil's learning goals have been laid down. As the lesson progresses a better understanding of their needs may emerge. What is being looked for here is:

- Is the PDI encouraging the pupil to say what they want from the lesson?
- Asking questions to ensure understanding?
- Checking understanding as the lesson progresses?
- Listening to what the pupil is saying?
- Taking note of body language?

In an ideal world the pupil will set their own goals as to what they wish to achieve. However, as driving is new to them, unless they have had several lessons, they may not know what it is they wish to achieve. They may therefore need leading and the 5 bullet points above are therefore very pertinent. For example, the ADI/PDI might say "Today we are going to help you with crossroads. What would you like to achieve by the end of the lesson?"

However, whatever goals are set, they need agreeing by the pupil. This way of learning should be used to encourage the pupil to make choices and therefore take some responsibility for their own learning. If the ADI/PDI follows all of the above and reacts positively to each point then they are likely to score 3. If, for instance, they do all the listening bits but fail to spot the learner becoming nervous or tense, then they would probably score 2 because they had good listening skills but failed to spot non-verbal clues. Indications of a lack of competence could include:

- Making assumptions about understanding or experience.
- Failing to note negative or concerned comments or body language that demonstrates discomfort.
- Undermining the pupil's confidence by continually asking questions clearly beyond the pupil's knowledge or understanding.
- Pushing the pupil to address issues that they are unhappy talking about, unless there is a clear need, such as an identified risk or safety critical issue.

Was the agreed lesson structure appropriate for the pupil's experience and ability?

The lesson should allow the pupil to progress their learning at a manageable rate – stretching them but not overwhelming them. For example, if a pupil is concerned about entering roundabouts, they should not be asked to enter fast-flowing, multi-lane, multi-exit junctions at the first attempt. At the same time, they should not be restricted to very quiet areas that do not stretch them unless the ADI/PDI identifies a potential risk that needs checking out first.

Indications that all levels of competence are in place are:

Did the ADI/PDI ensure that the pupil understood what they planned to do and agree with that plan?

- Provide a lesson that reflected the information given by the pupil and the learning goals they wanted to tackle?
- Build-in opportunities to check statements made by the pupil before moving on to more challenging situations?
- Check theoretical understanding?

Indications of a lack of competence include:

- Delivering a pre-planned, standard lesson that doesn't take into account the pupil's expressed needs or concerns.
- Failing to build in a suitable balance of practise and theory.

Were the practice areas suitable?

The area or route used by the ADI/PDI should allow the pupil to practise safely and help them achieve their goals. It should provide some stretch and challenge without taking them out of their competence zone.

Indications that all elements of competence are in place could include choosing an area or route that provides:

- A range of opportunities to achieve the agreed learning opportunities.
- Challenges, but is realistic in terms of the pupil's capabilities and confidence.

Indications of a lack of competence include the ADI/PDI going to an area that:

- Takes the pupil out of their competence zone so that they are under such pressure that they cannot address their learning goals.
- Exposing pupil to risks that they cannot manage.

It may be that on the way to a suitable area, for instance to look at a reversing manoeuvre, the pupil needs to drive in an area busier than they are used to. For instance, they need to deal with roundabouts. The ADI needs to mention that and, dependent upon circumstances, offer to help them deal with that. Check that the pupil is happy with that though before proceeding.

Was the lesson plan adapted, where appropriate, to help the pupil work towards their learning goals?

The ADI should be ready to adapt if the pupil appears to be uncomfortable or unable to deal with the learning experience set up for the lesson or, indeed, suggests that it is not providing what they were looking for. It is important to keep the balance of responsibility in the pupil's court because people learn best and more effectively when they are in charge of their own learning goals. For instance, in the last example (above) the pupil was to deal with reversing but had to deal with some busy roundabouts on the way. The ADI/PDI has already agreed to give them help and it is therefore your responsibility to keep the car safe so that the pupil has the opportunity of dealing with the reversing and you have therefore kept your part of the agreement about roundabouts.

If, in the core part of the lesson, the pupil's inability is creating what may be a possible risk situation, the ADI/PDI should adapt quickly. The situation may be that a few more questions are needed to clarify the problem. It may be that the teaching and learning style used by the ADI is wrong. However, whatever the reason for changing and adapting the plan the ADI must ensure that the pupil understands what they are doing and the reason for it. Indications that all elements of competence are in place could include:

- Comparing the actual performance of the pupil with their own feedback and clarifying any differences.
- Responding to any faults or weaknesses that undermined the original plan for the session.
- Responding to any concerns or issues raised by the pupil.
- Picking up on any non-verbal signs of discomfort or confusion.

Indications of lack of competence include:

- Persisting with a plan despite the pupil being clearly out of their depth.
- Persisting with a plan despite the pupil demonstrating faults or weaknesses that should lead to re-thinking the plan.
- Changing the plan without reason.
- Failing to explain to the pupil why the plan has been changed.

Risk management

It should be noted that the risk management competency is closely linked to the previous one, lesson planning. As a result of setting goals or objectives for the pupil, the agreed lesson plan, and a suitable route to achieve the goals, the way in which risk will be managed and who is responsible for what during the lesson needs to be considered.

Managing risk competently is vital to ensure that the goals set for the lesson can be achieved. Each of the competencies in the Standards Check are inter-related and the examiner's assessment process will take the whole lesson into consideration.

So, let's deal with each competency indicator in turn:

Did the trainer ensure that the pupil fully understood how the responsibility for risk would be shared?

Once the lesson goal has been agreed the ADI/PDI must consider how to share the responsibility for risk. For example, the pupil might say that they would like to practice something on their own, in which case you might simply tell them that you are happy to let them do that and all you will do is make sure that the car is kept safe. For example, the pupil might want to practice emerging from junctions independently after last week's lesson. You agree a fairly quiet route so that they can concentrate on the MSPSL routine approaching the junctions, getting the approach speed right and looking to see whether they are open or closed, as well as looking for gaps into which they can be properly be prepared to emerge safely. You agree on a period of time they can practice this for but you must allow them to do this independently whilst remaining alert and ready to step in with instructions or to operate the dual controls to keep the car safe if necessary.

Similarly, if the pupil has agreed that the goal for the lesson is the left reverse and that they will have achieved their goal if they can get the car into the new junction under control and with accuracy, then it may be agreed between you that you will keep a careful look out all around for other vehicles and pedestrians. In this way you are both sharing the responsibility for risk. The pupil will be able to concentrate on the control and accuracy aspects of the manoeuvre, whilst you will look after the safety aspect.

In both of these examples the risk is shared, agreed and understood by both the ADI and the pupil to ensure that they have the best possible chance of achieving their agreed goal.

Indications that all levels of competence are in place could include:

- Asking the pupil what is meant by risk.
- Asking the pupil what sort of issues create risk, such as the use of alcohol or drugs.
- Explaining clearly what is expected of the pupil and what the pupil can reasonably expect of the ADI/PDI.
- Checking that the pupil understands what is required of them when there is a change of plan or if they are asked to repeat an exercise.

Indications of a lack of competence include:

- Failing to address the issue of risk management.
- Giving incorrect guidance about where the responsibility lies for management of risk.
- Failing to explain how the dual controls will be used.
- Undermining the pupil's commitment to being safe and responsible, for example agreeing to risky attitudes towards speeding, alcohol abuse etc.
- Asking the pupil to repeat a manoeuvre or exercise without providing an understanding of the role the ADI/PDI will play.

Were directions and instructions given to the pupil clear and given in good time?

If your verbal directions and instructions are given clearly and in good time then you are managing the risk effectively and enabling the pupil to focus on achieving the agreed goal. In some lessons your pupil may want to practice independent driving and either choose the route for themselves, drive on a previous route without directions, or follow the signs for, say, "Anytown". This is perfectly acceptable and in such circumstances you would not be expected to give directions. However, you may still need to give instructions if the pupil becomes confused, if this is what has been agreed, or if a safety critical incident occurs. In these situations you must ensure that you are giving your instructions clearly and in good time. "Right, turn left here" is a confusing instruction! Instead, the trainer should have clearly stated "At the end of the road turn left" so as to avoid the pupil taking a wrong turning right, or turning into a private drive. Similarly, the timing of instructions and directions can be very distracting especially if given late. This can increase the risk of being involved in an accident because the pupil can become distracted, confused, and make mistakes.

Indications that all levels of competence are in place:

- Clear, concise directions.
- Ensuring that the pupil understands and agrees what they plan to do.
- Directions given at a suitable time so that the pupil can respond well.

Indications of a lack of competence include:

- Giving confused directions.
- Giving directions too late.
- Giving unnecessary directions.
- Failing to recognise when the ADI/PDI's input is causing overload or confusion.

Was the trainer aware of the surroundings and the pupil's actions?

Being able to observe the road ahead and behind as well as watching the pupil's eyes, hands and feet is essential for risk management. It is your responsibility to ensure that the pupil is able to safely deal with whatever presents itself on road, and to do this you have to be constantly assessing the whole of the surroundings and evaluating any risk factors that may affect you. For example:

The pupil has agreed that they would like to concentrate on dealing with 'meeting traffic' situations in a busy street. At the start of the lesson you have looked at the responsibility for risk and agreed that you will share the risk by ensuring that the pupil can focus on their goal whilst you manage any other hazards; on the route there is a toucan crossing which, at first glance on approach, looks safe. There is no need to mention the crossing because the pupil's goal is specifically adequate clearance to parked cars. However, if someone now walks or rides up to the crossing and presses the button to cross, there is now a potential safety critical incident and the examiner may well use the next 2 competency indicators to assess how effectively this risk is managed. Any serious lapses in awareness are likely to lead to a 0 mark.

Was any verbal or physical intervention by the trainer timely and appropriate?

It is not necessary to mention the toucan crossing if the pupil appears to be happily dealing with it and there is clearly no risk (unless pedestrian crossings are part of the goal for the session, or perhaps the pupil has particularly said that they want to be alerted to hazards outside of their main goal).

Many ADIs/PDIs don't fully understand how people learn and frequently disrupt their pupil's learning by giving partly-trained instruction. In many situations the learner will achieve far more understanding about how to apply their driving skills and assess the risks involved if they can carry out the task in silence; this raises their awareness of both their personal strengths and limitations and thus builds their responsibility. The use of constant verbal instruction whilst the car is moving can lead to confusion and frustration through sensory overload. Consequently, this overload (or over-instruction) can actually result in increased risk. Nevertheless, if you do need to intervene to keep the car safe then it really doesn't matter if there has been sensory overload.

So, in the example cited above where a pedestrian or cyclist approaches the crossing, you must now assess whether you will need to step in and take control in some way. There are 4 possible options to choose from:

1. There is no need to do anything. The pupil has already checked their mirror and eased off the gas in case the lights change.
2. The pupil has made no response and the lights have started to change. You need to say something and a timely Q&A may mean the pupil keeping responsibility for a little longer. You could ask

"Do you think you need to slow down for the lights ahead?" This is a leading question which demands action.

3. You decide to wait a little longer to see what response you get from your pupil. Interfering too early may compromise achievement of their goal – meeting traffic. However, if it becomes clear that the pupil is not responding then a direct instruction is necessary: "Slow down for the lights!"

4. You decided not to give any verbal instruction and must now take physical action. The lights have turned red, a pedestrian is crossing the road, and the pupil is not responding. You stop the car using the dual controls.

Indications that all levels of competence are in place could include:

- Intervening in a way that actively supports the pupil's learning process and safety during the session.
- Allowing the pupil to deal with the situations appropriately.
- Taking control of a situation where a pupil is clearly out of their depth.

Indications of a lack of competence include:

- Ignoring a developing situation and allowing the pupil to flounder.
- Taking control of a situation where the pupil is clearly dealing with it appropriately.
- Constantly intervening when unnecessary.

Was sufficient feedback given to help the pupil understand any potential safety critical incidents?

In each of the situations described above you must now decide how much feedback to give to the pupil. If, as in option 4 you have had to use the dual controls, it will probably be necessary to ensure that the pupil understands that you have taken action, reassure them, and ask if they are okay to continue until it is safe to pull up and discuss what has happened. In options 1 and 2 (and possibly 3) above, it may well be sufficient to continue with the agreed route and discuss the potential safety critical incident (the toucan crossing incident) as part of your lesson debrief on the main goal for the lesson, which was 'meeting traffic'.

Whatever the safety critical, or potentially safety critical situation that has occurred, it is vital that the pupil fully understands what has happened and how it could have been dealt with or avoided altogether.

Ideally the pupil should be supported to analyse the situation for themselves. However, feedback is necessary where, for instance, the pupil failed to identify the particular problem, and in those circumstances that feedback needs to be provided as soon as possible after the incident.

Indications that all levels of competence are in place include:

- Finding a safe place to stop and examine the safety critical incident.
- Allowing the pupil time to express any fears or concerns that the incident may have caused.
- Supporting the pupil to reflect in a clear and logical way about what happened.
- Providing input to clarify aspects of the incident that the pupil does not understand.
- Support the pupil to identify strategies for future situations.
- Providing input where the pupil does not understand what they should do differently.
- Checking that the pupil feels able to put the strategy in place.
- Agreeing ways of developing the competence if the pupil feels the need.

Indications of a lack of competence include:

- Failing to examine the incident.
- Taking too long to address issues generated by an incident.
- Not allowing the pupil to explore their own understanding.
- Telling the pupil what the solution is and failing to check their understanding.
- Failing to check the pupil's ability to put in place the agreed strategy.

Teaching and learning strategies

It is important to remember when considering your teaching style that this is not just about coaching. We are talking client-centred learning here. The DVSA are looking to see whether the ADI/PDI is helping the pupil to learn in an active way.

There are many times when a coaching technique will prove both useful and effective. The principle that underpins coaching is that an engaged pupil is likely to achieve a higher level of understanding and that self-directed solutions will prove to be far more relevant and effective.

Another way of looking at this (aside from jargon such as 'client-centred' or 'coaching') is to ask yourself whether or not you are **involving** the pupil in the learning process; if you do not ask them, for instance, what they know or how they feel about a particular subject, then how do you know what they already know or feel? You could easily be making some assumptions that are completely wrong and therefore, instead of involving the pupil, you are inadvertently erecting a barrier between you and them. This applies in every situation, including instruction. Direct instruction helps a pupil in early stages of their learning to cope with new situations as well as a struggle in a particular situation. Good coaching uses the correct technique at the correct time to match the pupil's needs. An ADI/PDI may sometimes need to give direct instruction through a difficult situation and that instruction forms part of the coaching process so long as the ADI/PDI encourages the pupil to analyse the problem and learn from it; thus it follows that a good ADI takes every opportunity to reinforce learning.

Was the teaching and learning style suited for the pupil's level of ability?

Every pupil is different and the trainer should understand their own pupil and how they prefer to be taught. This may take a few lessons to establish because some pupils may prefer the active way of teaching, whilst others wish to have the opportunity to reflect before taking the next step in their learning. The trainer should be able to make a judgmental response to their pupil's sensitivity and be able to adapt their approach if evidence emerges of a different preferred style.

Think back to your own school days. Did you have a favourite teacher or subject? What about teachers and subjects that you disliked? Why was this? Was it because some teachers just lectured to pupils whilst others 'involved' their pupils in the lessons much more? Think carefully about that! Learning cannot be forced on a pupil, and progress should be determined by what the pupil is comfortable with. There is a skill to recognising when a pupil stops learning, and the pace of a lesson needs to be determined by the pupil. At the same time, a pupil shouldn't be discouraged from experimenting (within safe bounds, of course!)

When coaching, the trainer should ensure that their method is suitable for the pupil. If a Q&A technique is used then match it to the level of the pupil's level of ability and encourage them to use a higher level of thought to give a response. Closed questions used with a pupil demonstrating a high level of ability are unlikely to be of much use unless, for example, you are checking knowledge. On the other hand, asking open questions of a pupil with limited ability who is struggling to achieve the set task for themselves may only serve to confuse and thereby have a negative effect. There are no hard and fast rules here. The ADI/PDI should be able to judge which method is the most effective to use in particular circumstances. Try experimenting with the way you teach in the car; try and be creative and consider whether your pupil is engaged in the lesson or is bored and 'switched off'.

Indications that all competencies are in place could include:

- Actively working to understand how they can best support the pupil's learning process (they might not achieve a full understanding during the lesson – it's the attempt that demonstrates competence).
- Modifying their teaching and method when, or if, they realise there is a need to do so.
- Providing accurate and technically correct instruction, information or demonstration (giving technically incorrect information or instruction is an automatic fail if it is likely to lead to a safety critical situation).
- Using practical examples and other similar tools to provide different angles to look at a particular subject.
- Linking learning in theory to learning in practice.
- Encouraging and helping the pupil to take ownership of the learning process.
- Responding to faults in a timely manner.
- Providing sufficient uninterrupted time to practice new skills.
- Providing the pupil with clear guidelines on how they might practise outside the lesson.

Indications of a lack of competence include:

- Adopting a teaching style which is clearly at odds with the pupil's learning style.
- Failing to check with the pupil if the approach they are taking is acceptable to the pupil.
- Failing to explore other ways of addressing a particular learning point if the initial method is not achieving the desired result.
- Concentrating on delivering their teaching tools instead of looking for learning outcomes.
- Ignoring safety issues.

Was the pupil encouraged to analyse problems and take responsibility for their learning?

This is a key part of the client-centred approach, and is basically the development of active problem solving by the pupil. The trainer needs to provide time for this to happen and therefore has to stop talking long enough for the pupil to do the work! However, the key thing to remember is that different pupils will respond to the invitation in different ways. Some can do it instantly following discussion, other may need to go away and have time to reflect upon a particular problem. You may need to point them toward the issue e.g. reading up the appropriate section of the Highway Code or another reading source in order to help them to get to grips with the problem. Pushing a pupil to come up with an immediate answer, on the spot, may prove unproductive.

At the same time, simple errors may occur and if the pupil knows what they have done and why, there is no need to push them on such a point. For example, they may have just stalled because they wrongly tried to pull away in 3rd gear. The pupil realises their error, quickly engages 1st gear and pulls away successfully. There is no need to mention this unless they repeatedly make the same mistake because, for instance, they are failing to use the palming method.

There is an expectation that instructors will encourage learners to reflect on situations that happen and consider how they can apply the skills they are learning now to use them after passing their test when driving solo. They may also need to reflect on what are currently unfamiliar situations that may prompt distractions, such as driving at night or carrying passengers.

Indications that all competencies are in place could include:

- Providing time, in a suitable location, to explore any problems or issues that arose during the lesson or were raised by the pupil.
- Providing timely opportunities for analysis, in the case of safety critical incidents these should be as prompt as possible.
- Taking time and using suitable techniques to understand any problems the pupil had with understanding a particular issue.
- Suggesting suitable strategies to help the pupil develop their understanding, such as practical examples or pointing them toward further reading.
- Giving clear and accurate information to fill the gaps in a pupil's knowledge or understanding.
- Leaving the pupil feeling responsible for their own learning situation.

Indications of a lack of competence include:

- Leaving the pupil feeling that the ADI/PDI was in control of the teaching process.
- Failing to explore alternative ways of addressing a problem – in response of evidence of different learning preferences.
- Providing unsuitable or incorrect inputs.

Were opportunities and examples used to clarify learning outcomes?

Whilst training in technique is core to the learning process it is important to reinforce this input and link it to theory. The best way of achieving this is to use real world situations in a lesson. Every lesson will provide plenty of opportunities for this. The use of practical examples where possible, or scenarios, gives the pupil a much better understanding of when, how and why to use a particular technique. For instance, the skills required for planning and anticipation can be developed in many situations. A goal may have been set to deal with roundabouts but the skills involved in both planning and anticipation can also be developed when dealing with a meeting situation or an area where there are many pedestrians about during the same lesson.

Indications that all competencies are in place could include:

- Using examples identified during a lesson in a suitable way at a suitable time to confirm or reinforce understanding.
- Exploring different ways in which to use examples that best respond to differences in the pupil's preferred way of learning.
- Using examples that match the pupil's ability and experience to understand.
- Recognising that some pupils are able to respond instantly, whereas others need time to think about an issue.

Indications of a lack of competence include:

- Using examples that the pupil doesn't understand because of their lack of experience.
- Using complex examples that the pupil doesn't have the ability to respond to.
- Failing to provide the pupil with time to think through issues and come to their own conclusion.
- Imposing an interpretation.

Was the technical information given comprehensive, appropriate and accurate?

As mentioned previously, giving incorrect or insufficient information, with the result that a safety critical situation may occur, will result in an automatic fail. It should be remembered that good information is:

- Accurate.
- Relevant.
- Timely.

Failure to meet any one of these criteria makes the others redundant.

Trainers will recognise that nearly every lesson requires some technical input from them to either help a pupil solve a problem or to fill a gap in knowledge. This input must be accurate and appropriate. If a pupil keeps making the same error it is insufficient to just keep on telling them that they are doing something wrong. The trainer's input needs to be comprehensive to help them overcome the problem. Any practical demonstration of technique must be both clear and suitable. The pupil must be engaged during the demo and encouraged to explore their understanding of what is being shown. Information given needs to be helpful. For example, continually telling a pupil what to do without giving them an opportunity to take responsibility. Unclear or misleading advice should be avoided. Comments such as "you're a bit close to those parked cars" could be used to introduce coaching on a weakness, but are of little benefit on their own as they are unclear. How close is "a bit" and is it significant?

Indications that all competencies are in place could include:

- Giving clear, timely and technically accurate explanations or demonstrations.
- Checking understanding and, if necessary, repeating the explanation or demonstration.
- Finding a different way to explain or demonstrate if the pupil still doesn't understand.

Indications of a lack of competence include:

- Providing inaccurate or unclear information, too late or too early in the learning process.
- Failing to check understanding.
- Failing to explore alternative ways of presenting information where the pupil doesn't understand the first offering.

Was the pupil given appropriate and timely feedback during the session?

Feedback is an essential part of the learning. Pupils need to have a clear idea of how they are performing in relation to their learning objectives throughout the lesson. When they are doing well they should be encouraged, and coached when a problem or learning opportunity occurs. However, constantly talking at an unsuitable time may prove demotivating or even dangerous. Sitting quietly and letting them get on with it can also be powerful feedback at times in an appropriate situation.

All feedback should be relevant, positive and honest. It is unhelpful to provide feedback that is unrealistic as it gives the pupil a false sense of their own ability. Try not to give negative feedback. Weaknesses should be expressed as learning opportunities. However, if something is wrong or dangerous, do not waffle – tell them! The pupil should have a realistic sense of their own performance.

Feedback should be two-way. In an ideal world the ADI/PDI should respond to comments and questions by the pupil. Feedback should never be overlooked or disregarded.

Indications that all competencies are in place could include:

- Providing feedback in response to questions from pupil.
- Seeking appropriate opportunities to provide feedback that reinforces understanding or confirms achievement of learning objectives.
- Providing feedback about failure to achieve learning objectives that help the pupil achieve understanding of what they need to improve.
- Providing feedback that the pupil can understand.
- Providing consistent feedback that is reinforced by body language.

Indications of a lack of competence include:

- Providing feedback so long after an incident that the pupil cannot remember what actually happened.
- Providing feedback that overlooks a safety critical incident.
- Providing continuous feedback that may be distracting the pupil.
- Failure to check the pupil's understanding of the feedback.
- Providing feedback that is irrelevant to the pupil's learning objectives.
- Refusing to listen to feedback on the ADI/PDIs own performance.

Was the pupil encouraged to ask questions and were these queries followed up and answered?

Direct questions by the pupil need dealing with as soon as possible. The ADI/PDI may give information or direct the pupil to another source. Wherever possible the pupil should be encouraged to discover answers for themselves but if the ADI/PDI does give information then they must check that the pupil understands the information provided. Pupils don't always have the confidence to ask direct questions. In these cases the ADI/PDI should be able to pick up on comments or body language that indicate uncertainty or confusion and be flexible enough to use different ways to tease out possible issues.

Sometimes a pupil may ask a question at an inappropriate time, for instance when dealing with a busy junction. A good response might be to say "Good question, I'll deal with that in a few minutes when we can pull up to the roadside."

Indications that all competencies are in place could include:

- Responding openly and readily to queries.
- Providing helpful answers or directing the pupil to suitable sources of information.
- Actively checking with pupils if their comments or body language suggest that they may have a question.
- Encouraging the pupil to explore possible solutions for themselves.

Indications of a lack of competence include:

- A refusal to respond to queries.
- Providing inaccurate information in response to queries.
- Avoiding the question or denying responsibility for answering it.

Did the trainer maintain an appropriate non-discriminatory manner throughout the session?

The trainer should maintain an atmosphere in which the pupil feels free to express their opinions. An open, friendly environment for learning should be created regardless of the pupil's age, gender, sexual orientation, ethnic background, religion, physical abilities or any other irrelevant factor. This implies respect for the pupil, their values and what constitutes appropriate behaviour in their culture. The trainer must not display inappropriate attitudes or behaviour toward other road users and should challenge the pupil if they display such behaviour.

A pupil may be a slow learner and lead to the trainer feeling frustrated or impatient because they are not picking up the skills being taught. Remaining non-discriminatory and non-judgmental encourages the trainer to consider a different approach, which may be required to achieve the learning goals.

Indications that all competencies are in place could include:

- Keeping a respectful distance and not invading the pupil's personal space.
- Asking the pupil how they wish to be addressed.
- Asking a disabled driver what the ADI/PDI should know about their condition so that they can best adapt their teaching style for the pupil.
- Adopting an appropriate position in the car.
- Using language about other road users that is not derogatory and that does not invite the pupil to collude with any discriminatory attitude.

Indications of a lack of competence include:

- Invading someone's physical space.
- Touching the pupil (including trying to shake hands) unless it is necessary for road safety reasons.
- Using someone's first name unless they have said it's acceptable.
- Commenting on a pupil's appearance or any other personal attribute unless it has a direct impact on their ability to drive safely (e.g. wearing footwear that makes it difficult to operate the foot pedals properly).

At the end of the session, was the pupil encouraged to reflect on their own performance?

At the end of the lesson the pupil should be encouraged to reflect on their performance and discuss their feelings with the trainer. Reflecting on one's own performance helps to embed learning and clarify whether the learning goal has been achieved. This also helps to develop self-evaluation skills and the ability to recognise one's own strengths and weaknesses. If you think about that statement, how essential is that to ensure that the pupil is able to reduce their own risk when driving on their own after passing their test?

The ADI/PDI should encourage honest self-appraisal and use client-centred techniques to highlight the areas that need development if the pupil has failed to recognise them. Once development areas have been identified the pupil should be encouraged to make them part of future development. You could, for example, ask the pupil to tell you 3 things that they were pleased with during that lesson. Ask them why that was, and encourage them to think along the same lines and ask what else they would like to develop, thereby setting goals for the next lesson.

Examiner's review

In most situations an ADI/PDI will maintain their awareness of all that is going in around them and thus be able to give clear and timely directions and be able to intervene in an appropriate way to ensure that no safety critical incident occurs. Their instruction may have its shortcomings but it is safe. However, from time to time situations will arise in which their action or instruction is of such poor quality that the examiner may decide that they are putting themselves, the pupil or any other third party in immediate danger.

For example: The pupil is approaching a closed junction. They ask the trainer whether they should stop at the give way line. The trainer is unable to see down the joining roads, but nevertheless tells the pupil to "go, go, go!"

In these or similarly dangerous situations the examiner would be entitled to stop the lesson and mark it as an immediate fail.

(ADI) part 3 summary

DURATION OF TEST	1 HR (approx.)
COST OF TEST	£111 PER ATTEMPT (as of Sept 2018)
NUMBER OF ATTEMPTS ALLOWED	3
PASS MARK	31
	Minimum of 8 in risk management
ABOUT PART 3	www.gov.uk/adi-part-3-test
UP-TO-DATE FEES	www.gov.uk/approved-driving-instructor-adi-fees
DVSA CUSTOMER SUPPORT	0300 200 1122 (Mon–Fri 8am–4pm)
BOOK PART 3 TEST	www.gov.uk/booking-driving-test

Chapter 5

LESSON PLANS AND TOPICS

In this section we will be exploring in greater detail how lessons should be structured. The topics will include lessons from the very first basic controls lesson to the complexities of manoeuvering, positioning and the meeting of other road users as you steer your pupils toward test standard and beyond.

Controls lesson

This will be the first time that you will have met your pupil so an eyesight and licence check will be required. Carry these out after you have introduced yourself, but before you drive your pupil to a suitable location for their first lesson as it is not unusual for pupils to leave their licence and glasses (or both!) in their house. As a recap, the requirements for eyesight are as follows:

- Minimum distance is 20 metres (65.5 feet) for new-style plates.
- Minimum distance is 20.5 metres (67.25 feet) for old-style plates.

A licence check can be carried out at www.gov.uk/view-driving-licence.

For new drivers the first lesson you will be carrying out will be a controls lesson. At this stage your pupil is unknown to you as is their history. We covered 'first impressions' in the lesson structure chapter, so take another look at it and always try to make the best first impression that you can.

The likelihood is that you will be driving to a suitable location (a quiet road) for the first lesson. This first meeting is the best

opportunity to get to know your pupil, so on the drive to the site use the time to establish a good rapport. You should be asking them about any previous driving history; this could include knowledge of the Highway Code as a result of having driven a scooter, for example, and will also mean they have dealt with other road users before. It would be a mistake to drive to the site in silence. Imagine how your pupil may be feeling at this time and indeed how they have felt prior to your arrival for this first lesson. At the very least, they will probably be feeling nervous excitement; a silent drive to the site will almost certainly expel that excitement and rack up the nerves to an uncomfortable level.

Conversing with your pupil should help to reduce their nerves, and will certainly increase their comfort in your presence. Always keep in mind that it is quite likely that you will be working with this person on a one to one basis for the next few months; instructors who tend to lose pupils early on probably didn't use these early lessons well enough to sell themselves. Who would want to spend months in a confined space with a misery guts, and have to pay for the privilege?

Use this first lesson wisely, and talk to your pupil about their hopes and desires for their driving life, which is about to commence on arrival at this first location. Most people are most comfortable talking about themselves so this is your chance to discover their expectations, hopes, attitude and dedication to their driving. Invest in it with them as much as you can!

On arrival at your chosen location it is time to get your pupil into the driving seat for the first time. Swap over at the back of the car so that you are both facing oncoming traffic once you are out of the car. When your pupil gets into the car tell them not to touch any of the controls and make sure that the ignition keys are in your possession when you swap seats. If you have established from the pupil any previous driving knowledge you will already know at what level to pitch the lesson. The majority of pupils will probably not have prior knowledge but it is worthy of note that some people may have already ridden scooters or motorbikes, whilst others could have driven vehicles on farms or private land; a proportion may have driven cars illegally, assisted a friend or parent who is a mechanic and therefore have knowledge of the workings of a vehicle. Never assume. Always ask, and deliver a suitable lesson.

Handbrake
Since safety is the most important aspect of any lesson, the first check to carry out is ensuring that the handbrake is fully secured for the manual variety, and switched on for the electronic variety.

Doors
The doors need to be closed and secured when driving. It is good to point out to your pupil at this stage that it is the driver who is responsible for the car even though you will be providing full supervision. There are various ways of checking that the doors are secure – the rattle of a partially open door, the interior light remaining on, an audible warning, a warning light on the instrument panel and a break in the symmetry down the side of the car. Ensure that your pupil knows how to look for each of these and that they understand the risks of driving without securing doors.

You should also show pupils how to open a door safely so that it does not blow open in the wind. This may sound a little ridiculous to them but once you explain the implications of striking a pedestrian or passing vehicle they should realise the importance of this issue. Show the pupil what observation precautions to take when opening the passenger door at the side of the footpath and opening the driver's door at the roadside.

Seat

It is most likely that the seat will need to be adjusted when you swap with your pupil, but even if they are the same height and size as you, it is important that you still cover this aspect in detail since they will require the knowledge at some point. Explain how to adjust the height (eye level half way up the windscreen) and the position relative to the pedals (with the clutch pushed down there should still be a slight bend in the left knee). Explain how to adjust the seat back so that all the controls can be comfortably reached, and advise how to adjust the head restraint and it's function.

Steering wheel

These days, most cars have an adjustable steering wheel, so explain to your pupil how this works so that they can set the wheel to a comfortable position at approximately 'ten to two'; this way their hands are balanced on the wheel and this gives them the ability to steer equally both to the left and the right. With power steering it is very easy to steer the wheel and it is therefore easy for pupils to develop their own individual style of driving.

On test, examiners are more focused on the outcome rather than the delivery and they will not be over-critical of individual steering styles. However, for safety reasons of balanced steering, the ten to two position should be strongly promoted alongside a push-pull method of steering. This should be explained and demonstrated if required. Ensure that, when the steering wheel has been set in place, the instrument displays are fully visible.

Seatbelt

It is highly likely that your pupil will have used a seatbelt as a passenger on many occasions. Therefore, using a client-centred approach, pitch your level of instruction to suit the pupil's experience. Get them to explain how they put their seatbelt on and what precautions should be taken. Watch and listen to the answers filling in any missing gaps, ensuring the pupil secures it in the correct side that it's not twisted and it fits correctly across the shoulder and waist. For safety reasons, before moving off, check that the mechanism will release and then reapply the seatbelt.

Mirrors

When the seat is correctly set up the mirrors can then be adjusted. Do not adjust the mirrors first as when the seat is then adjusted the mirrors will be out of position. Mirrors are used frequently when driving and it therefore essential that your pupil is shown how to set them correctly along with an explanation of the different types of glass. Firstly, get your pupil to look out of the rear windscreen over their left shoulder to see what the view looks like, then get them to look in the rearview mirror; the size and distance of objects behind the car should be the same and you can explain that this is because they are looking at flat glass and that his mirror should always be used first. Then, you can get them to look in the two door mirrors (resist the temptation to refer to these as 'wing mirrors' – they went out of service in the 1970s!) and describe to you how this view differs from the one in the interior mirror. The door mirrors are convex. Explain what this is to your pupil, adding how important it is to not use these mirrors first as it is easy to misjudge the distance and speed of approaching vehicles.

Once the mirrors have been set up, explain the location of the 'blind spots', particularly the roadside one. Get your pupil to look over their right shoulder and compare that view to what they can see in the offside door mirror. Explain to them the associated safety implications of the differences.

You should explain to your pupil how the M-S-M (mirror-signal-manoeuvre) routine should be used, and when, i.e.:

- When moving off from the side of the road.
- When slowing down, stopping and pulling in at the side of the road.
- When signalling.
- When changing direction.

Foot controls
Ask your pupil what they know about the 3 pedals and work with them and their existing knowledge. Quite a few new learners are aware of the reverse ABC for accelerator, brake and clutch where, when looking at the pedals, they are laid out CBA.

Accelerator – show your pupil which pedal this is and which foot to use to control it. Explain that you will be calling it the gas pedal ('gas' as an abbreviation of the word gasoline) because it is shorter and easier to call it gas rather than accelerator when you are giving instructions on the move where time is important. The pedal should be used lightly. The further the pedal is pressed, the more fuel goes into the engine and, when in gear, this will make the car accelerate. Releasing pressure on the gas pedal will have the opposite effect of slowing the car down. Safety is crucial, so the pedal should be used with care. Allow your pupil to practice using the pedal so that they can get a feel for its use.

Remember as a teaching style:

- I hear and I forget (tell).
- I see and I remember (diagrams).
- I do and I understand (practice).

Brake – Once again, run through the purpose of the pedal and how to use it. Allow your pupil to practice pivoting their right foot between the gas and brake pedals with their right heel secure on the floor. Advise your pupil that at slow speeds such as will be used on their first lesson, only light brake pressure will be required, but at higher speeds more pressure, progressively applied, will be required. It is quite likely that the pupil will use the brake too firmly when they use it on the move for the first time. Getting a bit creative with images is an excellent way of working with new learners, so for a first move off and stop, for example, when stopping get them to imagine that they are resting their foot on a balloon and to gently squeeze it. That is all the pressure needed to slow at slow speed.

The footbrake works on all 4 wheels to slow the car down. When applied, the brake lights come on. This way your pupil can use the brake light to control the following traffic. When driving at normal speeds use 3-pressure braking when slowing the car or stopping it:

1. First pressure braking involves coming off the gas pedal which will allow the car to slow. Apply light pressure to the brake pedal to illuminate the brake lights and start to manage the following vehicles with the aim of bringing their speed down as well.

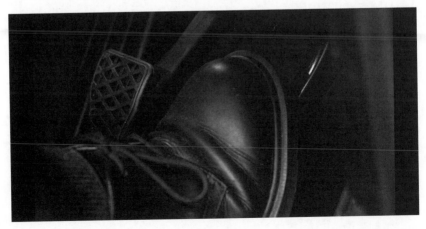

2. Second pressure braking is firmer and progressive and this stage is where your pupil will get the majority of the speed off.

3. As the second pressure braking brings the car towards a stop, so the third pressure braking is about releasing most of the brake pressure, using a small amount of braking in order to remove the remaining speed until the vehicle stops smoothly.

Clutch – Probably the most challenging of the 3 pedals for a learner driver! Explaining the function and operation of the clutch can be complex and technical but does need to be done. Try to keep your explanation relatively simple to avoid confusion and creating apprehension for your pupil. A good diagram as a visual training aid can simplify what could be a very complicated verbal explanation, so keep it simple where you can. Your pupil will need to know that the

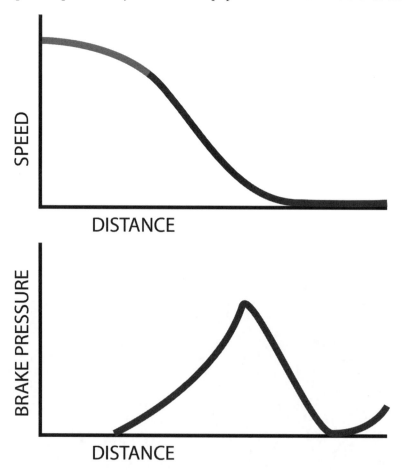

main purpose of the clutch is to connect the engine to the road wheels via the gearbox and needs to be used when setting off, stopping and changing gears and is operated using the left foot. Unless they express an interest in it, they don't necessarily need to know all the science behind it! You should explain to them the correct use of the pedal i.e. use the toe and ball of the foot to operate the pedal (a good image to assist with understanding of this is to ask them to imagine standing on their tiptoes – the part of their foot still on the ground is the ball of the foot). If your pupil uses the instep of their foot for this procedure then 2 things will happen:

1. They will not have full control of the clutch and will probably stall the vehicle frequently.
2. They are likely to catch their foot on the top of the plastic pedal box.

Practice is definitely the best way to understand how the clutch feels and works, and to develop use of the clutch until it is a smooth process. When changing gear, pause momentarily as the clutch engages during gear changes. The clutch can also be used to control low speed manoeuvering.

Gears

As part of the controls lesson, discuss the use of the gears explaining the layout that is relevant to the car you are teaching in. Explain neutral and the various techniques for working the positions of the gear lever. Diagrams of the gear layout will also assist the pupil in gaining a good understanding of the use of the gears. A 'palming' technique with the thumb down will be will be used for working against the spring-loading for gears 1 and 2, whilst a thumb up position is used to move to the higher number on the gear box. How to select reverse gear varies considerably depending upon the car manufacturer, so make sure that your pupil is fully aware of where all the gears are and how to select them before getting on the move. Allow them to move up and down the box, and remember that on the move they may well need to 'block change' from, say, gear 4 to gear 2 after several lessons, so show them this process too.

Horn

The horn should be operated using the hand rather than fingers in order to ensure sufficient pressure is applied to sound the horn the instant it is pressed. Demonstrate this for your pupil and allow them to practice as well. Explain what the horn should be used for. It is a warning instrument to make other road users aware of your presence on the road. It is NOT there for rebuking other road users and therefore should be used before an incident, not afterwards. Advise your pupil of the legality around when it can and cannot be used. If the area you are in is suitable, and the time is legal, then get the pupil to practice. It is important that pupils do not feel self-conscious about using the horn as this could put them at risk when driving.

Indicators

As with the other controls, you need to explain to your pupil how the indicators operate and be sure to let them practice their use. A lot of indicators these days have a nudge facility for use when lane changing where you just get 3 flashes of the indicator lights. Show your pupil how to press the stalk firmly so that the indicator stays on. Quite a lot of people have issues with left and right! When sitting at the side of the road it can be easy to identify left and right, but on the move, when there are many things to think about approaching a junction, any left/right issues will manifest themselves. You will need to find a polite and comfortable way of addressing this matter, as you need to be aware that at the start of teaching your pupil and not in the 'heat of battle', and one of the best ways to overcome it is to explain to your pupil that the stalk is pushed the same way as you steer and with an extended left finger.

Ancillary controls

There are a few other controls that need to be discussed and used in the future. These would include windscreen wipers and washers, demisters, heating controls, electric windows, the radio, and fog lights. So as not to overload your pupil on this first lesson, these ancillary controls can be explained as and when needed.

Common pupil errors

Now seems a good time to see the most common errors made by pupils at this stage of their learning, and it serves as a timely reminder of how important this first lesson is to instill in the pupil the foundations to their driving career.

- Failing to check blind spot before opening door.
- Walking around the front of the car, instead of the rear.
- Not closing the door.

- Failing to properly adjust the driver's seat to the correct position.
- Failing to properly adjust the head restraint to the correct position.
- Looking down at the pedals.
- Using the wrong feet on the pedals.
- Pressing the wheel arch instead of the gas pedal.
- Moving head/body whilst adjusting mirrors.
- Using both hands instead of just the left one to adjust the interior mirror.
- Putting fingers onto mirror glass.
- Changing into wrong gear – usually because 'palming' method not used.
- Fiddling with controls and car keys.
- Trying to turn the steering wheel when stationary.

Move off and stop (including mirrors and signals)

Having completed the controls lesson, it is time to get your pupil on the move for the first time. There are 2 key areas here:

- Moving off.
- Pulling in and stopping.

Make sure that you cover *both* of these areas on the briefing; getting your pupil on the move is *not* the time to realise that you haven't briefed them on how to get back to the kerb!

Initially you will need to establish any previous knowledge your pupil has on the subject such as, has your pupil moved off and stopped before? This information will be established during the RECAP.

Recap

During this part of the lesson make sure that you ask open questions to check any understanding of the subject. For example:

- What do you understand by the mirror-signal-manoeuvre (M-S-M) routine, and how would you apply it?
- Explain to me how you would use the 3 foot controls.
- When would a signal be necessary, and why would it be required?
- What is a blind spot and why is it essential to check it before moving off?

Objective

At this stage it is important to establish what the pupil wants to get out of the lesson. If the pupil is not sure what they want (as is often the case at this early stage) then you will have to tell the pupil what the lesson objectives are, but make sure that you get agreement and buy in from the pupil as this is their lesson.

Scaling is a good tool to use at this stage as it will establish a base point, and also can be used at the end of the lesson to see where the pupil thinks they are and what progress they have made. A typical question here would be:

'On a scale of 1–10 where 1 is the lowest level of knowledge, what score would you give yourself on your understanding of today's lesson. At the end of the lesson, what level would you like to have achieved?'

Briefing

If the pupil has previous experience, established through the recap, then the briefing session will involve more Q&A so that you use the skills that the learner already possesses allowing them to take some degree of ownership of their learning. If the subject is new, then guided instructions will be required following the briefing. The purpose of the briefing is to make sure that you can run through the lesson with the pupil before they actually drive. This allows you to check understanding and your pupil to ask questions. The briefing is, in essence, an overview of the lesson about to be taken.

Keep the briefing simple in nature and follow bullet points with a diagram. If you simply talk to your pupil then it is likely that they will forget, but if you use diagrams and ask good questions, then your pupil sees and starts to learn. By the time the briefing has finished your pupil should understand how to use the mirror, signals, observations, reference points, stopping position, and how to secure the car. Now is the time to assess the risk and get on the move.

Risk

During the briefing session and prior to the practical session, risk should be discussed to ensure a safe lesson and establish how the risk will be shared and handled between you, the driving instructor, and your pupil. Initially, this would include asking the pupil what they understand about the word 'risk', their definition of the word. People think in different ways and one person's definition of risk may be completely different from another's.

An early appreciation of the potential risks involved in moving off and stopping is required for safe driving. This is an excellent time for your pupil to understand that too often it is the other road users that can be the problem. The first time a pupil actually drives they are usually fully focused on themselves and the car, and without any real awareness of everyone else.

The risk, once established, needs to be shared out so that you and your pupil both know what to expect from each other. Naturally, at this stage, you will take on most of the risk, but not all of it. So, what risk should a new learner take on board when driving for the very first time? Well, they need to commit to listen to you, wait for instructions before doing anything, and not to do anything rashly. Make sure that your pupil understands what is required of them before they actually drive.

Practice
Always ask the pupil what help they would need from you. Their response will determine where the lesson goes next:

For a pupil with previous knowledge – Questions and guided instruction should be used to cover the preparation of the vehicle prior to moving off, such as setting the gas, practicing finding the biting point with the clutch, the decision as to whether to use an indicator when moving off, the use of the parking brake and all-round and effective observation to include the key area of blind spots. To check the blind spot of what can and cannot be seen, look over your offside shoulder and pick an object just behind the car that the learner cannot see in their door mirror but will once they have checked their blind spot. A driveway would be an ideal object to choose because of the obvious risk potential of emerging vehicles.

For a pupil with previous experience – For this pupil you will need to talk or guide them through the process of moving off and stopping. The recap will already have established what the pupil remembered but, more importantly, understood from the controls lesson.

Talk them through, and let them practice the following:

- What the M-S-M routine is.
- How to prepare the car – gear selection, setting the gas, finding and practicing the biting point.
- How to make all-round and effective observation using mirrors and blind spot,and confirm understanding of the different glass (flat or convex).
- Consider the use of a signal.

- How to move off away from the side of the road.
- Steering and road positioning.
- Use of gears appropriate for the lesson.
- Use of mirrors on the move.
- Using the M-S-M routine to pull in in a safe, convenient and legal place.

A full talk through would be needed with a new pupil where you, as the driving instructor, would have taken on most of the risk during the drive as previously discussed. As the lesson progresses, then the level of instruction can develop from guided instruction to prompted (by use of Q&A).

Examples of guided instruction would include the following:

- 'Apply gentle pressure with your right foot. Set the gas around 1200 revs and keep your right foot still'
- 'Lift your clutch the thickness of a pound coin at a time (show this measurement) until you reach the biting point (previously described) and then keep your left foot still'
- 'As you are about to move off, check over your roadside blind spot for anything you haven't seen in your offside door mirror, such as a cyclist'
- (When pulling in at the side of the road) 'Off gas, cover the footbrake and clutch. Gently brake with light pressure, clutch down and continue to brake gently to a stop'

All of the above instructions are examples of the type of words to use. When carrying out a move off and stop lesson, additional instructions would of course be required. Road positioning would be set with your guidance and once the car is in the correct road position the pupil can then set reference points on the front windscreen and thereby assist them in future lessons to attain the ideal road position. Remember, though, that whilst *you* let the pupil know where to position the car, it is the pupil who sets the reference point. You cannot set the reference points for them as they are personal to the pupil since those points change depending on the height of the driver and therefore their seating position.

As the lesson progresses you can test your pupil's knowledge by asking them questions to check what they have remembered and, more importantly, that they understand why they are doing certain things. This is prompted tuition.

Examples of prompted tuition questions would include:

- 'When setting off, what level of gas is needed and why would this be required?'
- 'Why is it important to keep your left foot still once you have got the biting point?'
- 'Where would your final observations be when leaving the side of the road, and what are you looking for?'
- 'What is the normal driving position, and what reference point would you use to find it?'
- 'When pulling in at the side of the road, at what point would you put the clutch down and why?'

Again, these are purely examples of questions to ask.

If your pupil progresses to the point where they are capable of carrying out an aspect of driving themselves then make sure that there is agreement between you and them by asking e.g. 'Would you feel confident trying this yourself now?' If the answer is yes, then you could also ask them to talk you through what they are doing in order that you can hear what they are thinking as they perform the task. Remember, however, that a pupil may tell you that they cannot talk and drive at the same time at this stage. This is fine, and you should assure them of that, and if so you can just watch what they are doing.

Common pupil errors

Again, it is worthwhile to look at the most common errors made by pupils when carrying out the moving off and stopping process and thereby reinforce the need for effective tuition to eliminate these:

- Not checking blind spots.
- Selecting 3rd instead of 1st gear.
- Setting gas – too much or too little.
- Trouble finding the biting point.
- Lifting both gas and clutch together.
- Paying little regard for approaching traffic.
- Failing to signal when necessary.
- Signalling the wrong way or not at all when they should.
- Jerky clutch and/or gas control.
- Looking at controls or bonnet instead of road ahead.
- Failing to use M-S-M on the move.
- Forgetting to put the clutch down before stopping.
- Braking either too hard or too softly.
- Failing to cancel the signal.
- Hitting the kerb or stopping too far from the kerb.

Approaching junctions

Once your pupil is capable of moving off and stopping using the M-S-M routine, it is time to introduce junction work to allow them to develop this skill to what can now be called the M-S-P-S-L routine. As can be seen in his new description, the second 'M'(i.e. manoeuvre) part of the M-S-M routine has been removed as a result of the development and increased skills of the learner and been replaced with P-S-L (i.e. position-speed-look) which are the key features of junction approach work.

Introduce your pupil to left turns first, and include a briefing on approaching turning left, emerging from junctions and in particular emerging left. At the start of the lesson recap their last lesson in order to check their knowledge of the M-S-M routine, set an objective for the current lesson and discuss risk and how this will be shared (covered in detail in the 'moving off and stopping' lesson). So much of this lesson is about the timing of your instruction, being concise, and keeping your pupil's approach speed down as they approach the junction. A very common mistake made by new instructors is using too many words, not starting their instruction early enough, and then not dealing with the pace of the approach to the junction.

Identify the junction

The first part of this lesson should be to work with your pupil to help them to identify the junction in the first place. This might sound straightforward but do not assume, because if your pupil cannot locate the junction, how can they prepare for it?

Explain how to identify junctions by the following visuals – give way lines, break in the kerb line, gaps in hedges or walls, detecting other

traffic in the junction, gaps in rows of houses, roof lines at 90 degrees to normal, and identifying the white road name signs.

Mirrors
Check that the mirrors are being used in the correct order, making sure also that your pupil is aware of following traffic. The mirrors should be used early enough in the process and effectively enough to give them enough time to deal with what they see. Use the 3 core competencies of identifying, analysing and correcting faults to deal with any issues your pupil may have.

Signals
Once the mirror work has been completed and your pupil is aware of what is around the vehicle, then a signal should be considered. The key rules with signals are that they should be applied in good time and should inform but not confuse.

Position of the vehicle
The position of your vehicle is also a signal to other road users, and therefore should not confuse them. Positioning of the vehicle should also be done in good time as a late or early change of position might cause confusion to other road users. The normal driving position would be used for left turns, and 'just left of centre' for right turns.

Speed
Based on the type of junction, other road users, and pedestrians, the approach speed should be appropriate to the above. In the early stages of learning it would be advisable to keep the approach speed a little slower than normal if traffic conditions allow, so that your pupil is not overloaded with information in an ever-shortening length of time on their first few attempts.

Gear
The gear selected should be appropriate to the junction and selected at the correct time with emphasis being on the use of the clutch; feeling for the correct gear, keeping eyes on the road, not gear watching, and avoiding coasting issues.

Look
As your pupil approaches the junction it is vital that they look around for other road users, pedestrians and obstructions (e.g. parked cars,

skips, roadworks etc.) before and during the turn. A good guide to this that you can use with your pupil would be:

- "look left – turn left"
- "look right – turn right"

You can imagine the consequences and potential risk of not looking until after the turn!

Approaching junctions to turn right

When your pupil has reached a satisfactory standard when turning left, then you can introduce them to turning right. So many aspects of the M-S-P-S-L routine are similar to turning left, so use Q&A to confirm that learning has been achieved with left turns and then guide your pupil through the differences when turning right. This would include mirror work and signals differing for a right turn. The road position would now need to be just left of centre on approach and there will now be the added difficulty of judging and crossing oncoming vehicles. Explanation and application of the 'walk across' rule will allow the pupil to judge oncoming vehicles and use their skills and knowledge as a pedestrian to help then to decide a safe gap in which to turn. You will need to work with your pupil to develop this skill.

Practice

As the sessions progress keep working on the core competencies, dealing with potential faults early rather than letting them develop into dangerous situations. Good guided tuition should prevent faults from happening. It is better to prevent fires from starting rather than priding yourself on being a good firefighter!

Guided instruction would be needed early on until the pupil becomes more familiar with the new parts of the lesson. Q&A should be used to prompt the pupil on what they already know from their moving off and stopping experience. As the lesson develops use more Q&A in order to check and clarify their understanding. Examples of prompted tuition questions would be:

- How would you identify a junction, and why is this important?
- Why is it important to check the interior mirror before the door mirror when approaching a junction?
- What road position would you take up when turning right, and why?
- Why is it important to look into the side road before turning, and what are you looking for?

Common pupil errors

This is a list of the most common errors that occur when approaching junctions to turn either left or right.

- Not checking both interior and appropriate door mirror.
- Checking the wrong door mirror.
- Checking the door mirror first.
- Not signalling on approach.
- Signalling too early or too late.
- Not reapplying a signal.
- Incorrect position – too close or too wide.
- Too fast or too slow on approach.
- Using gears instead of brakes to slow the car.
- Incorrect gear selection.
- Coasting.
- Missing point of turn.
- Steering too close to kerb.
- Swinging out over white lines in centre of new road.
- Poor observations at junctions.
- Failing to give way to pedestrians.
- Poor judgement (when turning right) of approaching traffic.
- Right corner cut.

Emerging at T-junctions

In the section 'approaching junctions' we talked about initially using a left circuit in order to get your pupil used to dealing with junctions; as their skills develop, the introduction of a right turning circuit will be a logical choice. Working on a left circuit will comprise of approaching junctions, turning left and then at T-junctions emerging left.

The briefing on emerging left has many similarities to the left turn regarding the M-S-P-S-L routine. Good Q&A will establish the level of knowledge that the pupil is at. The only real change is at the junction itself. The approach is the same. At the junction the final development of the M-S-M routine comes into play. This routine has already been expanded to M-S-P-S-L in order to deal with the approach to junctions. At the junction, the 'L' (i.e. look) becomes L-A-D-A (Look, Assess, Decide, Act). Guide your pupil through this new area with a full talk through, and use the level of instruction that is appropriate to your pupil's knowledge and ability to deal with the approach. Identify, analyse and correct any faults. Use guided, prompted and independent driving as appropriate as your pupil develops.

At the junction ensure that you work with your pupil on taking effective observation as this is a key area of the emerge. Discuss the difference between open and closed junctions and how to deal with each. Explain about the risks of stopping at open junctions if they are clear. Lowering a window to listen for traffic at a closed junction can be advantageous and this can be a tip to pass on to your pupil.

Once you have explained the differences between 'stop' and 'give way' junctions and you are happy that your pupil has understood them you can work on reference points so that your pupil knows where stop if required. You will need to show your pupil where to stop on their first attempt, and then the pupil sets their own reference points for future attempts.

Practice

As the lesson develops you will find that you are developing your teaching style, working mainly with guided and prompted tuition. Match your style to the pupil requirements, and ensure that learning takes place throughout the whole lesson. Use a scaling score of 1–10 both at the start and the end of the lesson so that your pupil can monitor their own progress too.

As always, risk must be discussed and shared out at the commencement of the lesson but as your pupil's skills develop you will probably find that they feel able to take on more of the risk in areas they have practiced well and gained confidence in.

Examples of prompted tuition questions would include:

- At a T-junction, which way should you look first, and why?
- What road position would you adopt at the 'give way' junction when emerging left, and why?
- What are the consequences of your car being over the hazard lines when approaching a T-junction?

Common pupil errors

The following list shows the most common errors made by pupils performing emerging from T-junctions and serves as a good indicator of the teaching/coaching areas most requiring attention in general:

- Not using M-S-P-S-L routing correctly on approach.
- Not signalling on approach.
- Signalling too late or too early.
- Incorrect road position on approach.
- Too fast or too slow on approach.
- Unnecessary use of gears on approach.

- Using gears, not brakes, to slow on approach.
- Selecting wrong gear.
- Coasting.
- Not having car prepared to move off before making effective observations.
- Failing to make effective observations before emerging.
- Not judging a safe gap.
- Either clipping kerb or steering too wide when emerging left.
- Cutting right corner.
- Steering too early emerging right and end up straddling white line.
- Failing to give way to pedestrians.

Crossroads

A logical progression from junctions, both approaching and emerging, is to crossroads as these are made up of both types of junctions with the addition of an extra road. In the recap for this lesson and during the briefing, you will be able to establish your pupil's existing knowledge of the M-S-P-S-L routine and how they intend to apply this. As usual, the use of diagrams will help with the learning process.

When you teach/coach the lesson you should be able to use prompting on the areas that your pupil is knowledgeable on, and guide them through the new ones. These new areas will be based around the crossroads themselves and the issues created by that extra road. Problems usually occur around the area of priorities and the observation skills required to cope. It is often the case that something a pupil can cope with when approaching a junction suddenly becomes an issue when tackling crossroads because there is more to think about and pupil becomes overloaded by the number of things they need to think about and carry out. Your guidance and assurance at these times will be essential in order that your pupil does not lose confidence in their abilities.

Turning right from the major road to the minor one is more complex on crossroads than a normal right turn into a side road because road users coming in the opposite direction may also be making a right turn so 'nearside to nearside' and 'offside to offside' passing will need to be discussed. Look at the advantages and disadvantages of both of these methods and how the road layout of the crossroads may well dictate which method to use. Remember, also, to discuss box junctions and unmarked crossroads in your briefing.

Your briefing should also consist of explaining priorities for the 6 different situations relating to crossroads driving; these being the 3 approaches from the major road i.e. turning left, turning right and straight ahead. Briefing on the straight ahead is vital as many drivers do not see this as crossroads because they are on the priority road and therefore 'switch off' and are unaware of the dangers of vehicles in the two minor roads emerging unsafely or simply travelling through the crossroads (minor to minor) without even stopping or slowing. The 3 emerges from the minor road need to be covered, these being left onto the major road, right onto the major road and minor to minor across the major road. As part of the briefing discuss with your pupil road-positioning, how to deal with other motorists flashing lights and waving, and how to predict the actions of other road users.

Practice

During the practice session, cover all the different approaches that you have explained during the briefing. Where possible, prompt the areas that your pupil is capable of dealing with and guide them through the new aspects. If Q&A doesn't work, then pull over and revise your style of teaching/coaching to suit better your pupil's capabilities.

As you will now see, the lessons are becoming more detailed and complicated as they progress from the initial 'move off and stop' one, and it is therefore more vital than ever that you are working closely with your pupil, tailoring your teaching to their preferred way of learning, and checking regularly what they can and cannot deal with; pull over as required and, using the client-centred approach, give your pupil the opportunity to explore and analyse any issues that they might be having and work with them to come up with solutions. Ensure that, when you both get back on the road, the risk and the sharing of it has been addressed and agreed.

Watch your pupil to make sure that their observation is effective when dealing with crossroads. As they develop their skills, watch how they respond to situations that arise. You will probably find that you can deal with any minor issues on the move, but if this is not possible, or a more serious issue develops, pull over to discuss further.

Examples of prompted tuition questions include:

- When turning right out of the minor road, who has priority?
- How would you deal with unmarked crossroads if there was another vehicle present?
- When would you consider a nearside/nearside pass turning right at crossroads?
- What precautions would you take when driving through crossroads on the major road and why?

Common pupil errors

The following is a list of the most common errors made by pupils tackling this area of driving:

- Not using M-S-P-S-L or using wrong sequence.
- Incorrect use of signals.
- Wrong approach speed.
- Looking down at gear lever.
- Wrong gear choice.
- Coasting.
- Not making effective observations before emerging.
- Looking in wrong direction when emerging.
- Flashing headlights at pedestrians or waiting traffic.
- Incorrect position either before or after turning.
- Failing to progress when safe to do so.
- Proceeding when unsafe.
- Not giving way to pedestrians.
- Right corner cuts.
- Incorrect use of yellow box junctions.

Emergency braking

By now your pupil will be managing a variety of roads as well as junctions (roundabouts we will deal with in a later section). Their use of gears should be at a reasonably good level and they will be driving at, or around, normal speeds appropriate to the road conditions. Therefore, being able to stop the vehicle in an emergency situation is important. Under the guidance of a driving instructor, most learner drivers are under control to a large extent. If taught correctly, once they have passed their test they should be driving according to the Highway Code. It has to be said that, usually, the problem when driving is other drivers on the road; the unexpected actions of these other road users and the new driver's lack of experience makes it essential that stopping in an emergency situation is a possibility that must be prepared for, and thus needs to be effectively covered during the learning process.

The best solution to the emergency stop is to not have the vehicle in a situation where one is required! Anticipation, therefore, is a vital aspect of driving whereby your pupil needs to look and plan well ahead. Since your pupil should be working toward their theory test preparation at the same time as taking driving lessons, they will be familiar with hazard perception video practice which will aid them in the development of their anticipation skills. The 'what if' scenario will get your pupil thinking of what might happen.

Stop!

The emergency stop session will be a practice session and therefore you are in charge of safety when carrying out these practices and you must make sure that any risk is reduced to a minimum.

Don't carry out an emergency stop if:

- You are being followed by another vehicle.
- Near junctions or bends.
- Meeting other traffic.
- When pedestrians are present.

Explain to your pupil that you will look over your right shoulder out of the back of the car to check for following vehicles. (This is **NOT** the signal to stop). You will then extend your right arm with you palm facing the windscreen and you will say "STOP!"

When in an emergency stop, mirrors are not a priority. This may seem an unusual thing to hear for your pupil as so far you will have been emphasising to them the need for use of mirrors, especially as the starting point for the M-S-P-S-L routine you have been teaching them. Explain to your pupil the typical stopping distances in dry and wet conditions, breaking this down to thinking and braking distances. With your help, your pupil should realise that there is no time to check mirrors for an emergency stop as quick reactions are essential. If you explain well to them the theory of stopping distances in such a way that they realise for themselves the lack of time for mirror checking, this is more likely to be retained in their memory.

Quick reactions are key and should be practiced at the side of the road to ensure that any issues arising are dealt with before getting on the move. You do not want to find out that there is a problem with your pupil's reaction times in a real emergency!

In an ideal situation when stopping the engine will be left running, but the most important aspect of the emergency stop is simply to stop, so if the clutch is a little late in being applied this is far better than getting the clutch down first and losing the benefit of engine braking. Emphasis MUST be on applying the brake first, quickly and with progressive, firm application. Over-enthusiastic application of the brake could lead to a skid. A firm grip of the wheel is required to keep control of the vehicle and to act as a brace to stop your pupil moving forward. Explain to your pupil how to secure the car once stopped and how all-round effective observation is essential before moving off again. On setting off, the nearside blind spot is an additional hazard that must be dealt with as your car is now in the normal driving position on the road as opposed to being parked at the kerb edge.

Skidding

As mentioned above, harsh use of the footbrake can induce a skid and therefore should be avoided. Skidding is usually caused by driver error, and good awareness and planning should help prevent skidding occurring in the first place.

Skidding occurs when the tyre grip on the road is less than forces that are acting on the vehicle such as braking, accelerating and steering. The amount of tyre that is in contact with the road when driving is around the same size as a CD (compact disc) and this has to share grip and the forces acting on the tyre. Discuss with your pupil the causes of skids, and talk them through the process of removing the cause of the skid by coming off the brake pedal and steering into the skid in order to straighten the car.

ABS (anti-lock braking systems)

Most modern cars are fitted with ABS. Explain to your pupil how this works and the need to keep firm pressure on the brake during an emergency stop. Make sure you advise your pupil that the ABS does not increase the grip and will not always prevent a skid, but importantly it will allow the driver to steer and brake at the same time as the ABS releases and re-applies the brakes just as the wheels are about to lock up; this is the point of maximum grip.

Examples of prompted tuition questions would include:

- Which pedal should you press first and why?
- Why are mirrors not a priority in an emergency stop?
- Where should you look when setting off after an emergency stop and why?
- Why should you keep a firm grip of the steering wheel?
- How would you correct a skid?

Common pupil errors

The following list shows the most common errors committed in the area of learner driving and reflects those areas where detailed and effective teaching is most required:

- Checking mirrors before braking in an emergency.
- Riding the clutch.
- Not braking hard enough.
- Clutch down before brake.

- Too slow to react.
- Braking with left foot.
- Letting go of the steering wheel (with one or both hands) before car stops.
- Easing off the brake just as the car stops.
- Skidding and failing to correct it.
- Releasing footbrake when ABS is activated.
- Poor observation or lack of observation when setting off.

Pedestrian crossings

Pedestrian crossings, in their various guises, present potential issues for learners and other road users so teaching your pupil how to deal with pedestrian crossings needs to be done in order to keep their driving safe. This will be an area that your pupil should already have a good deal of knowledge about since they will very likely have used several of these albeit as a pedestrian, so by means of a good Q&A find out what knowledge your pupil already has. By actively engaging your pupil in the recap and briefing sessions you are naturally putting them at the centre of the learning experience and keeping them actively involved in the whole lesson process, you just need to fill in the gaps in their knowledge.

Although there are 2 different styles of crossings (controlled and uncontrolled) the manner in which do deal with them is largely similar. Check with your pupil to find out how many different types of crossings they are aware of. A good way to brief this subject is to run through 'do's' 'don'ts' and 'differences'; the 'do's' are how to approach a crossing and the method is common to them all (this saves repetition for each type of crossing and the risk of losing your pupil's attention through boredom). Explain that once the crossing is identified, then the correct use of the M-S-M routine will be applied approaching the crossing. Explain and, if necessary, demonstrate where to stop. Advise the pupil how to progress if the crossing is clear so as not to cause a hazard to following traffic. Explain the 'don'ts' for all crossings regarding not waving pedestrians across, not parking in the zigzag area or stopping on the crossing, and not overtaking the moving vehicle nearest the crossing that has stopped to give way to pedestrians.

In the briefing run through the different types of crossings. These will be:

- Zebra.
- Pelican.
- Puffin.

- Toucan.
- Pegasus (equestrian).
- School Patrol.

Run through the 'differences' in the operation of each type of crossing including when pedestrians have priority and when your pupil should set off. Explain how central islands affect each type of crossing, and discuss how forward planning is essential for the safe use of crossings.

On the move you will need to guide your pupil through each type of crossing, and as they become more familiar with each and develop their skills you can progress to prompted tuition by asking questions to test their understanding. Remember, when prompting, it will take time for a pupil to take in what you have asked and then more time to process this and come up with an answer. Therefore, if you are prompting, do not wait until you can see the crossing as there may not be enough time to prompt correctly on the subject you are checking on; start early and give your pupil sufficient time to work with you. As always, use the core competencies to deal with any faults that may occur and when they feel they are ready, let your pupil try the crossings on their own as they talk you through them (if they are ok with this).

Your levels of instruction need to reflect how your pupil is dealing with the lesson, e.g. if they struggle when attempting a crossing on their own then you can drop back to prompted tuition.

Example of prompted tuition questions:

- How would you identify a pedestrian crossing?
- When does a pedestrian have priority on a zebra crossing?
- Which mirror would you check first on the approach to a crossing and what are you looking for?
- Why don't we wave pedestrians across at crossings?
- How would you deal with a flashing amber light on a pelican crossing?

Common pupil errors
The following is a list of the errors most often made by pupils for this subject:

- Not using M-S-M routine.
- Not approaching at appropriate speed.
- Not stopping when necessary.
- Not complying with white zigzag lines.

- Waving pedestrians across.
- Not making the car secure (footbrake or handbrake).
- Blocking the crossing.
- Failing to make effective observations when moving off.

Roundabouts

Since you have previously dealt with crossroads, including those controlled by traffic lights, a lot of the requirements for roundabouts will already have been dealt with. In your briefing check your pupil's understanding again of the M-S-P-S-L routine, and explain how roundabouts are designed to keep the traffic flowing at junctions. Compare this situation with your pupil's existing knowledge of sitting at a red light with nothing coming the other way. Use visual aids and explain lane discipline on roundabouts to them and include signs on approach and the paint markings on the road on approach too; this all ties in with early planning and anticipation. You will also need to discuss the use of mirrors and the timing of signals when exiting a roundabout, along with where to look on approach and how to look for gaps in the traffic with particular attention as to how the position of other vehicles using the roundabout can create gaps.

When you have finished the briefing check with your pupil to ensure that they understand what to do and how you have agreed the risk will be shared between you, then check that they fully understand how to put into practice the agreed strategy.

Practice on the move

Agree beforehand the level of instruction that you will be using (this will almost certainly be guided instruction). Start on more quiet roundabouts, initially turning left to allow the pupil time to study and understand how roundabouts work. Develop your instruction with them to move to prompted instruction as your pupil begins to understand. Roundabouts are probably most learners' major concern when driving because of the constant flow of traffic on and off them. Therefore, in the early stages, give your pupil plenty of reassurance and start your tuition early.

As the lesson develops change from turning left to following the road ahead (this is usually the second exit); watch for, and deal with, the possibility of your pupil 'straight lining' the roundabout instead of following lane discipline rules and using the left lane and the consequences of coming into conflict with right turning traffic in lane 2. One of the better word pictures I have come across to help with this problem is to ask your pupil to imagine that they are following the crust of a pizza!

This lesson can be quite an intense one, so it is advisable to pull over frequently to discuss progress. Try to get your pupil to analyse their own driving and ask them to advise you of the areas they find more difficult; good coaching from you should enable your pupil to come up with many of the solutions to their own problems. Re-assess the risks, then get back on road.

Once they have mastered the left and straight ahead aspects of roundabouts your pupil will be ready to tackle right turns. As their skills develop on this aspect too, you can agree with your pupil to work on more complex roundabouts, but if you find that they are now beginning to struggle with this it is a good idea to pull in somewhere between junctions on the roundabout, e.g. a petrol station and watch the traffic flow and then discuss it to assist the pupil in their understanding of how the roundabout works.

Throughout the session, ensure that your directions to the pupil are clear and concise. This will involve identifying and directing. It will include the exit number and any associated route direction.

Examples of prompted tuition questions:

- How early would you look to the right on approach and what are you looking for?
- What speed and what gear will you use on approach?
- Where would you stop if the roundabout was busy?
- When would you signal left to exit the roundabout taking the 2nd exit?
- Which lane would you normally use to follow the road ahead, 2nd exit?

Common pupil errors

The following is a list of the most common errors committed by pupils working on this subject in their driving lessons:

- Not using M-S-P-S-L on approach.
- Using M-S-P-S-L in wrong sequence.
- Incorrect timing of signals.
- Incorrect position/lane on approach.
- Incorrect position/lane on the roundabout.
- Too fast/too slow on approach.
- Too fast/too slow on roundabout.
- Selecting wrong gear.
- Late observations.
- Missing gaps in traffic.
- Late/missing signal when leaving roundabout.

Reversing exercises

As well as normal driving on the road, it is important for your pupil to be able to reverse the car under full control. There are a number of reversing exercises on the syllabus. These are:

- Reversing into a limited opening (side road) to the left and to the right.
- Turn in the road.
- Parallel park.
- Pull up on the right, reverse back and rejoin the traffic.
- Reverse into a parking bay and drive out forwards (left or right reverse).
- Drive forward into a bay and reverse (left or right).

All reversing exercises should be taught as these are skills required for safe driving for life. On test, some of these will be tested (see chapters covering the practical driving test). The key points that need to be taught are:

- A good standard of car control.
- Develop effective all-round observation skills.
- Develop a good standard of accuracy.
- To be able to deal effectively with other road users.

During the briefing and recap stages of the lesson find out what the pupil knows and understands about the above 4 key areas e.g. they may well have driven very slowly already in queues of traffic, for example, using 'peep and creep' at junctions, so Q&A can be used to establish the level of your pupil's knowledge and you can then fill in the missing gaps with guided tuition.

As already stated, it is far better to prevent faults from happening in the first place rather than dealing with them once they happened. Therefore, car control should be tested at the side of the road before moving off to carry out the manoeuvre and because of the change in seating position and observing out of the rear of the car, clutch control can be more difficult reversing than it is when slowly moving forwards. When looking out of the rear of the car (the direction of travel) the driver's left hip will move away from the clutch and the right hip will move nearer to the gas pedal. For many drivers, moving the seat slightly forwards will correct this and allow your pupil to retain control of the clutch. Although each of the 4 key skills are important, if your pupil cannot manoeuvre the car at slow speed at, say, a crawl, then it will be difficult to carry out the remaining 3 skills effectively.

Once you have established safe slow car control you can get your pupil to look at the reversing manoeuvre itself. Using your diagrams as a visual aid, run through with your pupil what is required. As well as slow car control, which has now been established, discuss the importance of effective all-round observation, looking for other road users and pedestrian activity paying particular attention to children as they are relatively small and very unpredictable.

Demonstration
In earlier lessons, you will have established your pupil's preferred learning style and alongside this, and especially with manoeuvres, it is often beneficial to offer a demonstration. A significant number of pupils will pick up things more quickly if they are able to actually see what to do by watching their instructor do it first. Explain to them the reference points that YOU are using and how THEY can set their own when they are driving. Show them where to look during the exercise and also what you are doing with your feet as you perform the manoeuvre. NB demonstration drives do not suit everybody, so do ask your pupil.

Practice
When getting on the move, so long as you have both discussed risk and how it will be apportioned during the manoeuvre, you may both agree that you (the instructor) will take responsibility for observations and allow your pupil to concentrate on car control

and accuracy as this will take a significant amount of pressure off your pupil in the initial stages. If you do see approaching traffic or pedestrian activity that will affect your drive, then get your pupil to pause and discuss what you both can see and then either tell or ask them how they are going to deal with the situation. Approaching traffic will either go past and not wait or will wait, but either way make sure that your pupil understands that it is the other road user's permission to give and not your learner's to take when you discuss priorities. If traffic is waiting then, to take some of the pressure off your pupil, it would be beneficial for you to wave the other driver on; when doing this, make sure that you have assessed the situation carefully. Do NOT allow your pupil to deal with other traffic unsupervised.

As the reversing exercise develops, using good coaching skills, re-assess the risk with your pupil and work with them as they take more responsibility for the manoeuvre. Prompted tuition will test your pupil's knowledge as you move away from guided tuition, and regular discussions during the lesson will confirm for you the amount of knowledge that your pupil is developing. Before moving on, check what your pupil thinks they are doing well and the areas where they feel they need more help.

Instructor's observations

It is very easy for PDIs to over-instruct and do all the observation work (unless, of course, it had been agreed with your pupil that you will do the observations!) As a teaching/coaching point, remember that it is the pupil who should be learning how to manoeuvre a car. Think of what they are learning if you do all the work! Therefore, your seating position needs to be reasonably square on to your pupil. You should be facing toward them and be able to clearly see all foot, hand and eye movements.

Ask your pupil what they can see *before* they move. Ask them where the kerb is, and how far away the vehicle is from the kerb. Ask them how they are going to control the car *before* they move. By these means, you should be able to keep the exercise well under control. Door mirrors can be lowered to check the kerb position, and reversing cameras can be glanced at to check the vehicle position. Reversing sensors can also be used. There is no issue with using technology, but they should only ever be a driver aid; full, effective, all-round observation by the driver (your pupil) is the *only* way to maintain full safety so long as they act correctly on what they see.

Examples of prompted tuition questions:

> Before moving, where would you look and why?
> If a vehicle approaches, who has priority?
> When would you give way to a pedestrian?
> Where are your blind spots and why must you check them?
> How would you control your car at a crawl downhill?
> How would you control your car at a crawl uphill?
> How much steering would you apply for this corner?
> Why must you look in the direction of travel?

Common pupil errors

The following is a list of the most common errors committed when performing a reverse manoeuvre:

- Failing to check blind spots.
- Failing to make effective observations.
- Failing to act on what is seen.
- Not releasing handbrake fully.
- Poor clutch control.
- Too much or too little gas.
- Steering too slowly.
- Not using large enough hand movements to steer.
- Hitting or mounting the kerb.
- Stopping too far from the kerb.
- Overhanging the kerb.
- Not looking the same way as they are steering.
- Not looking through the rear window whilst reversing.
- Inappropriate signalling to other road users.
- Selecting wrong gear.
- Stalling.
- Failing to make regular checks to the front and right (left reverse) or front and left (right reverse).
- Not seeing approaching traffic, cyclists or pedestrians causing inconvenience.
- Pulling up too close to the parked vehicle.

Interaction with other road users

As your pupil's driving develops they will be meeting and dealing with more and more traffic. We discussed earlier how anticipation of the actions of others allows more time to prepare, and 'buying time' in this way is important to all road users but is, in fact, essential for learner drivers.

Anticipation

Anticipation is not just relevant for other vehicles on the road, but is also vital for all pedestrians, cyclists, horse riders etc.

In the first instance check what your pupil understands by the term 'anticipation' and ask them for some examples e.g. "Give me some examples of what you might anticipate could happen when passing a line of parked cars." Once you have established what your pupil does and does not know about anticipation, you will know how much help they need. This learning will be client-centred so you will, of course, be asking what help they need from you as well as what they feel they can do themselves. This way the responsibility for risk is being shared.

Use diagrams to cover potential issues that may occur out on the road. These would include:

What unexpected things might **drivers** do?

- Emerge from junctions unsafely.
- Open doors or move off without warning.
- Take priority when they should give way.
- Contravene the Highway Code.
- Change lanes unexpectedly.
- Follow sat nav without taking account of other road users.
- Use mobile phones on the move and be unaware of other motorists.
- Stop suddenly without warning.

What unexpected things might **pedestrians** do?

- Children can be impulsive.
- Elderly people can be slow and over-cautious.
- Joggers often run across junctions without looking.
- Pedestrians can be in the road in rural areas.
- Dog walkers can have dogs off the lead and not under control.
- Pedestrians can step into the road between parked cars or areas other than crossings.
- School children wander across roads in groups.
- Areas around shops have a lot more footfall.
- Pedestrians getting off buses can cross without looking.

What unexpected things might **cyclists** do?

- Ride into the road without warning.
- Squeeze between traffic in queues.

- Be blown sideways by strong wind.
- Swerve to avoid potholes.
- Go through red lights.
- Turn without signals.

Examples of prompted tuition questions would include:

- Driving past parked cars, what might happen?
- How would you deal with it?
- When you are turning into a side road, what might a pedestrian do?
- How are cyclists affected by windy weather?
- How would you deal with this?
- Approaching a level crossing, what do you expect might happen and how would you deal with it?
- When driving on the major road at a crossroads, what are you looking for in minor roads?

Initially, you may have to give a talk-through with your pupil over any issues they are unfamiliar with. Questions asked in good time will test the areas with which they are more familiar. Make sure that, whatever level of coaching/teaching you are at, you:

1. Point out what to anticipate for.
2. How to deal with the situation.

Simply explaining that a pedestrian may walk out into the road without your pupil having a plan of action as to how to deal with the situation if it does arise, is a recipe for disaster. All the pupil would know is who they are going to hit!

The remedy for most anticipational issues is excellent observation and a reduction in speed in order to give time for the developing hazard to be dealt with. Racing headlong into a hazardous situation is never the answer! Teach your pupil to plan well ahead and for following traffic, keep a safe distance from other road users, and to expect the unexpected.

Meeting traffic

Anticipation needs to be a natural part of meeting traffic since these situations require good forward planning.

You will need to brief your pupil on the priority situation, which will depend on which side any parked cars are and the relative positions of your car and the oncoming vehicle. Legal issues may also come into play where traffic calming measures are in place. Your briefing should explain who has priority when there are parked cars on the left, the right, and when they are on both sides.

A 'meeting' situation is one where there is limited room and two cars cannot pass each other. In this situation, your pupil will need to position their car so that they can see oncoming vehicles and that oncoming vehicles can see them (see and be seen). Approach speed is important as this will affect which car gets to the restriction first, and also dictates how and where to stop.

If stopping to give priority it is important to control the pace of following vehicles so as to avoid incidents created by late, harsh braking.

Holdback position

If your pupil is required to give priority to the oncoming vehicle then they will need to stop at what is referred to as a 'holdback position'. This position should give them a good view of oncoming vehicles without causing an obstruction; therefore the position would normally be just left of the centre. Positioning too far left will block the view ahead and following vehicles may think that your pupil has parked and they could well attempt to pass them at the same time that your pupil sets off. The position should also be around two car lengths back to allow for smooth steering passed the parked vehicle; being too close to the parked vehicle would result in excessive steering in order to get past and may take your pupil too far across the centre of the road.

Talking your pupil through the first few meeting situations will eventually develop to prompted tuition as the confidence and competency of your pupil grows. You can pull over at the side of the road as required to run reflective sessions with your pupil and allow them to explore their development and further develop a plan of continued improvement with them. Ensure that your pupil understands and doesn't just remember, and when they become confident with meeting traffic in a variety of situations, and with their agreement, ask them to talk you through the process of meeting other traffic.

Examples of prompted tuition questions would include:

- Do we have enough room?
- With parked cars on the left, who has priority?
- With parked cars on both sides who has priority?

- How would you apply the M-S-M routine in these situations?
- How would you know if you had priority at traffic calming situations?
- What would you do if a vehicle forces its way through when you have priority?

Adequate clearance

Heavily linked to anticipation is dealing with adequate clearance to parked vehicles at the side of the road. When briefing this subject with your pupil check their existing knowledge with good Q&A, and in your briefing cover the following:

- Planning well ahead to anticipate and identify parked vehicles.
- Be aware of following traffic – where they are, and their relative speed to your pupil.
- Look for traffic approaching in order to decide available space.
- Adjust speed to suit the conditions (small gap = small speed).
- Moving out early to avoid late steering.
- Additional clearance for cyclists and horses – at least 2 metres. Pass wide and slow.
- An ideal minimum of a door's width for parked cars.

Use developing levels of instruction as your pupil improves to the point where they fully understand and can talk you through the subject. A point to be aware of here is that with learner drivers, unless you deal with this subject sufficiently, they have a tendency to move to the left when there are oncoming vehicles, especially larger ones such as buses. Make sure that your teaching/coaching has left them fully aware of the consequences of driving too close to parked cars.

Examples of prompted tuition questions include:

- Why is it important to maintain at least a 1 metre gap to a parked vehicle?
- If this gap was reduced, how would you adjust your speed and why?
- How much room should you leave for a cyclist or horse rider and why?

Crossing the path of traffic

As part of the process of dealing with other road users this lesson looks at turning right across the path of oncoming vehicles where your pupil does not have priority. This can be a challenge to a lot of learners as they probably have no previous experience other then turning right into minor roads on earlier lessons and the focus on those lessons was about how the basics of making a right turn and was most likely carried out on quieter roads where it is unlikely that there would be oncoming traffic to deal with. It may even have been done as a theory exercise using diagrams. Don't confuse this lesson with turning right. It is not. It is about judging oncoming vehicles. Right turns should have already been successfully dealt with before attempting this particular subject.

Q&A with your pupil will establish a starting point for the lesson. Use visual aids to explain what is required, and use the pupil's experience as a pedestrian to discuss the walk across rule. If your pupil could safely cross the road from left to right as a pedestrian across the path of the oncoming vehicle, then as a driver they can safely turn right from the normal right turning position.

- Ensure your pupil understands who has priority.
- Check into the side road first to ensure that the turn will be safe.
- Use the walk across rule to judge the speed and distance of oncoming vehicles.
- Observe oncoming vehicles to practice the above rule, whilst parked at the side of the road, so that you can see the level of understanding of the rule your pupil has and to enable them to practice it before putting into use on the move.
- If your pupil is in doubt about the gap then, in the same way they would as a pedestrian, don't go!
- Undue hesitation can also cause issues for following vehicles, so if the gap is there it really should be taken.
- The risk of corner cutting should have been covered in earlier lessons and should therefore not be an issue. However, if the gap is not there with oncoming traffic and your pupil decides to go, then a corner cut may result as they rush into a non-existent gap.

Practice

When practicing, initially guide and then later prompt your pupil. Ask them about their thoughts on gaps in traffic. Make sure that they only proceed if you also agree with their decision. It is strongly advised that you, the instructor, have your right foot set over the dual control brake just in case your pupil rushes a poor decision (remember, they are probably nervous, and this does happen!).

As the lesson progresses agree, and then hand over more responsibility to your pupil and ensure that an excellent level of communication remains in place throughout the manoeuvre.

Examples of prompted tuition questions would include:

- How would you know when it is safe to turn?
- Why must you look into the side road before considering the turn?
- If you are uncertain about the gap, what should you do and why?
- When using the walk across rule, which footpath would you set off from and why?

Overtaking

For clarity, overtaking refers to moving vehicles. You pass a stationary vehicle.

Overtaking tends to be a subject that does not receive enough attention when teaching learner drivers. The consequences of this becomes very apparent post-test when newly qualified drivers have to 'experiment' with this challenge and often with small engine cars (for insurance reasons) and often with disastrous results. Fatal accidents involve too many young drivers and rural roads tend to be the ones that most of these incidents occur on. One can visualise the scenario of a newly qualified driver in a 1.0 ltr car, friends onboard, trying to overtake a slower vehicle and having to be on the wrong side of the road... and they haven't been shown how to do it!

The rules for overtaking that should be uppermost in the mind of a driver are that it must be *safe*, *legal* and *necessary!* Discuss these 3 elements in your briefing.

Safe overtaking requires good observation and planning. If you cannot see, then it cannot be safe. Don't overtake approaching bends, the brow of a hill or where there is dead ground (dead ground is where there is a dip in the road over a reasonable distance that can hide oncoming vehicles). Dead ground can, on occasions, appear safe but as your pupil overtakes they could then be presented with a vehicle emerging out of the dip. It's called dead ground for a reason! Overtaking should not be done where there are junctions as vehicles may emerge out of these whilst your pupil is on the wrong side of the road.

Legal. There are a number of legal restrictions regarding overtaking:

- No overtaking sign.
- Solid white lines.

- Exceeding the speed limit in order to overtake.
- Zig zag area of pedestrian crossings.
- Overtaking on the left (unless the vehicle ahead is signalling to turn right).
- If you would have to enter a lane reserved for buses, trams or cycles during their hours of operation.

Necessary. Only overtake if it is necessary and the safe and legal boxes have been ticked. Think:

- Is there any benefit to be gained?
- Will you be turning off soon and therefore going to slow the vehicle down that you have just overtaken? (This would include the approach to roundabouts)
- Is the vehicle in front driving at a speed that matches the limit for the road and driving conditions?

On the move, if it is safe, legal and necessary, then guide your pupil through overtaking until they gain a good understanding. Discuss with them the use of mirrors, where to position so they don't end up close to the back of the vehicle they are overtaking, and possibly dropping a gear for more power. Once past the vehicle, discuss observations and possible use of signals to move back into the normal driving position. As the lesson progresses, prompted tuition will check knowledge prior to your pupil trying to overtake independently.

Examples of prompted tuition questions would include:

- Is it safe to overtake?
- Why wouldn't you overtake approaching a bend?
- What does a solid white line mean?
- What is the speed limit for this road and what speed is the car in front doing?
- Why shouldn't you overtake if you are approaching a roundabout?

Common pupil errors
The following represents the most common errors made by learner drivers on this subject and demonstrates the need for efficient, effective practiced teaching.

- Meeting
  o Incorrect use of MSPSL or using wrong sequence.
  o Incorrect holdback position.

o   Acting too hastily in tight situations.
o   Hesitancy or indecision.
o   Forcing oncoming traffic to change speed or direction.
o   Failing to give way when appropriate.
o   Failing to make progress when appropriate.
o   Flashing headlights at oncoming traffic.

- Clearance
  o   Shaving parked vehicles.
  o   Failing to leave cyclists a 2 metre gap.
  o   Not leaving 'tyres and tarmac' behind stationary vehicles in a queue.

- Anticipation
  o   Failing to anticipate the actions of other road users, including cyclists and pedestrians.

- Crossing path
  o   Not using MSPSL correctly.
  o   Approaching too fast or too slow.
  o   Hesitancy or indecision.
  o   Forcing oncoming traffic to change speed or direction.
  o   Not judging a safe gap.

- Overtaking
  o   Not using MPSL MSM routine correctly.
  o   Unsafe overtaking.
  o   Incorrect holdback position.
  o   Cutting back in too soon.
  o   Failing to use an overtaking opportunity.
  o   Incorrect use of gears.
  o   Incorrect use of signals.
  o   Failing to anticipate the actions of other road users.

Progress, positioning and hesitancy

By now your pupil will be making good progress with their lessons and should be capable of a good standard of driving. They will be driving with a reducing amount of help from you and will have developed a good degree of independence in their drive. Therefore, at this stage of driving, we are looking at making sure that your pupil's interaction with other road users is developing, is safe, and matches full licence holders'. Your pupil should be capable of judging gaps, taking opportunities to emerge without hesitation, position their car correctly at all times, be able to make progress and to be able to understand and read speed signs.

Progress

Progress is covered on the DL25 form used for the driving test in section 20 and states:

> On test, you need to show that you can drive at a realistic speed appropriate to the road and traffic conditions. You need to approach all hazards at a safe, controlled speed without being over-cautious or slowing or stopping other road users. You should always be ready to move away from junctions as soon as it is safe to do so. Driving too slowly can frustrate other drivers which creates danger to yourself and others.

In order to reach this standard your pupil should be aware of speed limits; relying on remembering where speed signs are does not work as there are too many distractions when driving. What you need to do is to work with your pupil so that they understand where speed limit changes come in, so discuss this with your pupil and check their existing knowledge.

Changes of speed would be as follows:

- At road junctions including roundabouts.
- Moving from a rural area to a built-up area.
- Moving from a built-up area to a rural area.
- Temporary restrictions such as roadworks.
- Managed motorways overhead signs.
- Specific areas such as outside schools.
- Where dual carriageways become single carriageways under the national speed limit and vice versa.

Work with your pupil to get them to plan ahead and expect to see signs whenever they see a change in driving conditions.

Remember, your pupil should always be able to stop well within the distance they can see to be clear, and speed limits are the maximum for the road and should never be considered as a target!

In order to maintain good progress, your pupil must be able to plan and scan, looking well into the distance, and behind, to assess traffic early, read road signs and road markings early and accurately, be aware of any positional changes with other road users, and keep a safe distance from other vehicles to the front, rear, and to the sides.

Hesitancy

The above can cause issues for your pupil and other road users, therefore your pupil should be able to drive with good progress (as detailed on previous pages) and also be prepared to move away from junctions as soon as it is safe to do so. When approaching junctions ensure that your pupil understands the problems that hesitancy causes, and therefore:

1. Starts their observation work early and looks for opportunities to move off as soon as it is safe to do so.
2. Has the car ready to move off by positioning it correctly and having the appropriate gear prepared as they approach the junction.
3. Applies the appropriate brake (usually the footbrake as it allows for less delay, but use the handbrake if a pause develops into a wait).
4. When moving away from the junction applies the correct amount of acceleration and moves up through the gearbox correctly.

Work with your pupil using varying levels of instruction appropriate to their abilities; pull over as required to discuss matters, and keep your pupil at the centre of the learning process, allowing them to explore issues they may have and encouraging them to come up with solutions.

Positioning

The correct positioning at junctions will help to prevent the hesitation we have just discussed, and for safe driving in general road positioning needs to be correct. There are a number of issues that that can be attributed in some degree to poor road positioning.

Positioning too close to the kerb can cause the following:

- Issues for pedestrians.
- Issues with traffic emerging at junctions.
- Damage to tyres by debris at the side of the road.
- Possibly inviting following vehicles to overtake.

Positioning too far away from the kerb can cause the following:

- Conflict with oncoming vehicles.
- Misleading following vehicles into thinking you are turning right.

Additionally, your pupil needs to know that positioning is vital at junctions, especially where there are various lanes, and that any required lane changes should be done in a timely manner. Maintaining lane discipline should also be covered in detail. Discuss with your pupil the consequences of poor road positions and look through possible solutions; your pupil may find one solution better than another. Solutions would include:

- Following the vehicle in front provided it is correctly positioned.
- Positioning equidistant between the centre lines and the kerb, using the door mirrors.
- Using a door's width or 1 m from the kerb if that works.
- Using road paint, such as arrows, to help position the car.

Once in the correct position, use the kerb position on the windscreen as a lock-in reference point.

Examples of prompted tuition questions would include:

- Why is it important not to hesitate at junctions?
- Where should you look when approaching a junction and why?
- What is the normal road position?
- On approach at roundabouts where would you find information about lane position?
- Where are speed signs located?
- How should you progress away from a junction and why?

Common pupil errors with progress/position/hesitancy

- Progress
  - o Not identifying changes of speed.
  - o Approaching hazards too fast or too slow.
  - o Moving away from junctions too slowly.
  - o Changing gear too early.
  - o Breaking speed limits.

- Positioning
  - o Incorrect road position at junctions.
  - o Poor lane discipline.
  - o Wrong lane approaching more complex junctions.
  - o Driving too close or too far from the kerb.
  - o Incorrect road position on bends.
  - o Turning right onto dual carriageway and using right-hand lane and staying in it on the new road.

- Hesitation
  - o Looking ahead only approaching T-junctions.
  - o Over-use of the handbrake at junctions.
  - o Not understanding filter traffic lights.
  - o Not using mirrors and unaware of other traffic.
  - o Unable to judge gaps.

Chapter 6

TRAINEE LICENCE

Application process

The Trainee Licence is an option that is available to you after you have passed your Part 2 test AND have completed the required number of hours of training. This option will allow you to gain experience working with real pupils whilst you prepare for your Part 3 test. *NB it is important to point out that this is NOT mandatory, and in fact many PDIs go to their Part 3 test without using the Trainee Licence option.*

In order to apply for a Trainee Licence you need to be able to fulfil the following requirements:

- Have passed your ADI part 1 test in the last 2 years.
- Have passed your ADI part 2 test.
- Are eligible to take the Part 3 test.
- Have had at least 40 hrs training from a qualified ADI in providing driving instruction (at least 10 hrs of which was done in a car) and recorded on the ADI21T declaration form.

Taking the option of the Trainee Licence allows you to be paid for giving instruction and helps you to gain experience instructing pupils to drive so that you can prepare for your Part 3 test. The licence lasts for 6 months.

Rules of use

You must:

- Be a fit and proper person.
- Get the required amount of supervision or extra training whilst your licence is still valid.
- Make sure that your advertising does NOT make it appear that you are a fully qualified driving instructor.
- Display your Trainee Licence on the nearside edge of the front windscreen of your car whilst you are giving lessons.

The trainee licence is pink and triangular on a square background.

Where you work

Your training licence will display the name and address of your training establishment. You are only allowed to give instruction from there, so you cannot work independently. If your trainee licence is with a national driving school etc. then you may work locally, but you must NOT set up your own driving school and you must adhere to the advertising rules as listed above.

Changing your driving school

Whilst you are operating under your trainee licence it may be that you change your driving school. This is allowed on a trainee licence, however you MUST apply for a new trainee licence. The DVSA will send you a new licence displaying the details of the new school. You will then need to send your old licence back to the DVSA. You are allowed to give driving lessons whilst you wait for the new licence. There is no fee for changing driving schools and getting a new badge but the trainee licence is still only valid for the 6 months that commence with the original badge and this period of time is not altered by the change to a new driving school.

Other trainee licence rules

Your licence can be taken away from you by the ADI Registrar before it runs out of you break any of the rules for having the licence, if the licence was issued by mistake or gained by fraud, or if you fail 3 attempts at the Part 3 test. If you should fall ill, or have other reasons why you are not using your trainee licence, then you should return it to the DVSA. You will not receive a refund for the period of time you haven't used it, but the DVSA will have a record of you only having partially used the badge and this may work in your favour if you apply for another badge in the future.

If your badge is lost or stolen you must inform the police immediately on 101 in order to receive a crime number. To replace the badge you will have to send the following to the DVSA:

- Crime reference number.
- A recent passport-style photo if you don't give the DVSA permission to use your photocard driving licence photo or you don't have a photocard licence.
- The fee (if you cannot furnish a crime number or if the licence was lost). Currently this fee is £3.00, as of September 2018).

Contact address: Approved Driving Instructor Registrar
Driver and Vehicle Standard Agency
The Axis Building
112 Upper Parliament Street
Nottingham
NG1 6LP

Options when on the trainee licence

Your trainee licence will last for 6 months from the date you wish to start (the start date must be a Monday).

As you will appreciate, to teach for 6 months unsupervised can lead to bad habits forming which are not checked, analysed or corrected; for example, a number of PDIs teaching on a trainee licence initially spend too much time looking out of the front windscreen and checking their rear-view mirror rather than watching the learner driver to see if he/she is checking their mirrors, scanning the road correctly or using their feet on the pedals correctly! PDIs also, initially, tend to 'over-instruct' and tell learners everything rather than using a variety of teaching and coaching styles based upon the learner driver's experience. When speaking to PDIs that are on a trainee licence receiving additional training, they often raise concerns about damaging their car or the feeling that they are not yet fully confident in their training abilities. Therefore, as a PDI requires further supervision whilst working on the trainee licence, the trainee licence application had been adapted to aid in addressing such issues.

When you apply for a trainee licence there are 2 options available to you. You need to choose only one of these and it is important to note that *you can only choose one option and can NOT change the option once you have made your decision.*

Option 1 – Supervision of lessons
Here, your sponsoring ADI needs to supervise 20% of all the lessons you give whilst on the trainee licence. You will be required to keep a records of these supervised lessons along with the number of hours of lessons you have given. These details are recorded on the ADI21S form which is signed by both yourself and the sponsoring ADI. This document must be sent to the DVSA when your trainee licence runs out and must be available for inspection at any time.

Option 2 – Extra training
For this option you are required to complete at least 20 hrs additional training on the topics in the training programme.
    You must:

- Do the training before you book your Part 3 test.
- Book the test within 3 months of getting your trainee licence.

At least 25% of the training must be practical in-car training. This training is recorded on the ADI21AT form. You must send this document to the DVSA before the end of the 3 months OR the day after you book your Part 3 test, whichever comes first.

If you fail an attempt at the Part 3 test or you do not book your test in time, you must complete an extra 5 hrs training before your next attempt. You are allowed 3 attempts to pass the Part 3 test.

Driver & Vehicle Standards Agency

ADI 21S (Rev. 02/17)
Licensed Trainee
Supervision Record

Record required by Regulation 15(2) of the Motor cars (Driving Instruction) Regulations 2005

Register of Approved Driving Instructors

Your Details (complete in BLOCK CAPITALS) **1**

Serial Number on Licence:

Your Personal Reference Number (PRN):

Name of Licence Holder:

Home address:

Postcode:

Telephone number (with area code):

Name of the Training Establishment on Licence:

Business Address:

Postcode:

Telephone number (with area code):

ADI Details – Who have signed overleaf **2**

ADI's Name:

ADI Certificate Number:

Signed:

ADI's Name:

ADI Certificate Number:

Signed:

ADI's Name:

ADI Certificate Number:

Signed:

ADI's Name:

ADI Certificate Number:

Signed:

Where to send your form:

At the end of the 6 months please send this completed record to:

The Register of Approved Driving Instructors,
Driver and Vehicle Standards Agency,
The Axis Building, 112 Upper Parliament Street,
Nottingham, NG1 6LP

Alternatively send a scanned copy to **PADI@dvsa.gov.uk**

Notes:

For the duration of your trainee licence, you must keep a record of the number of hours you spend giving driving instruction and the number of hours you are directly supervised by an Approved Driving Instructor. You must be supervised for at least one fifth of the time you give instruction during this period.

This form must be available to any DVSA official upon demand.

Remember it is an offence to make a false declaration. If you did not receive the supervision you should not sign.

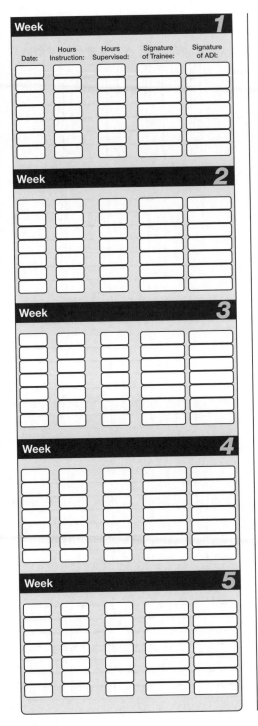

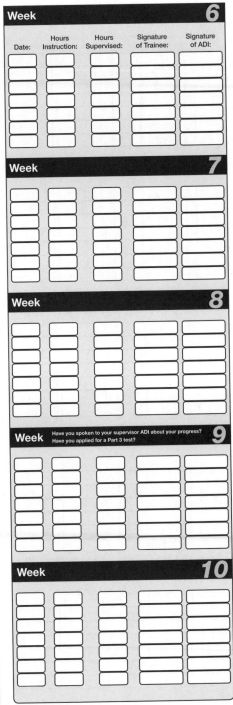

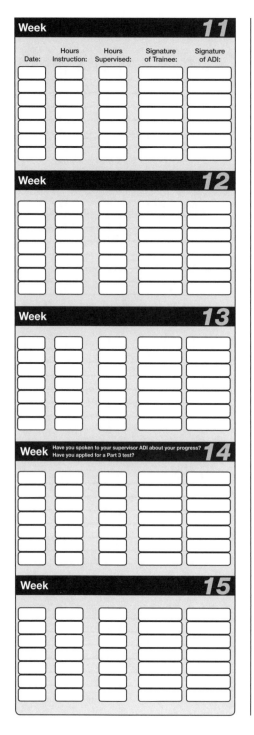

Week **11**

Date:	Hours Instruction:	Hours Supervised:	Signature of Trainee:	Signature of ADI:

Week **12**

Week **13**

Week **14**
Have you spoken to your supervisor ADI about your progress?
Have you applied for a Part 3 test?

Week **15**

Week **16**

Date:	Hours Instruction:	Hours Supervised:	Signature of Trainee:	Signature of ADI:

Week **17**

Week **18**

Week **19**
Have you spoken to your supervisor ADI about your progress?
Have you applied for a Part 3 test?

Week **20**

Trainee Licence

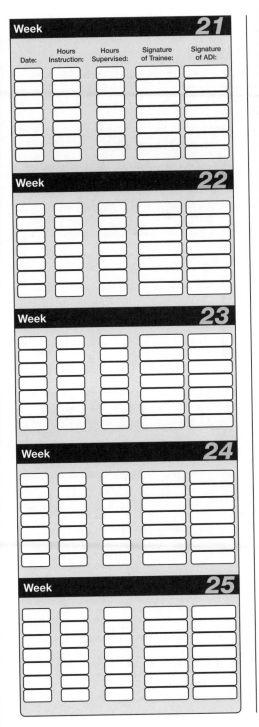

Week 21

Date:	Hours Instruction:	Hours Supervised:	Signature of Trainee:	Signature of ADI:

Week 22

Date:	Hours Instruction:	Hours Supervised:	Signature of Trainee:	Signature of ADI:

Week 23

Date:	Hours Instruction:	Hours Supervised:	Signature of Trainee:	Signature of ADI:

Week 24

Date:	Hours Instruction:	Hours Supervised:	Signature of Trainee:	Signature of ADI:

Week 25

Date:	Hours Instruction:	Hours Supervised:	Signature of Trainee:	Signature of ADI:

Week 26

Date:	Hours Instruction:	Hours Supervised:	Signature of Trainee:	Signature of ADI:

Week 27

Date:	Hours Instruction:	Hours Supervised:	Signature of Trainee:	Signature of ADI:

Week 28

Date:	Hours Instruction:	Hours Supervised:	Signature of Trainee:	Signature of ADI:

Processing your personal data:

The Driver and Vehicle Standards Agency (DVSA) directly manages all personal data it processes as an executive agency of the data controller, the Department for Transport. We use the personal data you give us to help run the Register of ADIs and practical driving test. We also use your details for statistics and analysis to assess equality and improve our customer service. We must ensure the integrity of the driving test. We may use the personal data you supply for the purposes of preventing or detecting crime and catching or prosecuting offenders. This may include hidden monitoring when appropriate.

We do not disclose or share personal data with any third parties other than in line with the Data Protection Act 1998. This may include, but is not restricted to, disclosure to the police, HM Revenue and Customs, local governments and DVLA. In the case of transfers from DVLA, this may include details of endorsements for the purpose of ensuring that registered ADIs continue to be fit to remain on the register. For further information, please see our website **gov.uk** or look for our notification document in the information commissioner's website: **www.ico.org.uk**. Our registration number is: **Z7122992**.

Qualified

Driver & Vehicle Standards Agency

ADI 21T (Rev. 5/16)
Instructor Training
Declaration

Register of Approved Driving Instructors

Please send this completed declaration to the Registrar *at the same time you submit an application for a Trainee Licence*. **If this is your first application for a trainee licence, apply online at www.gov.uk/instructors**

To be completed by the person applying for a Trainee Licence (in BLOCK CAPITALS).

Your Declaration **1**

Personal Reference Number:

Name of applicant:

Home address:

Postcode:

Name and Address of the Training Establishment:

Postcode:

I hereby declare that within the last 6 months I have received a total of not less than 40 hours training in the giving of driving instruction as required.

Signed :

Dated:

To be completed by the Approved Driving Instructor responsible for the training (in BLOCK CAPITALS).

Instructor's Declaration **2**

I hereby declare that within the last 6 months the above named trainee has been given a total of not less than 40 hours training in the giving of driving instruction as required. A record of such training is set out overleaf.

Name of Instructor:

Business Address:

Postcode:

ADI PRN:

Signed :

Dated:

Processing your personal data:

The Driver and Vehicle Standards Agency (DVSA) directly manages all personal data it processes as an executive agency of the data controller, the Department for Transport.

We use the personal data you give us to help run the Register of ADIs and practical driving test. We also use your details for statistics and analysis to assess equality and improve our customer service.

Processing your personal data: (cont.)

We must ensure the integrity of the driving test. We may use the personal data you supply for the purposes of preventing or detecting crime and catching or prosecuting offenders. This may include hidden monitoring when appropriate.

We do not disclose or share personal data with any third parties other than in line with the Data Protection Act 1998. This may include, but is not restricted to, disclosure to the police, HM Revenue and Customs, local governments and DVLA. In the case of transfers from DVLA, this may include details of endorsements for the purpose of ensuring that registered ADIs continue to be fit to remain on the register.

For further information, please see our website **gov.uk/dvsa** or look for our notification document in the information commissioner's website: **www.ico.gov.uk**

Our registration number is: **Z7122992**.

Trainee Licence

Record of Training | 3

Name and address of establishment from which instructor training was received:

Postcode:

Training objectives	Date training given	No. of hours	Signature of Trainee	Signature of ADI
Explaining the controls of the vehicle, including the use of dual controls				
Moving off				
Making normal stops				
Reversing and while doing so entering limited openings to the right or to the left				
Turning to face the opposite direction, using forward and reverse gears				
Parking close to the kerb, using forward and reverse gears				
Using mirrors and explaining how to make an emergency stop				
Approaching and turning corners				
Judging speed, and making normal progress				
Road positioning				
Dealing with road junctions				
Dealing with crossroads				
Dealing with pedestrian crossings				
Meeting, crossing the path of, overtaking and allowing adequate clearance of other vehicles and other road users				
Giving correct signals				
Comprehension of traffic signs, including road markings and traffic control signals				
Method, clarity, adequacy and correctness of instruction				
Observation and correction of driving errors comitted by pupils and general manner				
Attitude and approach to pupil				
Ability to inspire confidence in pupil				

Total Hours [ ] (Not less than 40 hours)

If you do not book your Part 3 within 3 months of getting your trainee licence, then you must also complete the extra 5 hrs training. This extra training needs to be recorded on the ADI21AT document. *NB If you do not record and send in the additional 5 hrs of training form, then the DVSA can revoke your licence.*

The purpose of this additional training is to allow you time to reflect on your test and to afford you the time to prepare for the next attempt. It is recommended that you contact your ADI and spend time with them on the result and feedback you were given by the examiner. It is important not to rush Part 3 attempts. It is often the case that a frustrated PDI who has failed an attempt at Part 3 then rushes the next attempt, believing they are ready. The result, invariably and sadly, is often another fail. It is better to invest quality time preparing and practicing before sitting the test again.

Chapter 7

LEVELS OF INSTRUCTION

Whilst coaching often makes use of open questions, there are occasions when open questions do not work and can, indeed, have a negative effect, e.g. if you continually use open questions that your pupil clearly is unable to answer, you can appreciate the negative effect that this will have on them. Therefore, it is quite acceptable to tell and instruct whilst still being client-centred on your coaching. If you have asked your pupil questions and listened to their answers, then guided instruction is a more than acceptable means of coaching in order to put 'books on the shelf' of the learner.

Guided instruction

First of all imagine that you, as a driving instructor, are akin to a library full of books; you are the person with the knowledge and resources to draw upon.

By the same token, a new learner driver with no knowledge to bring to the lesson is more like an empty bookshelf.

It would be difficult or impossible to get an answer from a pupil who has no 'books on their shelf' from which they can draw knowledge sufficient to answer the questions posed, leaving them at best embarrassed, and at worse demoralised.

For example, asking a new learner with no prior knowledge "How do you find the biting point?" can be an impossible question to answer if the pupil has never been taught or shown this process; to them, it is most likely a term they have never heard before, and their not having the answer can leave them feeling inadequate and in a negative mood.

Therefore, in the early stages of learning the 'books' need to be put 'on the shelf' i.e. the initial transfer of knowledge. This is guided tuition, but it is also worthy of note to remember that, whilst your pupil needs guided tuition at this early stage, it is still important to have an understanding of their learning style (this is covered in detail in a separate section). By using your pupil's preferred learning style, information is effectively transferred and 'books' are now beginning to be put 'on the shelves'.

As the 'shelves' are filled, this knowledge needs to be tested. So, for example, to put this back into driving terminology your pupil may have been taught the 'M-S-P-S-L' routine (mirror-signal-position-speed-look). You have explained the process and shown your pupil what this is. The pupil has said that their preferred learning style is visual and therefore diagrams have been used as well as watching the instructor as your pupil has also said that they learn best if given a demonstration. Your pupil has been guided through the M-S-P-S-L routine to the point where they now have a working knowledge of the process. It is important at this stage for you to ensure that the information that has been passed on using guided tuition is now in place in your pupil's mind i.e. there are now books on this shelf! Using this metaphor of a library shelf is powerful and memorable for learning since the brain works by metaphor as a matter of course and tapping into this produces strong and long lasting means of recall.

Prompted tuition

This tests the learner driver's knowledge and understanding. This is vital since the pupil must know:

- How to deliver an element of driving.
- Why they are doing this – the understanding behind the knowledge, and such a vital aspect of successful coaching.

One, without the other, will not work! It's okay having concerns about an issue, but pointless if the learner does not know how to correct their error.

Using the example in the diagram above of a corner cut, you and your pupil have pulled over at the side of the road to allow them to explore problems that arose from the corner cut. Your pupil is given the opportunity to analyse the corner cut to help them to understand the problem – all good so far. Your pupil reflects on what happened and with your assistance realises that the corner cut is potentially dangerous as there may have been traffic ready to emerge from the side road, or may be approaching the junction from the side road. As your pupil has discovered this for themselves (with questioning help from yourself), and realises that a collision is possible, they are now concerned about cutting corners. However, because you have only spent time with the pupil reflecting on the potential risks of cutting corners, your pupil is still in the dark about how to correct their fault. On the next practice, the potential consequences of the corner cut are fresh in their mind and this time they over-compensate and mount the nearside kerb in the side road (see the diagram on next page).

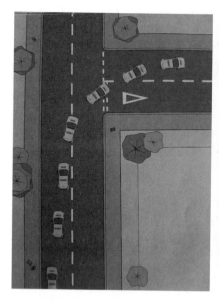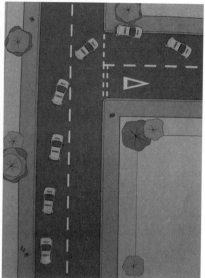

The pupil, although concerned, is missing the vital part of the solution – the how.

Similarly, if we look at this problem from the point of view where you, the driving instructor, helps the pupil with the how, but not the why, you then end up with a temporary solution which could be called a 'sticking plaster' solution as it is only a temporary fix.

Using the same fault of corner cutting, this time your pupil pulls over at the side of the road and following a period of reflection and allowing your pupil to explore the problem, the pupil realises that a corner cut is risky because of the potential danger of a collision with a vehicle emerging from the side road. The focus this time is purely about HOW to fix the problem. Back out on the road you help the pupil to find reference point, and the pupil now uses this method to avoid a corner cut.

All well and good you may think. Problem solved. But is it? Between lessons your pupil does some evening practice with a parent. They use the same estate roads that they used for their lessons. The practice session involves right-hand turns from the major to minor road. During the drive, they start to cut corners again and there is an incident with an emerging car whereby the parent has to grab the steering wheel to pull the car away from danger.

Parent: "I though your instructor had taught you how to right turn safely?"

Pupil: "Oh, sorry, I forgot"

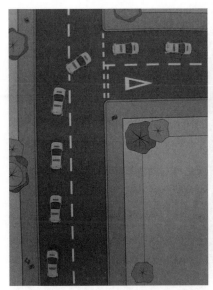 

In other words, your tuition worked well whilst you were present in the car, but failed to work as soon as you were not in the car! Why? Because there was no 'why'! Your pupil had only been taught HOW to fix the fault. They had no understanding of the risk or consequences of their actions i.e. *the sticking plaster solution*. Therefore, in order for the tuition and prompting to be effective, both the **how** AND the **why** need to be discussed in order to be effective.

A problem with prompted tuition

One of the main areas where a lot of trainee driving instructors struggle with this tuition is that they begin their prompting too late and usually at the point where they, as an experienced driver, would start to act on what they see when approaching a hazard. THINK! What is the purpose of a prompt, or prompted tuition? It is to refresh the memory, to bring to the front of the mind, the frontal lobes, what has been learned and how to deal with a subject. Therefore, this can be done well before the hazard since the intention is to get the pupil thinking about the hazard and how to deal with it.

If we use the example of a pedestrian crossing to demonstrate this point, the mistake would be to start prompting once the crossing has been identified.

Think about the process of the prompt. You, the instructor would need to ask a thought-provoking question about, for example, the use of the interior mirror on approach. This would involve both a how and a why question, firstly to check which mirror should be used

and when, and secondly to check why they are using it. At 30 mph the car is travelling 13.41 metres per second which is approximately 3 car lengths; it may well take 9–12 car lengths to ask your pupil the question. The pupil now has to process the thoughts in their mind, say 6 car lengths, and then they need to verbally respond to your questions, let's say 15 car lengths. That's a total of 33 car lengths or approximately 11 seconds to deal effectively with the first prompt, and without over-loading the pupil it may well be appropriate to ask a further question on the approach. We could, therefore, reasonably assume a further 33 car lengths (11 seconds at 30 mph) to deal with this further question.

Be aware, please, that we are using the speed of 30 mph here purely for calculation purposes rather than a recommended approach speed.

The total distance for effective prompts on just 2 questions on the approach to a pedestrian crossing has now taken up 22 seconds and 66 car lengths. That is almost 1/5th of a mile from our hypothetical crossing! Suddenly, we have a vivid demonstration of how early, as an instructor, you need to give your pupil the time to deal effectively with a hazard. The problem many PDIs experience when coaching for hazards is that they run out of time, therefore **start prompting earlier** for your pupils!

There's a further issue with prompting that needs to be discussed in order to make it effective. PDIs and indeed some ADIs struggle with prompted tuition by being too vague.

An example of what we're meaning here is for example prompting with the MSPSL routine, once a question has been asked about mirror work, a poor quality prompt to a new pupil would be "so what do we do next?" The reason why this is a problem is because the question isn't specific enough and the learner driver, your pupil, now has to use up valuable road distance and thinking time trying to work out quite what you mean.

We have already said that when prompting, driving instructors leave their prompting too late and therefore run out of time. Not being specific enough in the type of question you're asking simply compounds the problem.

Using the earlier example of the MSPSL routine, a better question to have asked would be "When would you consider applying a signal?"

Here the pupil's thought process is automatically drawn towards signals, thus saving valuable thinking time and allowing the pupil to concentrate on the topic of signals as the next part of the routine following the mirror work.

You are still developing the pupil's learning by testing knowledge with an open question, but you were saving time and helping the learner by being more specific here about what type of question you want them to answer.

A lot of trainee driving instructors are under the misapprehension that if you actually mention the topic in question such as the word signals, then this is guide instruction. It's clearly isn't. It is an open question with a question mark at the end and therefore a prompt. If you can imagine information being stored in the brain as a filing cabinet, then each topic the pupil has been taught since learning to drive is in its own filing cabinet stored away. Your job as a driving instructor is to test this knowledge to make sure it's in place and to make sure the pupil can recall and use the information correctly when asked. This is a natural stepping stone to independent driving.

If the prompted question is vague, then you could imagine the pupil having to go through a number of different filing cabinets in their brain to come up with the answer required. A specific or targeted question leads them to the correct filing cabinet at which point they simply have to open the drawer in their mind and find the correct piece of information.

Loaded questions can also be an extremely good form of prompt with new pupils or pupils who are new to a subject. A loaded question is one that gives the answer but requires an explanation of the reason why from the driver.

Once the pupil develops their knowledge further, a loaded question would not be required.

An example of a loaded question would be as follows: "Why do we not normally indicate when going past parked vehicles?"

Here you've told the pupil not to indicate going past a parked vehicle but you've asked them to explain why. This keeps it safe and simple for new drivers.

Independent driving

There will come a time in their learning that your pupil will have demonstrated knowledge as well as ability to handle a hazard, that you and they will both be confident in their ability to do so, and a stage arrives where the pupil would like to deal with the hazard themselves. It is crucial to discuss this with the pupil before allowing it, since an assumption by the driving instructor that the pupil is handling the hazard unaided could lead to confusion from the pupil who, if unaware of this decision, could well be still waiting for a prompt from you, the instructor.

If your pupil is comfortable talking whilst driving it may be beneficial for them to talk through what they are doing in order to be able to verbalise their thought processes. At this stage of learning, your pupil has the technical skills to carry out a particular aspect of driving and equally importantly they understand why they are doing what they are doing. Their 'bookshelf' on this subject, once empty, now contains books (knowledge) that have been checked and tested for content and understanding. From your pupil's perspective this data is now stored in their brain – both the how and the why. This section of the library is complete.

Multi-tasking

With a full library of driving knowledge consisting of many sections, the knowledge in each having been learned, tested, achieved and stored in the brain, your pupil now faces a new issue. Problems arise when they begin to multi-task, i.e. bringing together all the knowledge they have gained and applying it to every drive they perform; each task is achievable for them but parts can be forgotten due to an overload of information.

If you can imagine this in terms of a jigsaw (another very good metaphor), each piece is a task or skill learned. The problem is trying to put the pieces together efficiently to form a correct picture.

The skill required of the driving instructor here is to allow the pupil to build their jigsaw picture at a rate they can cope with, and for you to realise when they are beginning to overload. Talking with your pupil and asking good questions will help the learner to discover which part, if any, of the driving they feel is a step too far and outside of their coping zone. Once your pupil starts to reflect on what may have caused their learning to temporarily plateau, they are in a better position to start moving on from the hiatus. It may well be that they want you to take on an aspect of risk management to help them focus on the areas that they are capable of doing at that stage of their learning process.

If learning has taken place correctly, and the levels of instruction have created a progressive learning experience, then your pupil should understand what they are doing rather than just remembering what to do, and this is a vital skill as they commence to learn their roadcraft after passing the driving test and driving alone.

Again – you are teaching skills for life, not for passing a driving test!

Chapter 8

CLIENT-CENTRED LEARNING

With the changes to the way the ADI part 3 exam is conducted and therefore how the syllabus has changed, the DVSA are strongly in favour of a client-centred approach to the learning process.

Today, it is so much more about what the pupil has learned, rather than how much the instructor knows.

This change in approach is certainly welcome since, by using this method, there should be safer post-test driving whereby novice drivers are far more prepared for decision making and risk assessing situations.

On reading the examiner's marking sheet (see example on page 90), under the higher level competency section of Teaching & Learning strategies, the second lower level competency states "was the pupil encouraged to analyse problems and take responsibility for their learning?". This neatly sums up what we are talking about here.

The DVSA state their idea of client-centred learning in the National Standard for Driver and Rider Training.

This is covered in Role 6 Unit 3 (Deliver driver/rider training programs – Enable safe and responsible driving /riding).

Client-centred learning is not about the learner taking charge of the learning process and deciding what is going to happen. Instead it is about creating a conversation between the learner and the instructor that is based on mutual respect. The approach is based on the idea that people resist taking on new understandings and resist modifying their behavior if

- the person who is trying to teach them fails to respect and value their idea of who they are
- the person delivering the learning is not seen as 'genuine'
- the person delivering the learning is not seen as having legitimate authority

In the context of learning to drive and ride, the instructor brings to the learning process their hard-earned knowledge, understanding and experience. If they rely simply on telling the learner what they should do, they will probably be able to teach them enough to pass their test. However, all the evidence suggests that the learners in this sort of relationship do not really change the way that they think and quickly forget what they have been taught. There is a better chance of a long-lasting change in understanding and behaviour if the instructor

- presents their knowledge, understanding and experience clearly and effectively
- listens to the learner's reactions to that input
- helps the learner to identify any obstacles to understanding and change
- supports the learner to identify strategies for overcoming those obstacles for themselves

In the past, driving instruction was, to a large degree, a matter of the instructor passing on their knowledge and telling the pupil how to do each of the disciplines required to pass their driving test. It was often said that the pupil will then really learn to drive once they have passed their test! It is hardly surprising that newly qualified drivers who were taught this way would struggle to drive safely on their own once their driving instructor had "done their job"!

It can be argued that although the traditional method of driver instructor teaching worked to the extent that it got a pupil through their test, many pupils were really not capable of decision making to the levels they would require for long term safe driving.

So what is client-centred learning?

Client-centred learning involves putting the pupil at the centre of the learning experience. What it does not do is to put the learner in charge of the learning experience.

The common mistake driving instructors make when experimenting with client-centred learning as a new concept is to think that it is all about only asking questions and allowing the pupil to make all the decisions. This is seen all too often by the DVSA when unprepared PDIs go to test and allow the learner to run the show without guidance or direction. When on test the opposite is also seen frequently where by the PDI takes charge of the lesson and over instructs, not allowing the learner to develop their own problem solving techniques. Therefore, for client-centred learning to be effective a balance must be achieved.

So certainly the pupil should be involved heavily in the decision-making process, but you the driving instructor, the coach, should act as a facilitator, asking good questions so that the pupil can come up with their own solutions.

On the (ADI) part 3 marking sheet, under the higher level competency of Lesson Planning and the first of the lower competencies of – *Did the trainer identify the pupil's learning goals and needs?*, you should be encouraging your pupil to say what they want from the lesson.

Although you are encouraging your pupil, you still have to be in overall charge of the lesson, as your pupil's wants may well be unrealistic to their needs! Client-centred learning does not mean allowing a pupil to decide that they want to do a lesson on dual carriageways if, on the last lesson they were just learning moving off and stopping. It also doesn't involve telling them that they can't do that lesson. It is about facilitating a good conversation to allow the pupil to realise that the lesson is not suitable at this stage.

Earlier in this chapter we've had a look at the DVSAs idea of client-centred learning in the National Standard for Driver and Rider Training.

We can further develop this by looking at an extract from the ADI1. This document is the DVSA guidance for driving examiners carrying out instructor tests and checks.

The guidance notes under the title of teaching and learning strategies, the third of the high-level competences states the following:

> It is important to remember when considering your teaching or learning style that this isn't just about coaching. We're talking client-centred learning here. The DVSA is looking to see whether the ADI / PDI is helping the pupil to learn in an active way.
>
> There are many times when a coaching technique will prove both useful and effective. The principle that underpins coaching is that an engaged pupil is likely to achieve a higher level of understanding and that self-directed solutions will prove to be far more relevant and effective.
>
> Another way of looking at this (putting aside jargon such as 'client-centred' or 'coaching') is to ask yourself whether or not you are involving the pupil in the learning process. If you don't ask them for instance what

they know, what and how they feel about a particular subject, then how do you know what they already know or how they feel? You may be making some assumptions that a completely wrong and therefore instead of involving the pupil you are inadvertently erecting a barrier between both of you.

This applies in every situation, including instruction. Direct instruction helps a pupil in the early stages to cope with new situations when a pupil struggles in a particular situation. Good coaching uses the correct technique at the correct time to match the pupil's needs. An ADI / PDI may sometimes need to give direct instruction through a difficult situation and that instruction forms part of the coaching process so long as the ADI / PDI encourages the pupil to analyse the problem and learnt from it. Thus it follows that a good ADI / PDI takes every opportunity to reinforce learning.

Hopefully you're starting to see now what client-centred learning is and what client-centred learning isn't. Without direct instruction at key moments during the lesson, the lesson could potentially become highly dangerous and since we're talking about safe driving for life and keeping lessons safe at all times, client-centred learning must involve a variety of teaching methods, not just coaching to achieve this level of safety. Sometimes when studying new subjects or subjects you're revising again it is good to step back and look at the larger picture and remember what we are trying to achieve when teaching pupils.

What does client-centred learning involve?
The following gives you an indication of what's involved in client-centred learning and what you as a coach need to do when teaching pupils.

Client-centred learning or CCL involves:

- You, the coach, facilitating. In other words assisting in the learning process by using your knowledge and experience to make it easier for the pupil to develop their learning skills.
- Two-way communication.
- Providing an atmosphere that supports the pupil.
- Elicits the pupil's view.
- Not providing the answers unless the pupil is stuck and is unable to work out a problem themselves.
- Allowing the pupil to reflect on a situation and draw conclusions.
- Changing your approach where necessary to suit the pupils learning style.

- Learning styles tend to fall in to the acronym of VARK. These are **V**isual (diagrams etc.) **A**udible (listening), **R**ead & write (note takers) **K**inaesthetic (sleeves rolled up/do'ers).
- Allowing the pupil to explore different ways of dealing with a problem.
- Actively working to understand how you can best support the pupils learning process.
- Providing accurate and technically correct information to fill in missing gaps in the pupil's knowledge.
- Understanding of the pupil's preferred learning style.
- Using practical examples to reinforce the pupil's learning style when dealing with problems.
- Linking together theory and practice.
- Helping the pupil with guidance on how they may develop their skills outside of the lessons.
- Helping the pupil to achieve lightbulb moments.
- Using for example, a scaling system to allow the pupil to measure their own performance at the start of a lesson and at the end of a lesson.
- Using this scaling, allowing the pupil to look at areas that they want to develop and assisting them to come up with their own plan of action.

You can see from the above that the focus is on client-centred learning and has many advantages when teaching pupils.

However, this may well still prove ineffective if the client, your pupil is not made aware of how a client-centred approach will be a benefit to them.

When you first take your pupil out on a driving lesson they may well have a reasonable expectation that you are simply going to tell them everything they need to know and this is indeed what they've paid for.

Therefore it's essential that you talk to your pupil and explain how client-centred learning will be of benefit to them and to get their agreement on this. They need to know and agree that they will be taking a more active part in the learning process so that after they have passed their driving test they will still be actively thinking, assessing and problem solving for themselves. The emphasis being on driver safety, where your pupil will be aware to a high level and will be able to plan and think and deal with risk.

With this explained you should get the buy-in from your pupil, but you may well still come across pupils who are not interested in client-centred learning and simply want to be told what to do. Respecting the wishes of your pupil you will be able to vary or teaching style to suit their needs.

There will be times where the pupil is leading the session and also times when you, the instructor, are leading the session.

Because both the pupil and you the instructor are sharing the lesson to suit the needs of the pupil, in order to be safe the sharing of the management of risk is essential.

On the Standards Check marking sheet and the Part 3 test sheet, the DVSA naturally emphasise the importance of the management of risk as a sub section of the test that has to be passed on its own merits with a minimum score of at least 8 out of 15.

Hopefully you can see how essential this is. As a reminder the low-level competencies under risk management are as follows:

- Did the trainer ensure that the pupil fully understood how the responsibility of risk would be shared?
- Were directions and instructions given to the pupil clear and given in good time?
- Was the trainer aware of the surroundings in the pupil's actions?
- Was any verbal or physical intervention by the trainer timely and appropriate?
- Was sufficient feedback given to help the pupil understand any **potential** safety critical incidents?

Expanding on the first of these – did the trainer ensure the pupil fully understood how the responsibility of risk would be shared?

The following points are important:

- Ask your pupil what they understand by the term of risk. If it is a pupil you're familiar with, which is likely, then ask them to remind you what they understanding what risk is.
- Check with your pupil that they understand what sort of issues create risk and what risks they see in general driving.
- Ask them what risks they see specifically on the lesson there doing today.
- Explain clearly what is expected of the pupil of what the pupil can reasonably expect of you.
- Check that your pupil understands what's required of them when there's a change of plan or if they're asked to repeat an exercise.
- Make sure that the responsibility of risk is shared out so you and the pupil both know who's responsible for what.
- Check the pupil's understanding of this plan before starting out on the exercise – in other words, sign it off with your pupil.

HERMES Project
(High Impact Approach for Enhancing Road Safety Through More Effective Communication Skills)

It became apparent that ways had to be found to deal with the issue of teaching how to drive but missing out the all-important why, i.e. all the reasoning and understanding that form the bedrock of the basic skill of *how* to drive. One of the most significant projects entered into specifically to look at this issue was the HERMES Project (High Impact Approach for Enhancing Road Safety through More Effective Communication Skills). This is an EU project that looked mainly at how driving instructors could help reduce the number of fatal crashes on the roads by the way in which they deliver their training.

The HERMES project, a European coaching project started in March 2007, ending in 2010. The project looked at learning goals based around the Goals for Driver Education (GDE) matrix. This matrix is based upon accident research and looks at various of levels of learning goals and the reasons and influences that lead to accidents, especially with novice drivers.

In its simplest form it was found that vehicle crashes can be down to manoeuvering skills, but are more likely a lack of skills in managing traffic safely, influences on the driver such as peer pressure and distractions within the vehicle, e.g. mobile phones and finally the attitude and values of the drivers themselves.

One of the key issues discovered by the project was that, when learner drivers take their test, they are at a level whereby they can make their own decisions, can control the vehicle, and take responsibility for risk as well as complying with the Highway Code and dealing safely with other road users. However, all too often it is post-test that novice drivers tend to crash. So, what goes wrong? It appears that once the driving instructor (the conscience) is no longer in the car, then the decisions that are taken are down to the driver's attitude, responsibility, and their attitude to risk. All too often, teenage drivers have a feeling of invincibility.

The HERMES project looked at traditional driver training across Europe where the emphasis of this teaching was found to be more focused on the first level of the GDE matrix; the focus was more on teaching specific vehicle skills and manoeuvres. Pure skills training often leads to over-confidence with learner drivers and a failure to take the responsibility for their actions. In general, learner drivers are much younger than their instructor and often the learner is a teenager; they will usually have better eyesight and faster reaction times than their instructor and this adds to the problem of over-confidence and the feeling of invincibility – "it won't happen to me".

Novice drivers, post-test, involved in fatal crashes are often single vehicle crashes and tend to happen at 'vulnerable' times such as weekends and after midnight where the driver is sometimes tired, under the influence of alcohol/drugs (or both), with peer pressure from other people of similar age in the vehicle pushing the driver to drive beyond their ability to drive safely.

Responsibility, or rather a lack of it, seems to be a recurring theme with vulnerable drivers post-test.

GDE matrix

The GDE matrix (Goals for Driver Education Matrix) sets out the knowledge or skills/risk increasing factors/areas of self-evaluation necessary for driving at the four levels of competence. This will help learner drivers to develop an awareness of risks and to be able to assess their own driving.

The four levels of the GDE matrix are:

1. Vehicle and vehicle control.
2. Traffic situations.
3. The purpose and context of the journey.
4. Human factors that affect your driving.

Let's look at the 4 levels in a little more detail.

Level 1: The vehicle

It is crucial that you know and understand your vehicle and how to control it. This involves knowing what the vehicle is capable of, and what you are capable as a driver. Specifically, when you need to be able to brake, corner and accelerate safely and skillfully. You need to be able to reverse and manoeuvre your vehicle to good and safe levels.

Your vehicle must also be in good condition and safe to be driven. A useful checklist is the following P.O.W.D.E.R acronym:

Petrol – This refers to any fuel source (petrol/diesel/electric) and you should always ensure that there is sufficient fuel for the journey, or plans in place for refuelling if necessary.
Oil – This refers to engine oil and any other oil such as brake fluid or power steering fluid.
Water – These checks would include engine coolant and washer fluid levels.

Damage – This will involve an exterior check of the vehicle looking for loose bodywork and damage to exterior glass.

Electricals – This will involve all exterior lights, all emergency warning lights, horn, front and rear wipers.

Rubber – checking all tyres for damage such as cuts and bulges, objects stuck in the tyres, tread depth. Check wiper blades for damage too.

Level 2 – Traffic situations

Here, you will need to master your observation skills, scanning and planning the driving environment. Hazard perception skills are essential, as it is often other road users that are the cause of problems. You will need to use all these skills to negotiate your drive through traffic. Understanding and using safety margins will be required to keep you safe driving in these times. Risk management builds in here as a further essential.

Level 3 – The journey

Level 3 looks at the specific journey, looking at its purpose and the decisions that need to be made around the planning of the journey. Each trip needs to be evaluated, taking into account the necessity of the journey, the route that is planned to be taken, the types of roads and weather conditions likely to be encountered, the timing of the journey, and the effect that having passengers in the car is likely to have.

Level 4 – Human factors

Level 4 looks at you, the driver along with the type of issues that may affect your drive. These issues would include your attitude to risk, your state of mind at the time you are driving, your personality type, your own life goals and values, your approach to your own vulnerability and your attitude towards your passengers in the car. Also included at this level would be your attitude and approach to other road users; how do you feel about, for example, cyclists and van drivers?

Level 5? Social environment

Although the GDE Matrix shows 4 levels of driver behaviour, there is also an argument for a 5th level. This would look at areas such as group goals at work, the general social environment and cultural issues i.e. we are looking here at human factors, but more as a group than as an individual, but still looking at how these affect the driver.

What the HERMES project concluded was that coaching would help significantly with the problem of deterioration of responsibility in the driver post-test. Coaching would put the learner at the centre of

GDE Matrix

	Knowledge & skills to master	Risk Increasing factors you should be aware of	Evaluating yourself
Level 4 Personal goals for life and skills for living	• Your life goals and values • Personal style, values & situations • Personality type • How do these affect your driving?	• Peer pressure • Your acceptance of risk • Sensation seeking • Lifestyle dependences • Drug and alcohol use	• Attitudes towards risk • Are you impulsive? • Are you spontaneous? • What are the motives behind these impulses? • Examine <u>you</u>!
Level 3 Your specific trip, context and goals	• Be aware of each trip – purpose • Evaluate the trip • Specific needs, motives, goals and circumstances of the trip • Implications of passenger on the trip	• Why you are going on the trip • Is it necessary? • Are you under pressure? • Consider the driving environment • Relationship with passengers	• Have you planned adequately for the trip? • How are you feeling? • Expectations and goals of the trip • Why you undertook the trip • Self-critical thinking
Level 2 Mastering traffic situations	• Observation • Signalling • Scan and plan • Assessing safety margins • Keeping up with traffic rules and regulations • Anticipation skills • Positioning • Safe progress	• Specific driving conditions (weather/darkness) • Vulnerable road users • Your speed vs safety margins • Overload of information • Not following rules and regulations	• How is/are your driving style • Observation skills • Planning and anticipating hazards and how you react to them • Your own safety margins • Question your strengths and weaknesses for the trip
Level 1 Mastering specific vehicle skills and manoeuvers	• The physics of driving • Know your own vehicle and how to handle it • Specifically – Braking, cornering, acceleration • Technical details of your vehicle	• Lack of skill • Not understanding technology of the car • Poor use of speed • Bad road conditions • Poor vehicle maintenance	• How well do you handle the vehicle? • Consistency of car control • Assess your strengths and weaknesses • Understanding of your knowledge & skills

the learning experience. This process is recognised and referred to as 'client-centred learning', and the aim of the HERMES project was to put together a coherent package of coaching learner/novice driver training.

Coaching

What is coaching?

Quoting Sir John Whitmore in his book *Coaching for Performance*, he defines coaching as follows: "Coaching is unlocking a person's potential to maximize their own performance. It is helping them to learn rather than teaching them".

There is a significant difference between teaching someone and helping them to learn.

In coaching the coach is helping the individual to improve their own performance.

One of the most significant changes in the approach to coaching came about with the publication of Timothy Gallwey's book *The Inner Game of Tennis*.

There were limits to what tennis players and other sports professionals could achieve by technical skills teaching alone. The opposition wasn't on the other side of the net it was in fact inside the players head.

Timothy Gallwey suggested that the biggest obstacles to success in achieving potential were therefore internal and not external.

Significant improvements could be made in a person's performance by working and what was going on inside their head – the inner game. These are all the words we say to ourselves, or in a dialogue and the negative effect this has on us.

In tennis coaching, by distracting this inner voice it allow the tennis players body to take over in a relaxed state and therefore their tennis improved.

The principles in Timothy Gallwey's book can be applied in general rather than just specifically to sports players. So from a driving instructor's point of view learner drivers often have the answers to their own problems which can be realised through coaching.

Coaching allows people to help silence the inner voice and start to work more on instinct.

It could well be argued that term driving instructor is no longer relevant. By the very name of instructor this would suggest that it's the driving instructor that tells and instructs the pupil on what the lesson will be, how to plan a lesson, and tells the pupil what to do during the lesson...

It will be reasonable to assume that's our job title should be driving coach rather than driving instructor, as this is what client-centred learning dictates.

The HERMES project defined coaching as follows: "A learner-centred method that engages body, mind and emotions to develop inner and outer awareness and responsibility with an equal relationship between learner and coach."

What is involved in coaching?

The HERMES project in their final report list 13 principles of coaching as follows:

1. The coaching relationship is an equal relationship. The trainer is no longer the 'expert' in the hierarchical sense.
2. Coaching puts the learner in an active role.
3. Coaching encourages the learner to identify their goals and to meet these goals.
4. Coaching raises awareness, responsibility and self-acceptance of the learner.
5. Coaching raises awareness not only through rational thought but also through the learner's senses and emotions. It raises awareness of the learners' values, goals, motives and attitudes as well as their sensations and emotions, knowledge, skills in habits.
6. Coaching addresses the learner's internal obstacles to change.
7. Coaching builds on the prior knowledge and experience of the learner.
8. The coach is convinced of his / her role and of the benefits of coaching.
9. The coach communicates in an authentic neutral and non-judgemental manner.
10. The basic skills a coach uses are effective and precise questioning, listening and reflecting back.
11. Coaching and instruction do not mix. If instruction cannot be avoided, alternate with coaching rather than mixing them.
12. Coaching shall be experienced by the coachee as much as possible as a voluntary process. The learners should not be forced to participate in the coaching method.
13. Coaching is not just about asking questions. It is about using a method which is appropriate for the circumstances, insuring that the learner is putting the active role wherever possible.

Source: HERMES report (February 2010)

Explaining this in more detail:

1. Coaching is seen as a meeting of equals. There is no hierarchy of who's in charge although from a safety point of view the driving instructor is still there for that role. If the pupil feels that the driving instructor's in charge of the lesson then it is likely that they won't take an active part in the lesson to the same extent as they would if it was a meeting of equals. Coaching actively involves the pupil in the learning experience and puts them at the centre of it.

2. Following on from the first point above, coaching now puts the learner in an active role. They feel ownership of learning experience and see their driving instructor as a coach and a facilitator. If the pupil now has an active role they become energized if coached correctly. A pupil who has become active in this way now takes ownership of their learning experience leading to enthusiasm in creativity.

3. Allowing and encouraging a learner to identify their goals and to meet these goals, the goals puts ownership on to the pupil. This is important and links into the above 2 points. When coaching, a good discussion with the learner will insure the goals and needs are met but also importantly are done in a safe and legal manner. By goal setting with learners as a driving instructor it's important that the pupil buys into the goal and sets the goal. Instructors should try to make sure that they don't set the goal for them.

4. Because driving is a complex business it is important when goal setting that the pupil is both aware of the driving environment and is self-aware. They need to know how they're feeling both physically and emotionally and how that will affect their drive. They need to take responsibility for this. A good driving instructor will allow a pupil to take responsibility for their driving and decision-making is crucial both in the short term and long-term because at some point the pupil passes their driving test and they will not get the assistance of the driving instructor. It is fully understood that the driving instructor will often have to make decisions where the learner is not capable due to lack of experience. As time moves on, more responsibility should be given to the learner.

5. This section is more about the pupil's senses and emotions. The majority of drivers tend to be young teenage drivers who by nature tends to be emotional creatures. To an extent they are still

in the process of wiring up their brains and driving often has an emotional side to it, dealing with both other road users and mastering the complexities of physically driving the car.

6. Addressing learner's internal obstacles to change is important if lessons are to progress. The driving instructor, the coach needs to address these to make sure it doesn't have a negative effect on the lesson. internal obstacles could be there for a number of reasons which could include, previous held beliefs, the pupil's views on a subject such as their parents view point, irrational views, issues from previous lessons that haven't been cleared up and linking into the previous notes in this book on *The Inner Game* by Timothy Gallwey there will already be self-limiting beliefs preventing progress from taking place.

All the above points will have to be dealt with as part of the process of learning to drive.

7. Where possible it is good to build on prior knowledge and experience. Even young new drivers are able to bring some form of knowledge to driving lessons. When it happens there is a sense of achievement at the contribution from the learner. An example of this is when turning right from a major road into a minor road, the learner driver having never done this before can use their previous experience as a pedestrian to judge the speed and distance of oncoming vehicles before deciding when to turn.

8. This section is about the buying in of the driving instructor to actually being a coach. By the very nature of the name of instructor, that tends to suggest we should be telling and passing on our knowledge in that way and for many who have been on the register for years this can be a difficult process to change. "If it has worked well in the past and I have a good pass rate, so why should I change and become a coach?" 'Maybe it's some new fad that pass in time' is a view some driving instructors may hold. Hopefully the long-term effects of coaching learner drivers rather than telling them (instructing them) will prove beneficial and will change peoples minds.

9. It is vital when coaching that you come across as genuine and authentic. It's important that you show genuine interest in your pupil and share their desire to succeed. You must believe what you do in the coaching process. Make good eye contact and focus on positives. Check to make sure that your pupil understands and clarify any concerns and questions they may have. This section

also covers the requirement for the coach, the driving instructor, to be non-judgemental, so if something goes wrong it is better to ask the pupil what they think has happened rather than start attributing blame. Look on the positive rather than criticising their driving ability.

10. The very nature of coaching involves questioning and using Q&A techniques.

Quoting directly from the HERMES report, they say that a number of principles have been established for good coaching questions. These include the following:

- Question should follow the interests of the learner and use their words.
- Question should start broadly and then increasingly focus on detail.
- The coach should only ask one question at a time.
- Effective questions are clear open questions which require attention and thought and are non-judgemental.
- Questions can and should focus on the senses such as seeing hearing touching etc., emotions such as moods and feelings, attitudes such as opinions and values, goals and motives as well as cognitive factors such as knowledge and habits.
- Questions can relate current experience to prior experience.

Source: All the above points of direct quotes from the HERMES report (February 2010)

When asking open questions with words such as what, why, when, how, where, who etc, answers are required from the pupil to check that they have understood. Further drilling down of questions may well be necessary where there is ambiguity in the answer.

11. Section 11 on the principles of coaching according to the HERMES report suggest that instruction and coaching do not mix. Certainly when pupils are told what to do by the 'expert' they don't have inputs or ownership of the teaching process. Here the learner does not take responsibility for their learning. They may well pass their test, but post-test their driving starts to fall apart as they are not used to making their own decisions.

Coaching has the opposite effect allowing the learner to take responsibility for their learning, although it is possible that instruction may still be needed in some of the more basic levels and driving when the pupil is new.

12. Looking at the above point of not mixing instruction and coaching many teenage pupils may not have experience coaching in their lives particularly and have been more used to instruction. Therefore coaching can be a new subject and initially has to be explained to gain buy in. Section 12 looks at coaching as a voluntary process. Coaching should be sold as an excellent idea and an excellent way forward but the learner, the pupil cannot be forced in to accepting coaching.

13. The final principle of coaching deals with fact that coaching is not just about asking questions.

    For those who are new to coaching, simply asking questions might seem the obvious answer. In reality, questioning should be selective and appropriate. How do you think a pupil would feel if you continue asking questions and they are unable to give you answers? It will be demoralising to say the least and would certainly have a negative effect. The purpose of questioning when coaching is to put the pupil at the centre of the learning experience and to make the learning experience positive, therefore if questioning is continuously use this won't be reached.

Bricks and mortar

The title of this section may seem strange for a book about driving instruction.

But is it?

The photograph on the next page is that of an 800+ year old chapel. This building can truly be said to have stood the test of time, and has been around long enough to have remained standing through the reigns of 34 British monarchs, the Black Death, the Peasant's Revolt, the Battle of Agincourt, the War of the Roses, the English and Spanish Armadas, the Gunpowder Plot, the Great Fire of London, the Industrial Revolution, two World Wars, the Common Market, and now Brexit!

So, how has it lasted this long? What has held this structure upright for 8 centuries? Is it the bricks? The mortar? Or both?

Consider what would happen to unsecured bricks... The structure may appear perfect and may, initially, hold; but as soon as the structure is put under pressure it is more than likely to collapse, resulting in a failed structure and a pile of bricks. Great!

But how does this relate to driving instruction?

Relate this chapel metaphor to coaching pupils; think of the bricks as the process (how to) of doing something. Let's take the example of

emerging at a junction. The 'how' for observation instruction would be to look into the major road to the right first, then left, and check again to the right with further observations as required. Telling a pupil to do this works, and that is the BIG problem! Through repetition a pupil will remember what to do and may well pass their test. This is unfortunate. Why? If it gets the pupil through their test, how is this deemed unfortunate?

Think about it! Whilst the driving instructor is in the car, over time the pupil demonstrates good effective observations when emerging at T-junctions, so much so that this works when they take their test. Then, the pupil is on their own... The driving instructor is no longer there keeping an eye on the pupil's safety at the T-junctions by helping them to manage risk. Over a period of time, and usually a short one, the discipline of observation skills crumbles away, particularly if there have not been any safety critical incidents early on in the post-test driving. Then it all goes wrong, resulting in a collision with another road user or a pedestrian.

If we follow this example to a logical conclusion, this is one of the reasons why young/novice drivers experience accidents in their early solo driving careers. The 'how to do it' i.e. the bricks only scenario works for a while, but because there is little or no understanding, i.e. the mortar behind the 'how' the structure falls apart over time.

The key thing here is to ensure that not only does the pupil know what to do but, more importantly, they understand why they are doing what they are doing. The why, the mortar, holds everything together. It is vital when teaching/coaching that your pupil UNDERSTANDS rather than REMEMBERS.

So, to return to our earlier example of emerging from a T-junction; if the pupil fully understands that traffic from the right will be the most likely to impact an unsafe emerge rather than traffic from the left, but both directions are vital to observe, then they now understand why the initial and final observation needs to be to the right.

The key skill for the trainer is to use their knowledge, but also to allow the pupil to analyse the problems and take responsibility for their own learning; by doing this means pupils will be so much better prepared for driving once they have passed their test and are driving on their own. This should be a passion with trainers/coaches, not just a job requirement!

The human brain

The human brain is staggering. It is the most complex organ in the human body. Although, as far as size is concerned, it is not the largest brain amongst mammals, an accolade that belongs to the sperm whale.

The human brain is unique. It gives us the ability to speak, imagine, dream problem solve and sets us apart from all of the creatures on the planet.

As well as controlling normal body functions, our brain allows us to think, reason and problem solve.

The average human brain has around 100 billion neurons (nerve cells) which gather and transmit electrochemical signals.

The brain starts to develop in babies when they're still in the womb.

The brain is starting to get 'wired up' at this stage and it will be structured around hereditary genes and by the physical health of the mother. For example brain development in the foetus will be affected by nicotine, alcohol and other drugs.

Once born this wiring map is developed as the baby grows and is affected very much by its surroundings (level 4 on the GDE matrix).

This will include life goals and values often affected by the parents and close friends. It will include personal motives and ambitions. Many of these will be related to age will be affected by for example the journey through school and higher education. Opinions are affected by peer pressure and biases and prejudices can start to form. Group goals and values also become part of the wiring system in the brain. Many aspects of this wiring process can also have cultural backgrounds.

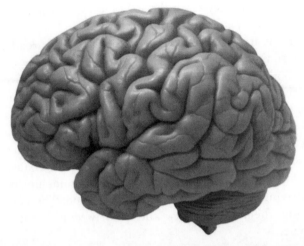

When you think of all the complexities of life from birth to the normal legal age for driving at 17, you can see that no two people could possibly be the same.

So as a driving instructor you can appreciate that each pupil is an individual who you must understand if you are to teach them effectively.

Taking this into account, do people learn to drive at 17 or is it earlier than this? It can be argued that people probably start learning to drive at the age of around about 2 or 3 when sat in the car with parents. It is their parents they look up to for life skills and advice and naturally start to take on board how their parents drive. Although not obvious at this age, by the time they reach the age of 17, their parents driving has formed an intricate pattern of wiring in the brain.

Therefore, is it possible for a new driver to have road rage on a controls lesson? Of course it is if this is the natural way one of their parents or both of them deal with other motorists.

As a driving instructor think about the challenges that are now ahead for you. Driving is the new challenge in life for these 17 year olds and it's you who are responsible for wiring their brain up for this new skill. Thinking of the dangers of driving post-test and the number of irresponsible motorists there are on the roads, then you better make sure that if you are wiring their brains up for this new skill of driving, that you get it right first time. The consequences of teaching them incorrectly and poorly could potentially be catastrophic.

Therefore make sure that you are teaching those skills for life and not how to pass a driving test!

So teach them correctly and understand who they are.

Make sure that you identify your pupils learning goals and needs. Ask the people what they want from their lesson. Ask questions to check understanding. Check understanding as the lesson progresses. Listen to what the pupil is saying and take notes of their body language. Make sure that the pupil understands what they plan to do and that they agree with the plan. Respond to any concerns that the pupil may have. Pick up on non-verbal signs of discomfort or confusion. Ask the pupil what is meant by risk and what sort of issues create risk. Make sure that the pupil understands how risk is going to be shared. Ensure that the pupil understands and agrees with what they plan to do. Allow the pupil to deal with situations appropriately. If there are any potential safety critical incidents, then allow the pupil time to express any fears or concerns that the incident may have caused. Supporting the pupil to reflect in a clear and logical way about what happened. Check that the pupil feels able to put any new strategies in place. Actively work to understand how you can best support the pupil's learning process. Use practical examples that would help the pupils learning. Link learning in theory to learning in practice. Provide time in a suitable location to explore any problems or issues that arise during the lesson or were raised by the pupil. Always leave the pupil feeling responsible for their own learning in a situation.

Explore different ways in which to use examples that best respond to differences in the pupil's preferred learning style. Recognise that some pupils are able to respond instantly where as others need time to think about an issue. Provide feedback that a pupil can understand and that helps them to improve. Respond openly and readily to pupils' queries. Encourage pupils to explore possible solutions for themselves. At the end of a session encourage of pupil to reflect on their own performance and discuss their feelings with them.

All the above come from the guidance notes for assessing driving instructors on their Standards Check or Part 3 test.

The key thing here is everything is about the pupil. In other words client-centred learning. Put another way – how their brain is wired up.

Coaching models

Coaching models allow you to put structure into the learning process. They help us clarify paths to learning.

The GROW model

The grow model has been around for some time.

The origins of the grow model are not exact although it was used as a coaching technique in Tim Gallwey's book *The Inner Game of Tennis* in 1974 and it was used in corporate coaching from the late 1980s.

Key figures in the use in introduction of the grow model can be attributed to Graham Alexander, Alan Fine and Sir John Whitmore.

The grow model has four key stages.

G goal. What do you want?
R reality. Where are you now?
O options. What could you do?
W will/way forward. What will you do?

Initially you need a topic. For example learning to parallel park.

Goal

The goal is about what you want from the session. What is the ideal end goal?

Here the example would be, by the end of the session to have a basic working knowledge of parallel parking, to be safe and reasonably accurate.

THR GROW MODEL

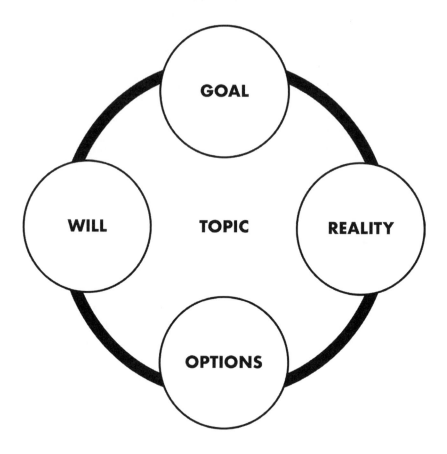

A footnote to the goal section is that goals should be SMART. In other words, Specific Measurable Achievable Realistic and have a Timeframe.

- Specific. What exactly do you want?
- Measurable. How will you measure success?
- Achievable. The goal with the time frame.
- Realistic. Based on current knowledge etc.
- Timeframe. Goals achieved by specified time.

Specific
Being specific targets what is required and adds clarity to the process. For example if the pupil wanted to work on manoeuvres, then this is

quite a general topic. The parallel park is specific and focusses the lesson on to a particular subject. This is useful if the pupil is uncertain about what they want to do, as is often the case.

Measurable

Once a specific goal has been set it needs to be measurable in order to understand when the goal has been achieved. This is where scaling will be of help using a scoring scale of 1–10 and asking your pupil initially where they think they are and at the end of the session, asking them what score they would now give themselves, and importantly asking them why. What help would they need from yourself to help them achieve their goal?

Achievable

As well as measuring a goal, the goal needs to be achievable. If the goal in somewhat unrealistic then it won't be achievable and will have a negative effect on your pupil. It may well be the case that your pupil has set themselves goals that are not achievable in terms of content and time. In the example we are using, then it would be unrealistic to be at test standard on parallel parking on a first lesson on the subject. A more achievable goal may be to have the car under full control and have a reasonable degree of accuracy with the risk being shared and you doing the observation initially.

Realistic

Goals need to be realistic and relevant to the pupil. In client-centred learning, when putting the pupil at the centre of the learning experience the pupil's expectations need to be realistic. This is the pupil's wants and needs. It may well be that their wants are not realistic when compared to their needs. This is therefore closely linked to the goal being achievable. An unrealistic goal with a pupil may well be that having done a controls lesson and moving off and stopping on their first lesson, to be doing dual carriageways on their next lesson (because their friend did dual carriageways last week!)

Timely

Goals need to be timely in order to put a time frame around the topic and goal. Left open ended, there is often no motivation and drive to achieve the goal. Putting a time frame on the goals keeps it focussed and leads to a sense of achievement, once reached.

Reality

Where are you now?

Here we're talking about practical and theoretical knowledge of the subject from the pupil's point of view. Has the pupil ever carried out a parallel park before? Do they understand what is required and therefore how far they are away from their goal and what is required by you to coach them?

Options

Here there are obstacles preventing the pupil from achieving their goal initially and therefore options are the ways of helping achieve their goal by making progress.

In the example, options would include an understanding of the level of accuracy required by the use of diagrams or a tutor demonstration, being able to control the vehicle at a crawl both forwards and in reverse, and the corresponding levels of instruction required. The key thing throughout the grow model is to facilitate and allow the pupil to do most of the decision-making and talking.

Will/way forward

By this stage of the model it should be fairly clear how to progress and the will or the way forward are the steps required to achieve the goal. Commitment from the pupil is required on the specific approach they are going to take to achieve their goal.

In the example we will be looking at practice during the session and possibly homework for the pupil to do to study up on the parallel park prior to the next lesson.

The OSCAR model

The OSCAR model was designed by Karen Whittleworth and Andrew Gilbert in 2002 and builds on the GROW model.

The model is built around 5 contributing factors:

- Outcome. What would success look like?
- Situation. What is the current situation and feelings?
- Choices. What choices do we have? What options can we choose from?
- Actions. What actions can we take? How will we do it? (Scale)
- Review. What steps will we take to review progress?

Outcome

What would success look like? Here we are looking at what the desired outcome of the coaching is. We are looking more towards the

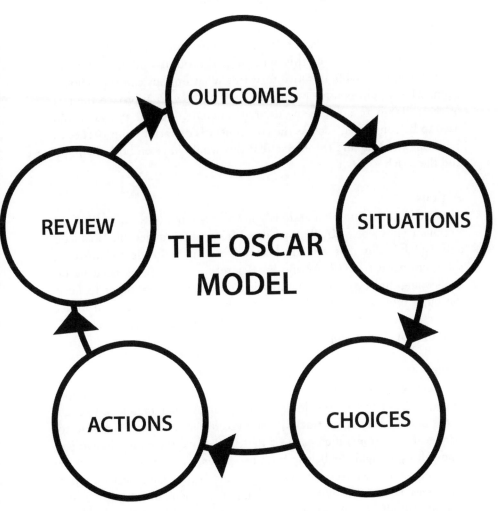

longer term goals of the pupil. So for example, the long term outcome of learning to drive would be safe driving for life and as a natural consequence of this, for your pupil to pass their driving test.

Situation
This is where we are now – the current situation and the pupil's feelings. So in assessing this in terms of learning to drive, the situation would include the level of skill that the pupil is at and what parts of the syllabus they have completed and also how they feel about what they have completed – their levels of confidence. It would also include their theory knowledge. Discussions with your pupil should be aimed at making the pupil aware of their current situation.

Choices

What choices do you have? What options can you choose from? Looking at this section, this will help the pupil understand what resources are available to move forward. What options can they choose from? This would involve planning ahead on how to approach the rest of the syllabus to achieve the desired outcome. Various things would need to be considered such as the consequences of various approaches to achieving the goal and the effects that this would have on both the pupil and the coach.

Actions

This section is about what actions you will take and how you will do it. Actions need to be SMART (Specific, Measurable, Achievable, Realistic and Timely). This has already been covered in more detail above in the section on the GROW model. Therefore the actions need to be challenging and positive without being too stretching in order to keep the pupil motivated. Again, scaling can be used to measure and target progress and to check if the progress is remaining on track. You will need to provide the support for your pupil to help them.

Review

The review stage of the OSCAR model is where you and your pupil can monitor progress and look at any changes that might be needed to the plan to keep it on track. If the overall plan is broken down in to manageable sections, then each of these will have their own individual timescales and again will help monitor progress. Reviews will also be able to look at the effectiveness of the details of the plan rather than just timescales. Discussions with your pupil, putting them at the centre of the process will allow them to come up with solutions to get the plan back on track, if this is what is required.

The diary of a potential driving instructor

In this section we are going to look at coaching skills in a practical environment.

Let's set the scene. You have passed your part 1 and part 2 exams and you have recently completed your basic 40 hour training (statutory minimum) with your ORDIT trainer (ORDIT – Official Register of Driving Instructor Training). In actual fact you did 47 hours as both you and your trainer agreed that after 40 hours you weren't quite ready for teaching learner drivers.

Teaching real learner drivers is the training route that you now want to follow, as you and your trainer both feel that gaining experience on a trainee licence will give you the best advantage when you take your Part 3 test, to get on the Register of Approved Driving Instructors.

You have sent off for your trainee licence a couple of weeks ago and this has now arrived. This gives you 6 months to develop your skills and take up to 3 attempts to get on the Register. Your instructor's driving school are sponsoring you and you have gone to pick your new car up from their office. You have an induction meeting during the morning at the school, collect your car at lunchtime and drive home.

It's Friday and you have the weekend off as your badge doesn't start until Monday. The school have been sending you pupils over the past few days and you have a total of 6 pupils from the school and a couple of your friends who want you to teach them to drive. 8 in total and you are hoping that the school will keep sending you more pupils over time. You don't want to overload yourself to start with and are happy teaching a couple of 2 hour lessons a day to start with.

You use the weekend to review your notes that you wrote up during your training. You keep going over in your head all the role plays you were involved in with your trainer and the other PDI who was in the car training with you. You go over your lesson plans so that these are clear in your head and you make sure that you have all the diagrams you need for teaching.

You remember numerous discussions you had with your trainer about coaching skills and client-centred learning. You remind yourself that you should be asking and not telling and empowering the pupil to analyse problems and take responsibility for their own learning. You go over the need for good risk management throughout every lesson you teach. You remember how useful feedback sessions were with your trainer when you were filling out reflective logs. You promised yourself that you would make sure you ran quality feedback sessions with all your pupils. You're prepared – Bring on Monday!

Monday arrives, time to put it all in to practice.

Your first pupil is one of the friends who you said you would teach to drive. You're prepared and ready. You run through a controls lesson without too many issues, then you get your friend setting off for the first time. This isn't role play anymore. As the lesson progresses your friend says he's confident with how you're teaching him and before the lesson ends, you try some junction work. A left emerge goes badly wrong with your pupil hitting the gas pedal before they have finished steering. The car shoots over towards the far kerb. You grab the wheel and hit the dual controls and come to an abrupt stop less than 1 metre from a parked car. The theory has gone out of the window now, this is real!

Your second lesson on your first day is with a pupil sent to you by the school. They took lessons a couple of years ago but stopped when they lost their job. They had done around 12 hours previously.

With this pupil, you decide to get out on the road after a few questions, the eyesight check and the licence check. You're nervous after the incident on the previous lesson, particularly since you know very little about your driver. You stay a bit quiet at first as your pupil seems to have remembered how to drive. They then stall 3 times setting off from traffic lights and the cars behind are all blasting their horns. This only makes matters worse, but eventually, your pupil gets underway. This is nothing like your training course and when you get home you tell your partner what happened and how your first day had gone.

They give you the advice that you need to take more control of what's happening and to speak more. You thank them and take this on board for tomorrow.

The next day you have 3 lessons. These go a little better, as you have now started looking ahead a lot more at what's going on out of the front windscreen. You find that if you talk a lot more and tell your pupil what to do, things start to get better and you can keep the learner under control.

The week progresses and there are a few more incidents, including slight damage to the front nearside alloy, but overall it wasn't too bad and you survived. You have a feeling that you have found a way of teaching and keeping safe.

You were going to look through your training notes at some point during the week, but as you were tired at the end of each day, you found yourself falling asleep in the chair a few times and you went to bed earlier than normal. You make a note to run through your training notes next week.

A couple of your pupils left you after their first lesson, but you are not sure why. These were both pupils who were quite experienced learners. You feel that you need to replace these and you could also do with one additional pupil. You phone the school and they send you another one during your second week. You decide to do some local advertising, but you remember from your training that you are not allowed to advertise in any way that would mislead people in to thinking that you are a qualified driving instructor.

You spend some of the following week dropping off leaflets as well as teaching pupils. You promise yourself that you will have a look through your training notes soon, when you get some more time.

The weeks roll by and after a few weeks, one of your pupils has their driving test. This is an exciting time for you as it's your first test and you think that your pupil should do well as you have been telling her what to do and how to pass her test for the last 5 weeks. Both of you are confident of a good first time pass.

Your pupil comes back and has failed with 12 driver faults and 2 serious faults. The atmosphere in the car on the way back from the test is a little frosty. Eventually you both have a chat about what went wrong. Your pupil tells you that she was nervous and had forgotten everything you told her to do.

A similar situation occurs with your second pupil you take to test. Again they say that they have forgotten what you told them. Your third pupil to test passes which is brilliant news for you and you are delighted, even though they got 14 driver faults. But whatever, a pass is a pass!

The driving school get in touch with you and remind you that you are booked in for your 20 hours additional training and you get in touch with your ORDIT trainer. The office ask you to bring any notes with you and any questions that you may have.

You meet up with your trainer to start your 20 hours of additional training. You start off having a debriefing session with your ORDIT trainer and run through everything that's happened since you picked your car up. You tell them how excited you were to get a first pass and mentioned that your first two people who you took to test didn't pass but they were a little bit nervous.

Your ORDIT trainer asks you why you think they didn't pass. You have a careful think and tell your trainer that you thought it was because they didn't listen to what you told them to do. Your trainer asks you why you are telling them what to do when they were driving all the time and you reply telling them that after a few incidents in early lessons it was the only way to keep the car under control.

You then both get out on the road to do some role-play sessions so your trainer can have a look at how you're teaching. It soon becomes very obvious to your trainer that as a trainee driving instructor you've started looking out of the front windscreen all the time and not noticing what your pupil, the driver is actually doing. Your trainer also notices that you're over instructing all the time, telling the driver what to do and not taking any time out to ask any questions. Therefore you're not providing any opportunities to check any form of understanding.

You go back into a classroom environment and spend a couple of hours reviewing your coaching and how you can progress forward. Your trainer has got an extract from the ADI 1 document covering what the examiners are looking for in each part of the 17 lower competences on the marking sheet. You both go through these in detail and you remember that this is what you should have done in the first week or two when you're out on a trainee driving licence. You explain to your trainer that this is what you had intended to do, but everything got busy and a little bit chaotic and you were tired at the end of each day. You had intended to read your notes but I guess you just forgot.

During the two hour discussion everything started to become a lot clearer when you realised that originally when you were doing your 47 hours training you had been taught how to coach a pupil, but when you got out in the real world teaching learners you had forgotten this and had started doing things your own way in order to try and keep the car safe, you safe and your learner safe.

Your trainer runs through your roleplay session and discuss it with you how this relates to the Part 3 marking sheet.

Regarding lesson planning, it is clear that you didn't identify the pupils learning goals and needs and therefore the lesson structure was not appropriate for the pupils experience and ability.

Regarding risk management, there was none and this hasn't been discussed at all during the lesson. You are not aware of the pupil's actions, your verbal intervention was not timely or appropriate and you're not conducting any feedback sessions (something you had promised yourself you would do with all your pupils in those more relaxing days before you actually started teaching learners).

Regarding teaching and learning strategies, your teaching style wasn't suited to the pupils learning style and current ability, the pupil wasn't being encouraged to analyse problems and take responsibility for their own learning because you were doing it all, there was no feedback and at the end of the session the pupil wasn't encouraged to reflect on their own performance.

So overall you're a long way away from where you should have been if you wanted to pass your Part 3 test.

You get back out on the road working with your coach / trainer.

Over the next few hours you work hard on developing your skills the way you have been taught originally when you did your 47 hours.

All the original training starts coming back to you and you find that when you're watching the pupil more you start to see the faults developing inside the car before they actually manifest themselves outside the car.

You start dealing with risk management correctly. At the start of each session you talk about risk, asking the pupil what they understand by the term risk, what type of risk they think is associated with the lesson and how the risk is going to be shared out. You asked your pupil what help they're going to need from you during the training session. Both you and your trainer work together on making sure that your directions and instructions to the pupil are clear and given in good time, that you are now fully aware of both the surroundings and the pupils actions, that verbal or physical intervention is timely and appropriate and also that feedback is given to help the pupil understand any potential safety critical incidents if they happen.

You conclude your training session with your trainer and go back out to teaching your learners.

This time after each lesson, you allow yourself time to make notes and prepare for your next lesson.

You decide not to replace the two missing pupils yet and use the spare time to improve the quality of what you're doing rather than dealing with volume. You were reminded by your trainer that the purpose of the trainee licence that you've got for 6 months is to allow you to practice in preparation for taking your ADI part 3 exams rather than turning it into a commercial venture.

You start to notice the quality of your tuition improving and surprisingly to you the lessons are starting to become safer because you are spending more time watching the pupil rather than spending all the time looking out of the front windscreen.

You notice what the pupil is doing with their eyes, their hands and their feet. You see the faults starting to develop inside the car before they start to develop outside the car.

You have remembered that feedback sessions are vital to the pupil and pull over as required to discuss progress. With practice you start putting the pupil at the centre of the learning experience. You start asking them questions and try your best not to provide the answers but to help them provide their own solutions to issues and problems.

This is by no means perfect yet, and you have further practice sessions with your trainer to refine your coaching.

Over the next few weeks you take 3 more pupils to test. Two out of the three of them pass, but the key thing here is that the number of driver faults is averaging around 4 and the one person who failed picked up one serious fault and only two minor faults. All your pupils are now saying that they actually understand what's happening when they're learning to drive rather than just trying to remember and they find that the question and answer sessions and the discussion of risk management are really helpful.

Taking on board the advice of your trainer you have booked your first attempt at the ADI part 3 exam and have that coming up in a couple of weeks. Again taking your trainer's advice you have selected a pupil who's done around about 15 to 20 hours so that they have got a reasonable amount of experience but still have plenty to learn. You have decided what the lesson is going to be as you feel you would be good at teaching roundabouts.

On the day of the test you turn up in good time and have ensured that you've got your training notes with you, as the examiner will want to see these prior to the test. Both you and your pupil are feeling a little bit nervous but confident that the lesson will be ok. Once the test has started, before long, you forget that the examiner's actually in the car and carry on with your lesson on roundabouts around a route that you've carefully selected and practiced over the last 2 weeks.

You consider it important to get back within the hour and manage to come back within 57 minutes and are pleased with how the test is gone.

The examiner has a brief word with you and says that it will be about 15 minutes before they have got the result, at which point they can have another discussion with you.

When you meet up with the examiner he says that on this occasion you haven't passed your part 3 exam. You have scored 27 marks and this is broken down as follows – 7 on lesson planning 9 on risk management in 11 on teaching and learning strategies. You're naturally disappointed as you were certain you have got a pass.

Although you'd listened to the debrief you haven't taken it all in and phone your trainer to meet up the following day. When you meet up with your trainer you have a question and answer session and you both have a good look through the marking sheet. Once you've talked through everything you realised that the lesson wasn't appropriate for the pupil and, in actual fact, had being chosen by you because you are comfortable with it. The level of instruction was also incorrect and you had guided them through everything rather than allowing them to take more responsibility as the lesson developed using questions and answers and eventually allowing them to practice independently if this is what they felt was appropriate. On a positive note the risk management section had achieved a reasonably good pass mark.

Although you had taken on board most of what your trainer told you, you had made the mistake of teaching the lesson that you wanted to do rather than the one that your pupil needed.

Remember when you were teaching pupils, the lesson should be based around what they want and importantly learning must take place.

Over the next week you review your teaching with your pupils and start to prepare for your second attempt at the ADI part 3 exam. Your second attempt is booked in in 6 weeks time and you choose a different pupil to take to test this time. In preparation you ask your pupil what they want to do on the lesson and base your lesson around this rather than what you want to teach.

You prepare well for your second test and on the day of the test you feel better prepared. When you ask your pupil what they want to do on the lesson, they say that they would like to carry out some practice on dual carriageways and faster roads. This is what the lesson is now based on.

During the test you ask your pupil to pull over at the side of the road a couple of times to reflect on how the lesson is going and in particular to deal with a potential safety critical incident that occurred part way through the drive. You allow the pupil to analyse and reflect on what happened and to come up with a solution to the incident. They ask you a couple of questions about areas they were uncertain of and you fill in the missing gaps in their knowledge.

At the end of the test, the examiner lets you know that you have passed your ADI part 3 test with a score of 38 and the risk management score of 11.

You are delighted and can now call yourself an Approved Driving Instructor.

Summary

As you can see from the notes from the diary of the PDI, the path to becoming a qualified driving instructor is not as straightforward as it may first appear.

Initially there is the minimum 40 hours training which may well end up being in excess of this basic minimum requirement depending upon how well the training goes and the requirements of the pupil. Although not essential the trainee licence offers PDIs the opportunity to practice their skills with learner drivers.

Theory and practice don't necessarily go hand in glove although you would think that they should. Problems start once the PDI is unsupervised following their initial training. When on a trainee licence you have the situation of a trainee driving instructor running lessons with a learner driver. Therefore the additional 20 hours or the 20% of supervised tuition is essential to keep the trainee driving instructor on track.

As a trainee, teaching real learners will be new to you, you have the pressure of trying to get enough people to teach and you will also be trying to put into practice everything you've been taught by your trainer. This is not an easy task and you should look for as much support as you can find. In addition to the help that your trainer can give you there are many online forums where fellow PDIs and also ADIs can share information.

Don't fall into the trap of over teaching, looking out of the front windscreen and not paying any attention to what the pupil's doing. Remember that it is the pupil who is driving the car. They're using the steering wheel the gear lever the indicators and the pedals and unless you can keep a check on what's happening with the pupil doing these tasks you'll never be in a position to keep the car fully under control. Taking your eyes off the road is a leap of faith to an extent, and once you realise that you can glance at what's happening in front of you and behind and at the same time watch what the pupil is doing then you will find that that you're teaching and their driving is becoming safer.

When it comes to the Part 3 test of instructional ability, try to forget that the examiner is in the car and focus on delivering a normal lesson that you would teach to a pupil rather than putting on a show for the examiner. Be as natural as you can be. During the test focus on the pupil and what they learn.

So good advice for the test is as follows:

- Prepare well during your training.
- Don't practice routes but know you're training area.
- Make sure that the lesson is suitable for the pupil and is a lesson that the pupil both wants and needs.
- If there are any incidents during the lesson make sure that you adapt the lesson to deal with this instead of persisting with the original plan.
- Ensure that you discuss risk and that the risk is shared out so both you and your pupil know who is responsible for what.
- Make sure that you are aware of your surroundings and also watch your pupil.
- Put your pupil at the centre of the learning experience.
- Use any opportunities that you see to emphasise points you're trying to make. Actually seeing an example of what you're talking about is so much more powerful than purely using diagrams.
- Do your homework and make sure that your own technical information is up to date and accurate.

- Be prepared to make sure that you answer all your pupils' queries and that you run feedback sessions to allow the pupil to explore their own lesson.
- Use the scaling system whereby your pupils are scoring themselves between 1 and 10 both at the start of the lesson and again at the end for comparison and put structure to the scaling, rather than arbitrary numbers.

Chapter 9

THE ESSENTIAL REQUIREMENTS OF A DRIVING INSTRUCTOR

In this chapter we will look at the essential requirements and skills of a successful driving instructor. We will look at the competencies that are required to be a safe and competent instructor/coach.

Looking at the exams that PDIs are required to undertake, these are done in a set order for good reason. First of all you need to demonstrate that your theoretical knowledge is to a high standard. This is the (ADI) part 1 exam. Here, your knowledge is tested to make sure that you fully understand the theory behind safe driving. Essential reading when studying for the (ADI) part 1 exam will include:

- *The Official Highway Code*
- *Know Your Traffic Signs*
- *The Official DVSA Guide to Driving: the Essential Skills*
- *The Official DVSA Complete Learner Driver Pack*
- *The Official DVSA Guide to Hazard Perception*
- *The Official DVSA Complete Theory Test Kit*
- *The Official DVSA Theory Test for Car Drivers*

The next stage is the ADI part 2 exam of practical driving ability where you will be able to use your theoretical knowledge whilst driving to a high standard.

The final and third stage in the process is the ADI part 3 exam of teaching ability, where you'll be able to put all your theoretical knowledge and practical driving experience to good use for passing on your knowledge in the examination of teaching ability. This exam is designed to test your coaching skills.

Safety

Safety is the key essential of all driving whether it's you driving the car or you teaching a pupil to drive the car. Safety must never be compromised for any other aspects of driving.

Safety will involve the management and sharing of risk with your pupil throughout the lesson and as we have previously alluded to, risk management is dynamic and therefore changes throughout the lesson. It is essential that both you and your pupil understands who is responsible for what elements of risk and that there is an agreed structure to the lesson regarding risk. This can be done by asking the pupil to identify what risks might be involved in the subject you're working on as well as risk in general, then asking the pupil how much help they would like from you.

As a driving instructor you need to be aware of the surroundings and also of your pupils actions.

You need to be aware of everything that's happening around you, how your learner's dealing with it and be prepared to help them deal with difficult situations. Whether this is done by verbal or physical intervention instruction or by prompt will depend on the situation and the current ability of the pupil. You need to be able to choose the correct method in good time.

Your verbal or physical intervention needs to be timely and appropriate. If you need to take control of the vehicle don't leave it too late so that this develops into a high risk situation. On the other hand don't take physical control if a simple instruction would do the job or if the pupil is capable of dealing with the issue of themselves.

Other areas of safety which are essential include the following:

To be able to come to an informed judgement that the driver's physical and emotional state are suitable for driving.
That the same applies to the passengers in the vehicle. In both examples of the driver and the passengers, we looking at things such as fitness to drive and also making sure that the driver and the passengers are not under the influence of drugs or alcohol, thus compromising safety.

The current legal limit for alcohol are as follows:

England and Wales

- 35 micrograms of alcohol per 100 ml of breath.
- 80 mg of alcohol per 100 ml of blood.
- 107 mg alcohol per 100 ml of your urine.

Scotland

- 22 micrograms of alcohol per 100 ml of breath.
- 50 mg of alcohol per 100 ml of blood.
- 67 mg alcohol per 100 ml of your urine.

Obviously the ideal level of alcohol when driving is zero. Alcohol and drugs have a number of different effects on the body and can therefore affect driving in different ways. Some people become more aggressive whilst others become more relaxed. Many people under the influence of drugs and alcohol have got a very unrealistic sense of their own ability.

That the vehicle you were using is roadworthy safe and legal.
Routine maintenance checks need to be carried out to check the roadworthiness of the vehicle. These would include checking that the tyres are in good condition correctly inflated, checking that all the lights work, that the fluid levels are all correct. This would include engine oil, water coolant, power steering and brake fluid levels. Other checks would include that there is no damage to the vehicle and the windscreen isn't damaged and the seatbelts are all working correctly.

The importance of planning a journey before setting off, taking account of road traffic and weather conditions.
When planning a journey before setting off, check your route for accidents, roadworks, heavy congestion and queues. This may well be affected by the time of the day you decide to travel. Using online communications there are so many different ways of checking all these, these days, and so if planned correctly there cannot be excuses. Always allow plenty of time for your journey.

Multitasking

As you can see by taking the ADI part 1, 2 and 3 exams in order you are building up detailed theoretical knowledge, detailed practical driving experience and passing this on to your pupil whilst you're coaching and teaching them.

As a driving instructor your ability to multitask while carrying out all these features is essential and not always easy. You have to scan the road ahead, scan the road behind, watch what your pupil's eyes hands and feet are doing and be fully aware of the position of your vehicle and other vehicles around you. Although not easy this is an essential requirement of the job that we do.

The journey

Regarding the journey you will need to plan a suitable route and calculate the time required for the journey:

- Choose roads that are suitable for your vehicle and not badly affected by weather conditions traffic volume or roadworks.
- Choose a suitable alternative route if appropriate.
- Choose locations for rest breaks and refueling if on a long journey.
- Memorise key references where necessary.
- Be prepared for unexpected delays and breakdowns.

All this information when planning a journey can be ascertained using maps, the internet, weather reports, sat nav, radio and TV news and traffic reports etc.

Therefore with the well-planned journey allowing extra time for unexpected events such as delays and queues of traffic, drivers will not put themselves in a situation where they have to rush compromise safety. Remember when travelling to a destination that is far more important to get there than to arrive on time, although with good planning arriving on time should not be too difficult. You can be travelling on a 6 hour journey and a sat nav taking into account road conditions will tell you within a minute what time are you likely to arrive.

The ability to guide and control a vehicle safely (Taken from the DVSA car and light van driving syllabus (Category B))

As a driving instructor you should be able to guide and control your vehicle safely responsibly taking into account road traffic weather conditions.

Learner drivers need to deal with the complexity of controls of the vehicle and therefore need to be able to master the basic skills. As a driving instructor we have to manage this process whilst at the same time taking account of everything around us. Acquiring vehicle control skills will give a learner driver the basic skills on which they can build.

As a driving instructor one of the important things to recognise is that you need to keep up to date with changes in the driving environment such as:

- Changes in the Highway Code and other rules and regulations that get updated.

- Changes and improvements to vehicle and road technologies. This is also so true for your pupils who will be in the process of studying for their theory test whilst learning to drive.

This is a continuous process for both yourself as a driving instructor and also for your pupils.

The following is a list of basic skills that a driving instructor will need to ensure their pupil can carry out safely

A pupil needs to be able to carry out pre start checks in line the vehicle handbook.

This would also include POWDER checks as discussed earlier in the book.

As a reminder this is P for petrol or any other fuel source to include diesel or electric, O for oil. This would include engine oil, brake fluid reservoir and power steering fluids. W for water. This would include engine coolant and the windscreen washer reservoir. D for damage. This will include damage to the alloys the bodywork mirrors windscreen front back side windows. E for electrical. This will include all the lighting system, the hazard lights and anything on the instrument warning panel. R for rubber. This will mainly involve the tyres but will also include windscreen wiper blades.

When starting the engine, your pupil needs to be aware of any instrument panel failure lights that may remain on. They also need to know what the warning lights mean in how to deal with a problem.

Your pupils will also need to know how to operate light switches in the vehicle referring to the vehicle handbook if required. Your pupils should understand what type of lights to use and when to use them such as dipped headlights, full beam, hazard warning lights and fog lights.

Your pupils need to be able to coordinate the use of the controls to move off safely and under control in different situations. Your pupil should check their brakes when first moving off to make sure that these work. They also need to understand how to recover quickly and effectively if the vehicle stalls and understand why they have stalled. You need to teach pupils to only move off when it's safe to do so, taking all-round effective observation including blind spot areas.

Pupils need to be able to move off safely and under control at an angle from behind a parked vehicle or obstruction. They also need to be able to move off under control and safely on a gradient. They need to pay particular attention to vulnerable road users such as:

- Elderly pedestrians.
- Children.
- Deaf or partially sighted pedestrians.
- Cyclists.
- Motorcyclists.
- Horse riders.

Once on the move pupils also need to be taught how to stop the vehicle in a safe legal and convenient position. They need to learn how to apply the parking brake effectively taking into account the different types of tuition needed for normal manual handbrake and also electronic handbrake.

They also need to consider whether to select a gear to hold the vehicle safely when parked particularly on a gradient. Additionally when parked on a gradient the front wheels may need to be turned towards or away from the kerb depending whether they're parked up or downhill.

Pupils need to consider whether parking lights would be required depending on the speed of the road and the time of day.

Once switched off the vehicle needs to be securely locked to secure against theft.

With modern cars and immobilisers it's worth considering where you leave the keys once in the house as keys can be cloned if left near windows or close to outside walls of the house.

Whilst driving pupils need to learn how to monitor and respond to information from:

- Instrumentation.
- Driving aids.
- The environment.

Pupils need to learn how to use switches and other controls in response to changes in the road surface and weather conditions as required, such as the use of wipers, demisters and fog lights etc.

When driving safely on the road your pupils need to be taught a safe and systematic routine such as mirrors-signal-manoeuvre whenever maneuvering.

Pupils need to be able to learn how to effectively indicate there intentions to other road users, insuring that signals are used in good time and inform but do not confuse.

Whilst driving it is essential that your pupils learn how to use the accelerator smoothly and effectively to maintain and change speed. Make sure when teaching that your pupils are aware of the risks of poor use of the accelerator.

Brakes should be used safely using appropriate techniques. This will involve training your pupils to apply appropriate break pressure and to understand how overall stopping distances change depending on weather conditions speed and how these distances are broken down into thinking and braking distances.

Pupils need to be taught how to stop accurately as and when necessary, to make appropriate use of the parking brake and also to be able to stop the vehicle safely and under control in an emergency.

As well as effective use of the pedals, teach your pupils to steer the vehicle smoothly and effectively to maintain and change position on the road, on a straight course and in corners or bends. You also need to teach how to hold a steering wheel so that when your pupil is steering this is done with full control. Pupil should also be able to change gear and operate the controls whilst keeping the steering under control.

You also need to teach pupils how to use steering lock where necessary when maneuvering.

Gears need to be used smoothly and effectively to maintain speed and minimise environmental impact. Inappropriate gear use can result in excessive fuel consumption and higher exhaust emissions.

Pupils need to be taught how to change gears smoothly and in good time. They also need to use a suitable gear for speed and driving conditions and use selective gear changing.

If you're teaching in a vehicle with an automatic gearbox, then the use of the automatic gearbox needs to be explained carefully and effectively used.

Manoeuvres

Maneuvering will involve the coordination of the clutch, the gears, the accelerator, brakes and steering to carry out the following manoeuvres safely, responsibly and accurately with consideration for other road users and awareness of blind areas:

- Left reverse.
- Right reverse.
- Parallel parking.
- Turn in the road.
- Forward bay parking.
- Reverse bay parking.

- Pulling up on the right-hand side of the road, reversing and rejoining the carriageway.
- Performing controlled stops.

When teaching safe driving for life, which is what we should be doing, then ensure that you teach all the above even though not all of the syllabus is tested during the learner driver test.

Driving in accordance with the Highway Code

Pupils need to be taught to deal with all types of junctions and roundabouts safely and in line with the guidance given in the Highway Code.

Pupils need to use a safe and systematic routine such as mirror-signal-manoeuvre to deal with junctions and roundabouts.

Pupils need to be able to carry out the following:

- Turn left.
- Turn right.
- Go ahead at junctions.
- Cross the path of oncoming traffic safely when turning right.
- Emerge into traffic streams correctly from both left and right sides.
- Interact safely and appropriately with other road users.

Pupils need to be taught how to maintain a suitable position on the road. This will include keeping to the left in normal driving conditions unless otherwise instructed and using lanes as described in the Highway Code. It also includes how to keep a safe position in the lane, change lanes safely and responsibly when necessary.

Whilst driving, pupils need to be taught how to respond correctly to:

- Warning signs.
- Information and direction signs.
- Comply with mandatory and prohibitive signs giving orders.
- Comply with all lights that control traffic.
- Deal legally and safely with all types of pedestrian crossings and also railway or tram crossings.

Driving within the rules of the Highway Code will also involve complying with all markings on the carriageway and therefore pupils will need to understand the meaning of:

- Lines in the centre or along the side of the roads.
- Lines at junctions.

- Segregation markings for buses trams and cycles.
- Ghost islands (these are islands with markings but not raised kerbs).
- Traffic calming measures.
- Written signs.

Your pupils also need to be taught how to comply with signals given by authorised persons such as:

- Police officers.
- Traffic wardens.
- School crossing wardens.
- Highways Agency traffic officers.
- DVSA officials.

Driving safely and efficiently

When interacting with other road users, pupils need to be taught how to give timely clear and correct signals according to the Highway Code.

They need to know how to position their vehicle to support the signaled intentions.

They also need to know how to use the horn and lights correctly to communicate with other road users and they should avoid showing aggressive or negative behavior towards other road users.

Pupils need to be taught to actively scan the road space all around both close-up and into the distance.

They need to make sure that they are aware of all of the road users, including pedestrians, cyclists and motorcyclists, and have time to plan what they going to do.

Pupils must show awareness of other road users anticipate what they are likely to do and give them time and space to manoeuvre.

Pupils need to look out for other road users who may not react as quickly as you would expect or in a way that you would expect. They need to allow for others mistakes.

Both you and your pupil need to manage the way they react to other road users, identifying and responding correctly to vulnerable road users and respond correctly to emergency vehicles.

When making progress on the road pupils need to be able to drive at a suitable speed for the road and conditions and only overtake when it's safe legal and necessary. Also, pupils should allow others to make progress where required.

Defensive driving

Driving defensively means that your pupil needs to:

- Judge speed and distance correctly and effectively.
- Create and maintain a safe driving space around the vehicle.
- Not encroach unnecessarily on other road user's space.
- Stop safely within the distance you can see to be clear.
- Always use a safe and systematic routine when driving including effective scanning.
- Look for clues for potential hazards and anticipate situations that might turn into a hazard.
- Prioritise hazards and potential hazards effectively.
- Ensure that their vehicle is in an appropriate position on the road in the right gear and travelling at the right speed so that you can respond appropriately to any hazard.
- Maintain their attention to the driving task when faced with distractions.

Pupils need to be aware of their physical and mental fitness and assess whether it is affecting their fitness to drive.

Eco driving

Teach your pupils the principles of eco-safe driving by:

- Removing excess weight including roof racks and storage boxes from the vehicle when not needed.
- Planning well ahead so they make progress on the road and can accelerate and decelerate and brake smoothly and progressively to minimise fuel consumption.
- Ensuring they can use the highest gear appropriate for the road and traffic conditions.
- Teaching them to use cruise control where appropriate as this will help minimise fuel consumption.
- Instructing them to make appropriate decisions about the use of ancillary equipment such as air conditioning.
- Teaching your pupils to turn off the engine when appropriate. In traffic queues many modern cars have an automatic facility for this.

Dealing with incidents

Make sure that you teach your pupils how to deal with a vehicle that breaks down.

Teach them how to stop the vehicle in a safe place to minimise future risk and switch off the engine.

Where appropriate they should get out of the vehicle.

They should be taught how to make sure any passengers and animals and managed safely.

Teach them to make sure where practical and safe to do so do they provide adequate warning to other road users to minimise risk.

Explain to them how to get appropriate help.

If they are involved in an incident or witnessing an incident, then all the above are applicable and in addition pupils need to be taught how to comply with legal requirements accurately and in good time.

Business person

You could possibly be the best driving instructor in the world but without a business brain that talent will be wasted and your career will be a short one.

Good driving instructors need to be business savvy.

For many people this may well be the first time that you've been self-employed and had previously been part of the corporate world. In the corporate world you're told what time to come in, when you can have breaks, and how much you're paid, but as a driving instructor you're now self-employed and the master of your own destiny. This can be fantastic and very rewarding or for those who are unaware can be quite catastrophic. Your car and your home become your office. You can take breaks when you want. You don't have to go in to work if you don't want to. Nobody will chase you. As well as good business knowledge self- discipline is also a key requirements of the job.

For example, if you have 4 pupils pass in a week, then are you a genius or a fool. A genius you may well say until you look at next week's diary. This may change your mind. If driving instructors are good at what they do they lose customers when their pupils pass their test. It's a natural consequence of doing our business well. Therefore it's essential to have driving tests spread out particularly if the assumption is that they will pass first time. Therefore make sure you manage your own diary and don't allow test congestion to take place.

Sales

Once experienced as a driving instructor a lot of your business will come through personal recommendation from people who specifically want you to teach them based on your reputation. This is an excellent situation to be in were quite possibly the only problem you then have is not being able to fit everybody in and having to manage people's expectations in a queue.

However there will be plenty of times when this business is not available and you need to generate it yourself. Here are some suggestions:

Social media.

Create yourself a Facebook profile if you don't already have one. Let your friends know that you're offering driving lessons and in what areas and then ask your friends to share this with their friends. The multiplication effect of this can be quite staggering. Rather than asking people if they want to learn to drive, ask if they know anyone who wants to learn to drive. They may well say yes me, or will know somebody who does want to drive.

Quite often your best sales people will be those who just passed their test and they will be delighted to recommend you. Make good use of this.

Also with pupils, you could offer incentives such as a free lesson when someone starts with you to help boost your business.

Most towns and cities have sites for people to sell things these are usually connected to Facebook and have names such as "items for sale in Leeds" or any other town and city. Post on as many of these as you can find in the areas that you are working.

Business cards and leaflets

These are easy to get hold of from either your driving school or if you're an independent from printers online. Try local shops with leaflets and with business cards whenever you are parked up in supermarket car parks etc., then it's a good idea to leave these tucked into the outside of the windows or under windscreen wipers.

Remember that this is your business. The more you can do to promote yourself the more successful you will be. Quite often at the beginning when you're new, a disproportionate amount of effort goes into the early stages. It's a little bit like trying to get an aircraft off the ground. All the effort and thrust goes into the takeoff and getting airborne and then you can start to throttle back. Another metaphor we can use here is an example of filling a bucket of water from scratch. A lot of effort is needed in the early stages to get the water into the bucket from whatever source you can find, but once full its only needs a drop to overflow.

Regarding voicemail messages, make sure that your voicemail message is professional and explains who you are rather than just allowing a standard greeting from a telephone company such as EE, Vodafone, Virgin Mobile or any other telecoms operator.

Tax and the self-employed

When changing career to become a driving instructor this may well be the first time that you've been self-employed. For others who have been self-employed in the past then these notes are to be used for reference rather than being new.

Even if you're working for a driving school you will still be classified as self-employed unless you are an employee of the school, rather than a franchisee.

If you start working for yourself you're classed as a sole trader. This means you're self-employed even if you haven't told the Revenue and Customs (HMRC).

Running a business

You're probably self-employed if you:

- Run your business for yourself and take responsibility for its success or failure.
- Have several customers at the same time.
- Can decide how, where and when you do your work.
- Can hire other people at your own expense to help you do work for you.
- Provide the main items of equipment to do your work.
- Are responsible for finishing any unsatisfactory work in your own time.
- Charge agreed fixed price for your work.
- Sell goods or services to make a profit.

The above are all definitions of self-employed from the government website.

You could also be employed and self-employed at the same time, for example if you work for an employer during the day and run your own business in the evenings.

This may well be the case for any PDIs who are starting to work as a driving instructor but still use their main job as a source of income.

So you can see, as a driving instructor once you start work you need to register as self-employed with HMRC as soon as you start your new business. You need to register for self-assessment and Class 2 national insurance as a self-employed person.

To register as a self-employed person you need to create a Government Gateway account. Visit www.gateway.gov.uk

You will be sent a user ID.

Use this to sign in and then register as self-employed for self-assessment tax as a sole trader.

You will then need to provide a start date for your business. This is the day you started working for yourself. As a PDI this will be the date when your badge starts.

The HMRC will ask you what type of work you do and you will let them know you're a driving instructor.

Once your application has been received by the HMRC they will send you a 10 digit unique taxpayer reference which is referred to as a (UTR).

Your responsibilities

You'll need to:

- Keep records of your business sales and expenses (your expenses will include the franchise fee if that's what you pay, your fuel and any other expenses directly related to the business).
- Send a self-assessment tax return in every year.
- Pay income tax on your profits and class 2 and class 4 national insurance.
- Class 2 national insurance if your profits are £6,205 or more a year.
- Class 4 if your profits are £8,424 or more a year.

The rate for the tax year 2018 to 2019 is as follows:

- Class 2 national insurance is £2.95 a week.
- Class 4 national insurance is 9% on profits between £8,424 and £46,350. Additionally it is 2% on profits over £46,350.

*As these figures are used as examples for the above tax year please check online for the current rates for the year you're reading this book.

Most people pay their national insurance through self-assessment.

To work out your profits you need to deduct your expenses from your self-employed income.

You then pay tax on this profit, not on your turnover.

It is recommended that you take advice as to whether to employ an accountant which will cost you, or whether to do self-assessment online which is not as difficult as people think.

VAT

As a driving instructor it is unlikely that you will need to register for VAT as your turnover must be over £85,000, although this may be possible if you decide to start your own school then employ other driving instructors.

Legality

As a driving instructor you also have a number of legal obligations which you need to be aware of.

As far as the vehicle is concerned, legal requirements will include the following:

- Tyres are in good condition, legally compliant and correctly inflated.
- Lights in good working order and legally compliant.
- Engine oil level is correct.
- Water coolant in washer reservoir levels are correct.
- There is no damage to the vehicle that would impair roadworthiness.
- Windscreen in other areas of vision are clear and undamaged.
- Seatbelts are in working order and undamaged.

There also is a legal requirement for the driver to make sure that not only are you wearing a seatbelt but also you were legally responsible for any passengers under the age of 14 to make sure that they are wearing theirs.

As the driver of the vehicle you're also responsible for making sure you understand how the vehicle works. This will obviously change between manufacturers and different models. You need to be aware of all the information contained in the vehicle handbook such as fuel capacity, fuel type and how the onboard equipment works.

As well as the legal requirements regarding the vehicle itself you also need to be responsible for your documentation and the vehicles documentation.

This will include the following:

- Make sure your driving licence is current and up-to-date for the vehicle category be driven.

- Make sure you have valid insurance for the vehicle.
- Make sure the vehicle is taxed and up-to-date.
- Make sure the vehicle registration is updated if you change or sell the vehicle.
- Make sure the vehicle has a current MOT certificate where applicable.

Chapter 10

THE ADI STANDARDS CHECK

Booking and overview

Once you have qualified as an Approved Driving Instructor (ADI) and received your green badge, then you will be assessed on your ability to teach and coach a pupil. You will be assessed once in the lifetime of your badge, and the badge lasts for a period of 4 years. In order to remain on the register you will have to take a 'Standards Check' even if you do not have a car or are not working as an ADI.

The assessment has been in place since 7th April 2014 when it replaced the ADI Check Test and is based around the National Standard for Driver Training. The National Standard sets out what you need to know and the skills you require in order to provide training for drivers of cars, light vans, mopeds and motorcycles. During the test a senior examiner from the DVSA will sit in the back of the car and watch you deliver a normal lesson. You will probably have now started to realise that this is exactly the same test as you had to take in order to pass the ADI part 3 test, and you would be correct! Prior to 23rd December 2017 you would have qualified using the role play 10 pre-set test method of assessment. This test simply looked at the core competencies of fault identifications, fault analysis and fault rectifying; you would then have had to go through further training to prepare for and pass the Standards Check. The DVSA have now aligned the 2 tests so that the method of assessment is consistent and is based around a client-centred approach where the purpose of the assessment is to see if the instructor (the ADI) is teaching/coaching in a way that helps the pupil to learn effectively. As with the ADI part 3 test, the assessment is based around lesson planning, risk management and teaching and learning strategies.

It is worthy of note that you can be removed from the ADI register if you do not book or attend your Standards Check.

To book your test, initially you will receive a letter from the DVSA letting you know that you are required to book your Standards Check. You can then book your test online at: www.gov.uk/book-driving-test

The test type ('Other'....ADI), then from the drop down box select 'instructor and trainer tests – ADI Standards Check'.

When booking your test you will need to have to hand:

- Your driving licence number.
- Your ADI personal reference number (PRN).

Should you require any assistance with your booking you can contact the DVSA Customer Service Team at:

- customerservices@dvsa.gov.uk
- Tel: 0300 200 1122 (Mon–Fri 8am–4pm)

There is no charge for booking your Standards Check as the cost of this is covered in the £300.00 fee you have to pay for your badge renewal (price correct as of September 2018).

NB It is proposed by the DVSA that at some time in the future the £300 badge renewal fee will be scrapped and replaced with a charge for the Standards Check on an individual basis. Built into this proposal will be the ability of an ADI to rebook a Standards Check if they need to improve their pass score.

If an ADI fails the Standards Check they have 2 further attempts to pass.

What to take to the Standards Check

When you attend for your Standards Check you will need to take with you the following:

- Your ADI registration certificate.
- A car that meets the requirements.
- A pupil.

Your 'pupil' cannot be an ADI or someone who is preparing to take the ADI part 3 test. They can be a learner or a full licence holder.

Suitable car

The rules for the car you wish to use on the test are as follows.

Your car must:

- Be taxed.
- Be insured for a driving test (check with your insurance company).
- Be roadworthy and have a current MOT (if older than 3years).
- Be a saloon, hatchback or estate car in good working condition – convertibles cars are not allowed.
- Have full-size rear seats.
- Have no warning lights showing, e.g. airbag warning light.
- Have no tyre damage and be legal tread depth in each tyre. You cannot have a space-saver spare tyre fitted.
- Be smoke free – this means you cannot smoke in it just before or during the test.
- Have an ADI badge on display if you are charging for the lesson.
- Be fitted with L plates (or D plates in Wales) if your pupil is a learner.

The DVSA may remove you from the register if you keep bringing a car to test that does not meet the requirements.

Structure of the Standards Check

The Standards Test is a competency-based assessment that is in line with the National Standard for Driver and Rider Training. The standard sets out skills, knowledge and understanding that you will need to be an effective instructor/trainer. The test is the same as the ADI part 3 test.

Your pupil can be a learner or a full licence holder, but they can not be an ADI (Approved Driving Instructor) or someone who is preparing to take the Part 3 test (PDI).

During your Standards Check the examiner will sit in the back of the car and will observe you carrying out a lesson. They will be looking to see if your instruction helps someone to learn in an effective way; for this reason, you will need to present a normal lesson. The assessment is based on a client-centred approach and is intended to help emphasise the importance of risk management when teaching.

Before the start of the lesson, the Standards Check examiner will have a short chat with you, where they will ask you about your pupil and will want to know what development areas the pupil is looking for.

At this stage you should show the examiner any training records you have for your pupil. Once the examiner has the details of the driving history of the pupil and what the lesson will be about, they will ask you to be back at the test centre in one hour and won't take any further part in the lesson (Unless they intervene as they consider the lesson to be dangerous).

Your lesson should follow a normal structure. This will involve introducing the pupil to the examiner and explaining that the examiner is present to assess you and not the pupil. You then need to recap the previous session you had with this pupil. There should be good use of question and answer (Q&A) to establish a starting point for the lesson. Try to get the pupil to do most of the work here! Aims and objectives then need setting for the lesson which, again, should be led by the pupil. If your pupil is a beginner then you may well find that you will need to set the aims and objectives for them, but it is essential that, should you do this, you get the pupil's agreement. Either way, the pupil's needs should be clear. It would be useful here to use a 'scaling system' whereby the pupil can scale where they think they are between 1–10, and this can then be used again in the summary at the end of the lesson to see if progress has been made.

Risk management will need to be discussed, whereby an agreement of the level of help and instruction between yourself and the pupil must be agreed. Whilst you are out on the road you will need to use the 3 core competencies of fault identification, fault analysis and remedial action, to help the pupil achieve their aims and objectives. This may well include pulling up at the side of the road to assess how the lesson is progressing, what is going well and what needs to be improved; pulling up at the roadside is a bit like a 'timeout' where the pupil can focus on issues without being on the move.

When the lesson ends summarise and recap on what has happened during the lesson. Look at what went well and, again, the pupil needs to be at the centre of the process whereby you encourage them to reflect on the lesson. The use of scaling (1–10) can be compared to the aims and objectives. Finally, have a talk with the pupil about what they wish to cover on the next lesson.

Test result

If you pass, then you will remain on the register of Approved Driving Instructors.

If you do not pass then you can take the test again if this is your first or second Standards Check Test. If you fail your 3rd attempt:

- You will be removed from the ADI register.
- You will have to retake and pass the ADI part 1, 2 and 3 exams and register again.

Appealing your ADI part 3 test

There is a right to appeal your test result if you feel that the examiner didn't follow the regulations when carrying out the Part 3 test. The result of the test will NOT be changed, but you might get a free re-test if your appeal is successful. Appeals in England and Wales will be at a Magistrates Court within 6 months of the test. Appeals in Scotland are at the Sheriff's Court within 21 days of the test. Appeal a test at www.gov.uk/find-court-tribunal

Cancelled tests

If your test is cancelled for any reason, including bad weather (icy roads, fog, high winds, flooding), then the DVSA will:

- Automatically book you the next available date for your test.
- Send you the details within 3 working days.

You are allowed to change the date of the test given you if it is not suitable at www.gov.uk/change-driving-test

Should the DVSA cancel your test at short notice, for example if an examiner is unwell, then you can claim for out of pocket expenses at www.gov.uk/government/publications/application-for-out-of-pocket-expenses

Standards Check assessment form

The assessment form for the Part 3 test is based on 3 areas of competence:

- Lesson planning.
- Risk management.
- Teaching and learning strategies.

Putting these categories into everyday language:

- Was the lesson appropriate?
- Was it safe?
- Did it work/was it effective?

These 3 areas of competency are then further broken down into a further 17 lower level competencies.

Lesson planning

- Did the trainer identify the pupil's learning goals and needs?
- Was the agreed lesson structure appropriate for the pupil's experience and abiltiy?

- Were the practice areas appropriate?
- Was the lesson plan adapted, when appropriate, to help the pupil toward their learning goals?

Risk management

- Did the trainer ensure that the pupil fully understood how the responsibility for the risk would be shared?
- Were directions/instructions given to the pupil clear and given in good time?
- Was the trainer aware of the surroundings and pupil's actions?
- Was any verbal or physical intervention by the trainer timely and appropriate?
- Was sufficient feedback given to help the pupil understand any potential safety-critical incidents?

Teaching and learning strategies

- Was the teaching style suited to the pupil's learning style and current ability?
- Was the pupil encouraged to analyse problems and take responsibility for their learning?
- Were opportunities and examples used to clarify learning outcomes?
- Was the technical information given comprehensive, appropriate and accurate?
- Was the pupil given appropriate and timely feedback during the session?
- Was the pupil encouraged to ask questions and were the pupil's queries followed up and answered appropriately?
- Did the trainer maintain appropriate and non-discriminatory manner throughout the session?
- At the end of the session, was the pupil encouraged to reflect on their own performance?

The following document is the examiner's ADI part 3 test report form.

The form is designed to identify the strengths in the ADI's instructional ability and to highlight any areas that need development. The examiner will also give you verbal feedback to help you understand your own instructional ability. Your overall performance will be based on the markings shown against the lower competencies. For each of those competencies a mark is given on a score of 0–3.

- Score 0 = no evidence of competence.
- Score 1 = competence demonstrated in a few elements.
- Score 2 = competence demonstrated in most elements.
- Score 3 = competence demonstrated in all elements.

In order to pass as a satisfactory assessment a minimum score of 31 must be achieved.

In addition, in the section of risk management a minimum score of 8 must be achieved. Pass marks are graded into 2 categories:

- 31–42   Grade B
- 43–51   Grade A

As well as not achieving the required scores, you will also fail the test if the examiner believes that your behaviour is placing you, the pupil, or any third party in immediate danger. In these circumstances the examiner may well stop the test.

At the top of the examiner's marking sheet a number of recordings can be made.

Assessment criteria
The breaking down of the 3 main areas of competence into 17 lower competencies has been mentioned a number of times, and the following section shows how this is done:

Lesson planning
The purpose of all driver training is to assess and develop the learner's skill, knowledge and understanding of the National Standard for Driver and Trainer Riding. Research by the DVSA has indicated that the best way to achieve this is by placing the client at the centre of the learning process.

Did the trainer identify the pupil's learning goals and needs?
This would normally take place at the start of a lesson. In most cases it is envisaged that the ADI/PDI and learner have worked together for some time and the basic structure of the pupil's learning goals have been laid down. As the lesson progresses, a better understanding of their needs may emerge. What is being looked for here is:

- Is the ADI encouraging the pupil to say what they want from the lesson?
- Asking questions to ensure understanding?
- Checking understanding as the lesson progresses?

- Listening to what the pupil is saying?
- Taking note of body language?

In an ideal world the pupil will set their own goals as to what they wish to achieve. However, as driving is new to them, unless they have had several lessons, they may not know what it is they wish to achieve. They may therefore need leading and the 5 bullet points above are therefore very pertinent. For example, the ADI might say "Today we are going to help you with crossroads. What would you like to achieve by the end of the lesson?"

However, whatever goals are set, they need agreeing by the pupil. This way of learning should be used to encourage the pupil to make choices and therefore take some responsibility for their own learning. If the ADI follows all of the above and reacts positively to each point then they are likely to score 3. If, for instance, they do all the listening bits but fail to spot the learner becoming nervous or tense, then they would probably score 2 because they had good listening skills but failed to spot non-verbal clues. Indications of a lack of competence could include:

- Making assumptions about understanding or experience.
- Failing to note negative or concerned comments or body language that demonstrates discomfort.
- Undermining the pupil's confidence by continually asking questions clearly beyond the pupil's knowledge or understanding.
- Pushing the pupil to address issues that they are unhappy talking about, unless there is a clear need, such as an identified risk or safety critical issue.

Was the agreed lesson structure appropriate for the pupil's experience and ability?

The lesson should allow the pupil to progress their learning at a manageable rate – stretching them but not overwhelming them. For example, if a pupil is concerned about entering roundabouts, they should not be asked to enter fast-flowing, multi-lane, multi-exit junctions at the first attempt. At the same time, they should not be restricted to very quiet areas that do not stretch them unless the ADI identifies a potential risk that needs checking out first. Indications that all levels of competence are in place are:

- Did the ADI ensure that the pupil understood what they planned to do and agree with that plan?
- Provide a lesson that reflected the information given by the pupil and the learning goals they wanted to tackle?

- Build in opportunities to check statements made by the pupil before moving on to more challenging situations?
- Check theoretical understanding?

Indications of a lack of competence include:

- Delivering a pre-planned, standard lesson that doesn't take into account the pupil's expressed needs or concerns.
- Failing to build in a suitable balance of practice and theory.

Were the practice areas suitable?
The area or route used by the ADI should allow the pupil to practice safely and help them achieve their goals. It should provide some stretch and challenge without taking them out of their competence zone. Indications that all elements of competence are in place could include choosing an area or route that provides:

- A range of opportunities to achieve the agreed learning opportunities.
- Challenges, but is realistic in terms of the pupil's capabilities and confidence.

Indications of a lack of competence include the ADI going to an area that:

- Takes the pupil out of their competence zone so that they are under such pressure that they cannot address their learning goals.
- Exposing pupil to risks that they cannot manage.

It may be that on the way to a suitable area, for instance to look at a reversing manoeuvre, the pupil needs to drive in an area busier than they are used to. For instance, they need to deal with roundabouts. The ADI needs to mention that and, dependent upon circumstances, offer to help them deal with that. Check that the pupil is happy with that though before proceeding.

Was the lesson plan adapted, where appropriate, to help the pupil work towards their learning goals?

The ADI should be ready to adapt if the pupil appears to be uncomfortable or unable to deal with the learning experience set up for the lesson or, indeed, suggests that it is not providing what they were looking for. It is important to keep the balance of responsibility in the pupil's court because people learn best and more effectively when they are in charge of their own learning goals. For instance, in the last example (above) the pupil was to deal with reversing but had to deal with some busy roundabouts on the way. The ADI has already agreed to give them help and it is therefore your responsibility to keep the car safe so that the pupil has the opportunity of dealing with the reversing and you have therefore kept your part of the agreement about roundabouts.

If, in the core part of the lesson, the pupil's inability is creating what may be a possible risk situation, the ADI should adapt quickly. The situation may be that a few more questions are needed to clarify the problem. It may be that the teaching and learning style used by the ADI is wrong. However, whatever the reason for changing and adapting the plan, the ADI must ensure that the pupil understands what they are doing and the reason for it. Indications that all elements of competence are in place could include:

- Comparing the actual performance of the pupil with their own feedback and clarifying any differences.
- Responding to any faults or weaknesses that undermined the original plan for the session.
- Responding to any concerns or issues raised by the pupil.
- Picking up on any non-verbal signs of discomfort or confusion.

Indications of lack of competence include:

- Persisting with a plan despite the pupil being clearly out of their depth.
- Persisting with a plan despite the pupil demonstrating faults or weaknesses that should lead to re-thinking the plan.
- Changing the plan without reason.
- Failing to explain to the pupil why the plan has been changed.

Risk management
It should be noted that the risk management competency is closely linked to the previous one, lesson planning. As a result of setting goals or objectives for the pupil, the agreed lesson plan, and a suitable route to achieve the goals, the way in which risk will be managed and who is responsible for what during the lesson needs to be considered.

Managing risk competently is vital to ensure that the goals set for the lesson can be achieved. Each of the competencies in the Standards Check are inter-related and the examiner's assessment process will take the whole lesson into consideration.

So, let's deal with each competency indicator in turn.

Did the trainer ensure that the pupil fully understood how the responsibility for risk would be shared?

Once the lesson goal has been agreed the ADI must consider how to share the responsibility for risk. For example, the pupil might say that they would like to practice something on their own, in which case you might simply tell them that you are happy to let them do that and all you will do is make sure that the car is kept safe. For example, the pupil might want to practice emerging from junctions independently after last week's lesson. You agree a fairly quiet route so that they can concentrate on the MSPSL routine approaching the junctions, getting the approach speed right and looking to see whether they areopen or closed, as well as looking for gaps into which they can be properly be prepared to emerge safely. You agree on a period of time they can practice this for but you must allow them to do this independently whilst remaining alert and ready to step in with instructions or to operate the dual controls to keep the car safe if necessary.

Similarly, if the pupil has agreed that the goal for the lesson is the left reverse and that they will have achieved their goal if they can get the car into the new junction under control and with accuracy, then it may be agreed between you that you will keep a careful look out all around for other vehicles and pedestrians. In this way you are both sharing the responsibility for risk. The pupil will be able to concentrate on the control and accuracy aspects of the manoeuvre, whilst you will look after the safety aspect.

In both of these examples the risk is shared, agreed and understood by both the ADI and the pupil to ensure that they have the best possible chance of achieving their agreed goal.

Indications that all levels of competence are in place could include:

- Asking the pupil what is meant by risk.
- Asking the pupil what sort of issues create risk, such as the use of alcohol or drugs.
- Explaining clearly what is expected of the pupil and what the pupil can reasonably expect of the ADI.
- Checking that the pupil understands what is required of them when there is a change of plan or if they are asked to repeat an exercise.

Indications of a lack of competence include:

- Failing to address the issue of risk management.
- Giving incorrect guidance about where the responsibility lies for management of risk.

- Failing to explain how the dual controls will be used.
- Undermining the pupil's commitment to being safe and responsible, for example agreeing to risky attitudes towards speeding, alcohol abuse etc.
- Asking the pupil to repeat a manoeuvre or exercise without providing an understanding of the role the ADI will play.

Were directions and instructions given to the pupil clear and given in good time?

If your verbal directions and instructions are given clearly and in good time, you are managing the risk effectively and enabling the pupil to focus on achieving the agreed goal. In some lessons your pupil may want to practice independent driving and either choose the route for themselves, drive on a previous route without directions, or follow the signs for, say, "Anytown". This is perfectly acceptable and in such circumstances you would not be expected to give directions. However, you may still need to give instructions if the pupil becomes confused, if this is what has been agreed, or if a safety critical incident occurs. In these situations you must ensure that you are giving your instructions clearly and in good time. "Right, turn left here" is a confusing instruction! Instead, the trainer should have clearly stated "At the end of the road turn left" so as to avoid the pupil taking a wrong turning right, or turning into a private drive. Similarly, the timing of instructions and directions can be very distracting especially if given late. This can increase the risk of being involved in an accident because the pupil can become distracted, confused, and make mistakes.

Indications that all levels of competence are in place:

- Clear, concise directions.
- Ensuring that the pupil understands and agrees what they plan to do.
- Directions given at a suitable time so that the pupil can respond well.

Indications of a lack of competence include:

- Giving confused directions.
- Giving directions too late.
- Giving unnecessary directions.
- Failing to recognise when the ADI's input is causing overload or confusion.

Was the trainer aware of the surroundings and the pupil's actions?

Being able to observe the road ahead and behind as well as watching the pupil's eyes, hands and feet is essential for risk management. It is your responsibility to ensure that the pupil is able to safely deal with whatever presents itself on road, and to do this you have to be constantly assessing the whole of the surroundings and evaluating any risk factors that may affect you; for example:

The pupil has agreed that they would like to concentrate on dealing with 'meeting traffic' situations in a busy street. At the start of the lesson you have looked at the responsibility for risk and agreed that you will share the risk by ensuring that the pupil can focus on their goal whilst you manage any other hazards; on the route there is a toucan crossing which, at first glance on approach, looks safe. There is no need to mention the crossing because the pupil's goal is specifically adequate clearance to parked cars. However, if someone now walks or rides up to the crossing and presses the button to cross, there is now a potential safety critical incident and the examiner may well use the next 2 competency indicators to assess how effectively this risk is managed. Any serious lapses in awareness are likely to lead to a 0 mark.

Was any verbal or physical intervention by the trainer timely and appropriate?

It is not necessary to mention the toucan crossing if the pupil appears to be happily dealing with it and there is clearly no risk (unless pedestrian crossings are part of the goal for the session, or perhaps the pupil has particularly said that they want to be alerted to hazards outside of their main goal).

Many ADIs don't fully understand how people learn and frequently disrupt their pupil's learning by giving partly-trained instruction. In many situations the learner will achieve far more understanding about how to apply their driving skills and assess the risks involved if they can carry out the task in silence; this raises their awareness of both their personal strengths and limitations and thus builds their responsibility. The use of constant verbal instruction whilst the car is moving can lead to confusion and frustration through sensory overload. Consequently, this overload (or over-instruction) can actually result in increased risk. Nevertheless, if you do need to   intervene to keep the car safe then it really doesn't matter if there has been sensory overload.

So, in the example cited above where a pedestrian or cyclist approaches the crossing, you must now assess whether you will need to step in and take control in some way. There are 4 possible options to choose from:

1. There is no need to do anything. The pupil has already checked their mirror and eased off the gas in case the lights change.
2. The pupil has made no response and the lights have started to change. You need to say something and a timely Q&A may mean the pupil keeping responsibility for a little longer. You could ask: "Do you think you need to slow down for the lights ahead?" This is a leading question which demands action.
3. You decide to wait a little longer to see what response you get from your pupil. Interfering too early may compromise achievement of their goal – meeting traffic. However, if it becomes clear that the pupil is not responding then a direct instruction is necessary: "Slow down for the lights!"
4. You decided not to give any verbal instruction and must now take physical action. The lights have turned red, a pedestrian is crossing the road, and the pupil is not responding. You stop the car using the dual controls.

Indications that all levels of competence are in place could include:

- Intervening in a way that actively supports the pupil's learning process and safety during the session.
- Allowing the pupil to deal with the situations appropriately.
- Taking control of a situation where a pupil is clearly out of their depth.

Indications of a lack of competence include:

- Ignoring a developing situation and allowing the pupil to flounder.
- Taking control of a situation where the pupil is clearly dealing with it appropriately.
- Constantly intervening when unnecessary.

Was sufficient feedback given to help the pupil understand any potential safety critical incidents?

In each of the situations described above you must now decide how much feedback to give to the pupil. If, as in option 4, you have had to use the dual controls, it will probably be necessary to ensure that the pupil understands that you have taken action, reassure them, and ask if they are ok to continue until it is safe to pull up and discuss what has happened. In options 1 and 2 (and possibly 3) above, it may well be sufficient to continue with the agreed route and discuss the potential safety critical incident (the toucan crossing incident) as part of your lesson debrief on the main goal or the lesson, which was 'meeting traffic'.

Whatever the safety critical, or potentially safety critical situation that has occurred, it is vital that the pupil fully understands what has happened and how it could have been dealt with or avoided altogether. Ideally the pupil should be supported to analyse the situation for themselves. However, feedback is necessary where, for instance, the pupil failed to identify the particular problem, and in those circumstances that feedback needs to be provided as soon as possible after the incident.

Indications that all levels of competence are in place include:

- Finding a safe place to stop and examine the safety critical incident.
- Allowing the pupil time to express any fears or concerns that the incident may have caused.
- Supporting the pupil to reflect in a clear and logical way about what happened.
- Providing input to clarify aspects of the incident that the pupil does not understand.
- Supporting the pupil to identify strategies for future situations.
- Providing input where the pupil does not understand what they should do differently.
- Checking that the pupil feels able to put the strategy in place.
- Agreeing ways of developing the competence if the pupil feels the need.

Indications of a lack of competence include:

- Failing to examine the incident.
- Taking too long to address issues generated by an incident.
- Not allowing the pupil to explore their own understanding.
- Telling the pupil what the solution is and failing to check their understanding.
- Failing to check the pupil's ability to put in place the agreed strategy.

Teaching and learning strategies

It is important to remember when considering your teaching style that this is not just about coaching. We are talking client-centred learning here. The DVSA are looking to see whether the ADI/PDI is helping the pupil to learn in an active way.

There are many times when a coaching technique will prove both useful and effective. The principle that underpins coaching is that an engaged pupil is likely to achieve a higher level of understanding and that self-directed solutions will prove to be far more relevant and effective.

Another way of looking at this (aside from jargon such as 'client-centred' or 'coaching') is to ask yourself whether or not you are **involving** the pupil in the learning process; if you do not ask them, for instance, what they know or how they feel about a particular subject, then how do you know what they already know or feel? You could easily be making some assumptions that are completely wrong and therefore, instead of involving the pupil, you are inadvertently erecting a barrier between you and them. This applies in every situation, including instruction. Direct instruction helps a pupil in early stages of their learning to cope with new situations as well as a struggle in a particular situation. Good coaching uses the correct technique at the correct time to match the pupil's needs. An ADI may sometimes need to give direct instruction through a difficult situation and that instruction forms part of the coaching process so long as the ADI encourages the pupil to analyse the problem and learn from it; thus it follows that a good ADI takes every opportunity to reinforce learning.

Was the teaching and learning style suited for the pupil's level of ability?

Every pupil is different and the trainer should understand their own pupil and how they prefer to be taught. This may take a few lessons to establish because some pupils may prefer the active way of teaching, whilst others wish to have the opportunity to reflect before taking the next step in their learning. The trainer should be able to make a judgmental response to their pupil's sensitivity and be able to adapt their approach if evidence emerges of a different preferred style.

Think back to your own school days. Did you have a favourite teacher or subject? What about teachers and subjects that you disliked? Why was this? Was it because some teachers just lectured to pupils whilst others 'involved' their pupils in the lessons much more? Think carefully about that! Learning cannot be forced on a pupil, and progress should be determined by what the pupil is comfortable with. There is a skill to recognising when a pupil stops learning, and the pace of a lesson needs to be determined by the pupil. At the same time, a pupil shouldn't be discouraged from experimenting (within safe bounds, of course!)

When coaching, the trainer should ensure that their method is suitable for the pupil. If a Q&A technique is used then match it to the level of the pupil's level of ability and encourage them to use a higher level of thought to give a response. Closed questions used with a pupil demonstrating a high level of ability are unlikely to be of much use unless, for example, you are checking knowledge. On the other hand, asking open questions of a pupil with limited ability who is struggling to achieve the set task for themselves may only serve to confuse and thereby have a negative effect. There are no hard and fast rules here. The ADI should be able to judge which method is the most effective to use in particular circumstances. Try experimenting with the way you teach in the car; try and be creative and consider whether your pupil is engaged in the lesson or is bored and 'switched off'.

Indications that all competencies are in place could include:

- Actively working to understand how they can best support the pupil's learning process (they might not achieve a full understanding during the lesson – it's the attempt that demonstrates competence).
- Modifying their teaching and method when, or if, they realise there is a need to do so.
- Providing accurate and technically correct instruction, information or demonstration (giving technically incorrect information or instruction is an automatic fail if it is likely to lead to a safety critical situation).
- Using practical examples and other similar tools to provide different angles to look at a particular subject.
- Linking learning in theory to learning in practice.
- Encouraging and helping the pupil to take ownership of the learning process.
- Responding to faults in a timely manner.
- Providing sufficient uninterrupted time to practice new skills.
- Providing the pupil with clear guidelines on how they might practice outside the lesson.

Indications of a lack of competence include:

- Adopting a teaching style which is clearly at odds with the pupil's learning style.
- Failing to check with the pupil if the approach they are taking is acceptable to the pupil.

- Failing to explore other ways of addressing a particular learning point if the initial method is not achieving the desired result.
- Concentrating on delivering their teaching tools instead of looking for learning outcomes.
- Ignoring safety issues.

Was the pupil encouraged to analyse problems and take responsibility for their learning?

This is a key part of the client-centred approach, and is basically the development of active problem solving by the pupil. The trainer needs to provide time for this to happen and therefore has to stop talking long enough for the pupil to do the work! However, the key thing to remember is that different pupils will respond to the invitation in different ways. Some can do it instantly following discussion, other may need to go away and have time to reflect upon a particular problem. You may need to point them toward the issue e.g. reading up the appropriate section of the Highway Code or another reading source in order to help them to get to grips with the problem. Pushing a pupil to come up with an immediate answer, on the spot, may prove unproductive.

At the same time, simple errors may occur and if the pupil knows what they have done and why, there is no need to push them on such a point. For example, they may have just stalled because they wrongly tried to pull away in 3rd gear. The pupil realises their error, quickly engages 1st gear and pulls away successfully. There is no need to mention this unless they repeatedly make the same mistake because, for instance, they are failing to use the palming method.

There is an expectation that Instructors will encourage learners to reflect on situations that happen and consider how they can apply the skills they are learning now to use them after passing their test when driving solo. They may also need to reflect on what are currently unfamiliar situations that may prompt distractions, such as driving at night or carrying passengers.

Indications that all competencies are in place could include:

- Providing time, in a suitable location, to explore any problems or issues that arose during the lesson or were raised by the pupil.
- Providing timely opportunities for analysis, in the case of safety critical incidents these should be as prompt as possible.
- Taking time and using suitable techniques to understand any problems the pupil had with understanding a particular issue.

- Suggesting suitable strategies to help the pupil develop their understanding, such as practical examples or pointing them toward further reading.
- Giving clear and accurate information to fill the gaps in a pupil's knowledge or understanding.
- Leaving the pupil feeling responsible for their own learning situation.

Indications of a lack of competence include:

- Leaving the pupil feeling that the ADI/PDI was in control of the teaching process.
- Failing to explore alternative ways of addressing a problem – in response of evidence of different learning preferences.
- Providing unsuitable or incorrect inputs.

Were opportunities and examples used to clarify learning outcomes?

Whilst training in technique is core to the learning process it is important to reinforce this input and link it to theory. The best way of achieving this is to use real world situations in a lesson. Every lesson will provide plenty of opportunities for this. The use of practical examples where possible, or scenarios, gives the pupil a much better understanding of when, how and why to use a particular technique. For instance, the skills required for planning and anticipation can be developed in many situations. A goal may have been set to deal with roundabouts but the skills involved in both planning and anticipation can also be developed when dealing with a meeting situation or an area where there are many pedestrians about during the same lesson.

Indications that all competencies are in place could include:

- Using examples identified during a lesson in a suitable way at a suitable time to confirm or reinforce understanding.
- Exploring different ways in which to use examples that best respond to differences in the pupil's preferred way of learning.
- Using examples that match the pupil's ability and experience to understand.
- Recognising that some pupils are able to respond instantly, whereas others need time to think about an issue.

Indications of a lack of competence include:

- Using examples that the pupil doesn't understand because of their lack of experience.
- Using complex examples that the pupil doesn't have the ability to respond to.
- Failing to provide the pupil with time to think through issues and come to their own conclusion.
- Imposing an interpretation.

Was the technical information given comprehensive, appropriate and accurate?

As mentioned previously, giving incorrect or insufficient information, with the result that a safety critical situation may occur, will result in an automatic fail. It should be remembered that good information is:

- Accurate
- Relevant
- Timely

Failure to meet any one of these criteria makes the others redundant.

Trainers will recognise that nearly every lesson requires some technical input from them to either help a pupil solve a problem or to fill a gap in knowledge. This input must be accurate and appropriate. If a pupil keeps making the same error it is insufficient to just keep on telling them that they are doing something wrong. The trainer's input needs to be comprehensive to help them overcome the problem. Any practical demonstration of technique must be both clear and suitable. The pupil must be engaged during the demo and encouraged to explore their understanding of what is being shown. Information given needs to be helpful. For example, continually telling a pupil what to do without giving them an opportunity to take responsibility. Unclear or misleading advice should be avoided. Comments such as "you're a bit close to those parked cars" could be used to introduce coaching on a weakness, but are of little benefit on their own as they are unclear. How close is "a bit" and is it significant?

Indications that all competencies are in place could include:

- Giving clear, timely and technically accurate explanations or demonstrations.
- Checking understanding and, if necessary, repeating the explanation or demonstration.
- Finding a different way to explain or demonstrate if the pupil still doesn't understand.

Indications of a lack of competence include:

- Providing inaccurate or unclear information, too late or too early in the learning process.
- Failing to check understanding.
- Failing to explore alternative ways of presenting information where the pupil doesn't understand the first offering.

Was the pupil given appropriate and timely feedback during the session?

Feedback is an essential part of the learning. Pupils need to have a clear idea of how they are performing in relation to their learning objectives throughout the lesson. When they are doing well they should be encouraged, and coached when a problem or learning opportunity occurs. However, constantly talking at an unsuitable time may prove demotivating or even dangerous. Sitting quietly and letting them get on with it can also be powerful feedback at times in an appropriate situation.

All feedback should be relevant, positive and honest. It is unhelpful to provide feedback that is unrealistic as it gives the pupil a false sense of their own ability. Try not to give negative feedback. Weaknesses should be expressed as learning opportunities. However, if something is wrong or dangerous, do not waffle – tell them! The pupil should have a realistic sense of their own performance.

Feedback should be two-way. In an ideal world the ADI/PDI should respond to comments and questions by the pupil. Feedback should never be overlooked or disregarded.

Indications that all competencies are in place could include:

- Providing feedback in response to questions from pupil.
- Seeking appropriate opportunities to provide feedback that reinforces understanding or confirms achievement of learning objectives.
- Providing feedback about failure to achieve learning objectives that help the pupil achieve understanding of what they need to improve.
- Providing feedback that the pupil can understand.
- Providing consistent feedback that is reinforced by body language.

Indications of a lack of competence include:

- Providing feedback so long after an incident that the pupil cannot remember what actually happened.
- Providing feedback that overlooks a safety critical incident.

- Providing continuous feedback that may be distracting the pupil.
- Failure to check the pupil's understanding of the feedback.
- Providing feedback that is irrelevant to the pupil's learning objectives.
- Refusing to listen to feedback on the ADIs own performance.

Was the pupil encouraged to ask questions and were the pupil's queries followed up and answered appropriately?

Direct questions by the pupil need dealing with as soon as possible. The ADI may give information or direct the pupil to another source. Wherever possible the pupil should be encouraged to discover answers for themselves but if the ADI does give information then they must check that the pupil understands the information provided. Pupils don't always have the confidence to ask direct questions. In these cases the ADI should be able to pick up on comments or body language that indicate uncertainty or confusion and be flexible enough to use different ways to tease out possible issues.

Sometimes a pupil may ask a question at an inappropriate time, for instance when dealing with a busy junction. A good response might be to say "Good question, I'll deal with that in a few minutes when we can pull up to the roadside."

Indications that all competencies are in place could include:

- Responding openly and readily to queries.
- Providing helpful answers or directing the pupil to suitable sources of information.
- Actively checking with pupils if their comments or body language suggest that they may have a question.
- Encouraging the pupil to explore possible solutions for themselves.

Indications of a lack of competence include:

- A refusal to respond to queries.
- Providing inaccurate information in response to queries.
- Avoiding the question or denying responsibility for answering it.

Did the trainer maintain an appropriate non-discriminatory manner throughout the session?

The trainer should maintain an atmosphere in which the pupil feels free to express their opinions. An open, friendly environment for learning should be created regardless of the pupil's age, gender, sexual orientation, ethnic background, religion, physical abilities or any other irrelevant factor. This implies respect for the pupil, their values and what constitutes appropriate behaviour in their culture. The trainer must not display inappropriate attitudes or behaviour toward other road users and should challenge the pupil if they display such behaviour.

A pupil may be a slow learner and lead to the trainer feeling frustrated or impatient because they are not picking up the skills being taught. Remaining non-discriminatory and non-judgmental encourages the trainer to consider a different approach, which may be required to achieve the learning goals.

Indications that all competencies are in place could include:

- Keeping a respectful distance and not invading the pupil's personal space.
- Asking the pupil how they wish to be addressed.
- Asking a disabled driver what the ADI should know about their condition so that they can best adapt their teaching style for the pupil.
- Adopting an appropriate position in the car.
- Using language about other road users that is not derogatory and that does not invite the pupil to collude with any discriminatory attitude.

Indications of a lack of competence include:

- Invading someone's physical space.
- Touching the pupil (including trying to shake hands) unless it is necessary for road safety reasons.
- Using someone's first name unless they have said it's acceptable.
- Commenting on a pupil's appearance or any other personal attribute unless it has a direct impact on their ability to drive safely (e.g. wearing footwear that makes it difficult to operate the foot pedals properly).

At the end of the session – was the pupil encouraged to reflect on their own performance?

At the end of the lesson the pupil should be encouraged to reflect on their performance and discuss their feelings with the trainer. Reflecting on one's own performance helps to embed learning and clarify whether the learning goal has been achieved. This also helps to develop self-evaluation skills and the ability to recognise one's own strengths and weaknesses. If you think about that statement, how essential is that to ensure that the pupil is able to reduce their own risk when driving on their own after passing their test?

The ADI should encourage honest self-appraisal and use client-centred techniques to highlight the areas that need development if the pupil has failed to recognise them. Once development areas have been identified the pupil should be encouraged to make them part of future development. You could, for example, ask the pupil to tell you 3 things that they were pleased with during that lesson. Ask them why that was, and encourage them to think along the same lines and ask what else they would like to develop, thereby setting goals for the next lesson.

Chapter 11

THE LEARNER DRIVER TEST

If you are training on a pink badge training licence, then it is very likely that you will be training pupils to test standard and taking them to test. It would therefore be worthwhile to look at the L test to enable you to assist your pupils.

Application process

Applications for a first provisional licence are made through the Driver and Vehicle Licensing Agency (DVLA). In order to obtain the licence applicants must be:

- At least 15 years and 9 months of age.
- Able to read a number plate from 20 metres away.

A Government Gateway ID is also required. If the applicant does not have one, or needs to re-register, they will receive an ID as part of this application. Those people already in possession of a provisional licence do not need to apply again in order to drive a car, but will need to provide the following:

- An identity document (unless in possession of a UK biometric passport).
- An address at which they have resided for over 3 years.
- Their national insurance number.

Details of the documents required can be found at www.gov.uk/id-for-driving-licence.co.uk

Applications can be made by post using form DI (available at certain Post Offices) as well as online. The cost to apply by post is slightly more expensive, at £43, whilst the online application costs £34.

Learner drivers can commence driving a car when they are 17 years old. There is an exception to this for learners who have, or have applied for, the enhanced rate of the mobility component of Personal Independence Payment (PIP); these learners can commence driving at age 16.

Preparing for the test

The most efficient way to learn to drive is under instruction with lessons. If this is done, then anyone they pay to teach them to drive must be either:

- A qualified and approved driving instructor (ADI)

OR

- A trainee driving instructor (PDI)

To find the nearest driving instructor use www.gov.uk/find-driving-schools-and-lessons. The instructor's badge will be displayed in their windscreen. ADI badges are green, and PDI badges are pink. Prices are set by individual schools and instructors. There are no minimum or maximum prices.

Service from your instructor

Should learners have concerns about their instructor regarding issues such as repeated cancellation of lessons, providing short lessons, late arrival for lessons or non-provision of lessons paid for, and are not satisfied that their instructor or driving school has dealt with such matters when reported, then they can contact the DVSA Instructor Team at adireg@dvsa.gov.uk (online), or by post at DVSA, PO Box, Newcastle upon Tyne NE99 1FP.

Complaints with regard to an instructor deemed to be shouting, swearing, using inappropriate language, unnecessary physical contact or use of mobile whilst the learner is driving should be referred to DVSA counter-fraud and investigation team at atcfi@dvsa.gov.uk.

Practising with family or friends

Learner drivers may practice their driving with someone other than a driving instructor so long as:

- The learner does not pay them.
- They are over 21 years old.

- They have had a FULL driving licence for at least 3 years (from countries within the EEC).
- They are qualified for the type of vehicle the learner wants to learn in.

Theory and hazard perception test

In order to take the learner driving test pupils must firstly pass a theory and hazard perception test.

The test can be booked either by phone 0300 200 1122 or online at www.gov.uk/book-theory-test. Learners must have their provisional driving licence in order to book their theory test.

Booking tests for your pupil

An instructor can book the driving tests in behalf of their pupils. This will allow the instructor to manage their diary efficiently, allowing the ability to book tests up to 10 weeks in advance for their pupils. In order to this the instructor will need the following:

- Government Gateway user ID and password.
- Credit or debit card or a pre-funded account.
- The pupil's driving licence number.

To use this facility, the instructor needs to register with the DVSA at www.gov.uk/book-pupil-driving-test

Using this facility will also allow the instructor to change or cancel a booking (by giving 3 clear working days' notice) however **NB** you can be stopped from using this facility if you cancel 20% or more tests within 5 clear working days.

The test format

The theory test is in 2 parts:

- Multiple choice questions.
- Hazard perception.

These are taken as a single test. Candidates must pass BOTH parts in order to pass the overall one. Once successful, candidates will be given a pass certificate which is valid for 2 years. This certificate will be required when booking the driving test.

When can the theory test be taken?

Pupils can take the theory test once they have turned 17. However those who have, or have applied for, the enhanced rate of the mobility component of Personal Independence Payment (PIP) may take this test from their 16th birthday.

Pupils with reading difficulties

Reading difficulty issues MUST be stated when the theory test is booked. Pupils can ask for an English voice-over; this will allow them to listen to instructions and questions through headphones and they can hear questions and possible answers as many times as they like, and may ask for more time to answer the multiple choice questions.

It is a requirement that the pupil send proof of the reading difficulty to the DVSA. This proof can be in the form of an email or letter from a teacher, other educational professional, or a doctor or medical professional using the following addresses:

- Email DVSA theory test enquiries at 'customercare@pearson.com'
- Write to DVSA Theory Test Enquiries, PO Box 1286, Warrington WA1 9GN

Taking the theory test

On attending the test, candidates will need to produce their photo-card driving licence, or their passport if they have an 'old-style' paper licence. They should also bring their appointment letter.

The 2-part test consists of a multiple choice section which followed by the hazard perception section.

Multiple choice section

This consists of 50 questions on a multiple choice format. Candidates are required to select the correct answer from those shown. The time allocated for this part of the test is 57 minutes, and the pass mark is 43.

Before the test starts, candidates will get:

- Instructions on how the test works.
- A chance to do some practice questions to familiarise themselves with screen use.

How the test works

A question has several possible answers on a screen. Candidates have to select the correct answer.

Some questions are given as a case study. The case study will:

- Show a short story on which 5 questions will be based.
- Be about a real life situation that a pupil could come across when driving.

If a candidate is not sure of an answer for any of the 50 questions they can flag the question and return to it at the end of the test; in this way they are not held up on a question they do not know the answer for, and can proceed to other questions they can answer. If there is still uncertainty when they return to the flagged question(s) then, by a process of elimination, they can begin to delete in their mind any obvious wrong answers. Candidates are able to change any previously selected answer at any point during their test.

Although the maximum time allocated is 57 minutes, candidates can finish the test at any point that they have answered all the questions to their satisfaction.

There is a 3 minutes break upon completion of the multiple choice section of the test before commencing the hazard prevention section.

Revision for the multiple choice section

There are lots of excellent apps that candidates can use on their smart phones in order to practice for the test. Recommended reading for the test would be the following 3 books as it is from detail within these books on which the questions are based:

- *The Highway Code.*
- *Know Your Traffic Signs*
- *Driving – The Essential Skills.*

Examples of multiple choice questions

Q. Who can use a toucan crossing?
A. a) Cars and motorcycles.
     b) Cyclists and pedestrians.
     c) Buses and lorries.
     d) Trams and trains.
Correct answer is b) Cyclists and pedestrians.
Read more – Highway Code, Rule 199. *The Official DVSA Guide to Driving and Essential Skills* – section 7.

Q. What type of emergency vehicle is fitted with a green flashing beacon?
A. a) Fire engine.
     b) Road gritter.
     c) Ambulance.
     d) Doctor's car.
Correct answer is d) Doctor's car.
Read more – Highway Code Rule 219. *The Official DVSA Guide to Driving and Essential Skills* – section 7.

Q. Why should you switch off your rear fog light when the fog has cleared?
A. a) To allow the headlights to work.
   b) To stop draining the battery.
   c) To stop the engine losing power.
   d) To prevent dazzling following drivers.
Correct answer is d) To prevent dazzling following drivers.
Read more – Highway Code Rules 114 and 226. *The Official DVSA Guide to Driving and Essential Skills* – section 12.

Q. How should a load be carried on your roof rack?
A. a) Securely fastened with suitable restraints.
   b) Loaded towards the rear of the vehicle.
   c) Visible in your exterior mirror.
   d) Covered with plastic sheeting.
Correct answer is a) Securely fastened with suitable restraints.
Read more – Highway Code Rule 98. *The Official DVSA Guide to Driving and Essential Skills* – section 2.

The theory questions are based on the following topics:

- Alertness.
- Attitude.
- Safety and your vehicle.
- Hazard awareness.
- Vulnerable road users.
- Other types of vehicles.
- Vehicle handling.
- Motorway driving.
- Rules of the road.
- Road and traffic signs.
- Essential documents.
- Incidents.
- Vehicle loading.

The Hazard Perception Test

When the candidate has completed the multiple choice section of the theory test they will get a 3 minute break before the hazard perception test commences. Before the test begins the candidate will be shown a video about how it works.

When the test starts there are 14 computer-generated video clips to watch (computer-generated imagery has been used to add clarity to the clips). These 14 clips feature everyday road scenes and contain at least one developing hazard, but one of the clips contains 2 developing hazards. Candidates get 5 points for spotting the developing hazards as soon as they start to happen; up to 5 points can be scored if candidates respond early enough when the scoring window opens. The clip with 2 developing hazards is worth 10 points (i.e. 2 separate developing hazards each worth up to 5 points). As the hazard develops the available points reduce from

5 down to 0 dependent upon how early a response to the hazard is recorded. Candidates do not lose points if they click the mouse and get the developing hazard wrong. However, if they click continuously or in a pattern, then they will score zero for that clip and any others where this happens. Candidates only get one attempt at each clip and they cannot change their responses as they can on the multiple choice section.

The pass mark for the hazard perception test is 44 out of a maximum of 75 points.

Pass mark and test result

	Pass mark	Points available
Multiple choice questions	43	50
Hazard perception	44	75

If the candidate passes they will get a certificate that is valid for 2 years. The certificate is part of the booking process for the practical test and must therefore be kept safe. The practical test must be passed within 2 years of passing the theory test otherwise another theory test must be passed again.

Should a candidate fail this test then they will receive a letter at the test centre telling them the parts of the test on which they did not score sufficient points. Candidates must rebook and retake the full test again if they wish to progress to the practical test, and have to wait 3 days before taking the theory test again.

The practical driving test

When learners have passed their theory test they can book their practical driving test (if a driver is upgrading from an automatic licence to a manual one there is no requirement to pass another theory test).

To book a driving test use the following website: **www.gov.uk/book-driving-test** (service is available from 6am–11.40pm).

If a pupil needs help booking their practical test they should contact the DVSA driving test booking support on Tel 0300 200 1120 (Mon–Fri 8am–4pm) or email at customerservices@dvsa.gov.uk.

Once booked, if the pupil wishes to look for an earlier appointment then they can use the following website www.gov.uk/change-driving-test

The cost of the practical test is £62 for weekday appointments and £75 for evenings, weekends and Bank Holidays. It is important to note that pupils should use the official DVSA site for booking the test as there are now numerous websites that will book the pupil's test for them and then charge a commission fee on top of the standard test fee. It is therefore recommended that pupils DO NOT 'Google' "book driving test" but go directly to the DVSA official site and book from there. This will not attract a commission fee. To book the test pupils will require:

- UK driving licence number.
- Credit or debit card.
- Driving instructor's personal reference number (PRN) to check their availability.
- The candidate must have lived in England, Wales or Scotland for at least 185 days in the last 12 months.

What to take to the test
Pupils must take the following with them to the test:

- UK driving licence (bring valid passport if on the 'old' style paper licence).
- Theory pass certificate.
- A suitable car (usually the driving instructor's, but pupils can use their own if it meets the requirements).

It is worthy of note that the test will be cancelled and the pupil will lose the fee paid for it if they do not take the correct things (copies of documents are not acceptable) and therefore as a driving instructor it is good practice to ensure that the pupil has all the correct items with them when you pick them up for their test and even advise them to have the documents prepared a week before the test. Don't leave things to chance!

Should a pupil misplace their licence they can apply for a replacement one but this can take up to 15 days to arrive. If a pupil misplaces their theory certificate they can contact the DVSA and provide their name and driving licence number and they will then be provided with an official letter from the DVSA to be taken to their practical test in place of the pass certificate. Again, do not leave things to chance, advise pupils of the importance of keeping documents in a safe place ready for future use, so as to keep the whole test situation as stress-free as possible.

The practical driving test
The practical driving test is broken down into 5 parts:

1. An eyesight check.
2. 'Show me, tell me' vehicle safety questions.
3. General driving ability.
4. Reversing the vehicle.
5. Independent driving.

The test lasts for around 40 minutes and 70 minutes for an extended test. The 70 minute test is for people who have previously been banned from driving.

Eyesight check

At the start of the test the examiner will check the candidate's eyesight by means of reading a number plate from the following distance:

- 20 metres – for vehicles with new-style number plates.
- 20.5 metres – for old-style number plates.

Vehicle safety questions (Show me, tell me)

Candidates will be asked of the above style questions. These are vehicle safety questions. At the start of the test candidates will be asked a 'tell me' question before commencing their driving. They will be asked the 'show me' question whilst they are driving.

The 'show me' questions delivered on the move have proved to be one area where pupils pick up serious faults on their test as they are required, 'when it is safe' to operate car controls whilst the car is on the move. It is therefore recommended that instructors, when training/coaching their pupils, ensure that they can carry out the 'show me' actions competently and safely.

The following constitutes the 'show me, tell me' questions for the driving test.

Tell me questions

Q1 Tell me how you'd check that the brakes are working before starting a journey.
A. Brakes should not feel spongy or slack. Brakes should be tested as you set off. Vehicle should not pull to one side.

Q2 Tell me where you would find the information for the recommended tyre pressures for this car, and how the tyre pressures should be checked.
A. Manufacturers guide, use a reliable tyre pressure gauge, check and adjust pressures when tyres are cold. Don't forget the spare tyre, and remember to refit valve caps.

Q3 Tell me how you would make sure that the head restraint is correctly adjusted so it provides the best protection in the event of a crash.
A. The head restraint should be adjusted so the rigid part of the restraint is at least as high as the eye or top of the ears and as close to the back of the head as is comfortable. **NB** some restraints may not be adjustable.

Q4 Tell me how you would check the tyres to ensure that they have sufficient tread depth and that their general condition is safe to use on the road.

A. No cuts or bulges, 1.6 mm of tread depth across the centre three quarters of the breadth of the tyre, and around the entire outer circumference of the tyre.

Q5 Tell me how you would check that the headlights and tail lights are working. You don't need to exit the vehicle.

A. Explain that you'd operate the switch (turn on the ignition if necessary), then walk around the vehicle to check all lights. **NB** since this is a 'tell me' question there is no need to physically check the lights, an explanation is sufficient.

Q6 Tell me how you'd know if there was a problem with your anti-lock braking system.

A. Warning light should illuminate if there is a fault with this system.

Q7 Tell me how you would check the directional indicators are working. You don't need to exit the vehicle.

A. Explain that you would operate the switch (turn on ignition if necessary) and then walk around the vehicle and check each indicator. **NB** since this is a 'tell me' question there is no need to physically check the lights, an explanation is sufficient.

Q8 Tell me how you would check the brake lights are working on this car.

A. Explain that you'd operate the brake pedal, make use of reflections in windows or doors, or ask someone to help.

Q9 Tell me how you would check the power-assisted steering is working before starting a journey.

A. If the steering becomes heavy the system might not be working properly. Before starting a journey 2 simple steps can be made:

   1. Gentle pressure on the steering wheel, maintained while the engine is started should result in a slight but noticeable movement as the system begins to operate.
   2. Alternatively, turning the steering wheel just after moving off will give an immediate indication that the power-assistance is functioning.

Q10 Tell me how you'd switch on the rear fog light(s) and explain when you'd use it/them. You do not need to exit the vehicle.

A. Operate the switch (switch on the engine and dipped headlights if necessary). Check warning light is on. Explain use.

Q11 Tell me how you switch your headlights from dipped to main beam and explain how you'd know the main beam is on.

A. Operate the switch (with ignition or engine on if necessary). Check with main beam warning light.

Q12 Open the bonnet and tell me how you would check that the engine has sufficient oil.

A. Identify the dipstick or oil level indicator and describe how you would check the oil level against the minimum and maximum markers.

Q13 Open the bonnet and tell me how you'd check that the engine has sufficient engine coolant.

A. Identify high and low level markings on header tank (where fitted) or radiator filler cap, and describe how to top up to the correct level.

Q14 Open the bonnet and tell me how you would check you have a safe level of hydraulic brake fluid.

A. Identify the reservoir, check the levels against high and low markings.

Show me questions

1. When it is safe to do so, show me how you wash and clean the rear windscreen.
2. When it is safe to do so, show me how you wash and clean the front windscreen.
3. When it is safe to do so, show me how you'd switch on dipped headlights.
4. When it is safe to do so, show me how you'd set the rear demister.
5. When it is safe to do so, show me how you'd operate the horn.
6. When it is safe to do so, show me how you'd demist the front windscreen.
7. When it is safe to do so, show me how you'd open and close the side window.

Candidates will fail the test if they lose control of the vehicle whilst answering any of the 'show me' questions.

General driving ability

During the driving test candidates will be required to drive in various road and traffic conditions. They will NOT be required to drive on motorways. The examiner will give directions. Candidates will be asked to pull over at the side of the road; they will be marked on where and how they pull over and how they rejoin the traffic. The test will include:

1. Normal stops at the side of the road.
2. Pulling out from behind a parked vehicle.
3. A hill start.

The test may also include an emergency stop. The examiner's guideline is to carry out an emergency stop on one in three driving tests. This is shown as a guideline, however, and should not be taken as a hard and fast rule.

Reversing the vehicle (manoeuvres)

During the test, candidates will be asked to carry out one reversing manoeuvre from the following:

- Parallel park the vehicle at the side of the road. **OR** Reverse park the vehicle into a parking bay and drive out (this will be at the test centre).
- Drive forward into a parking bay and reverse out.
- Pull up on the right-hand side of the road, reverse for around 2 car lengths and rejoin the traffic.

Independent driving

During the drive candidates will be driving for around 20 minutes by following either:

- Directions from a sat nav.
- Traffic signs.

The examiner will tell them which one they will have to do.

The sat nav is provided by the examiner who will set it up for the candidate. The model used will be a TomTom Start 5 2; this has been chosen by the DVSA as it is the most adaptable to changing colour, contrast and volume to suit everyone's needs. Candidates will not be allowed to follow directions from their own sat nav during the test. If a candidate goes off route during the independent drive this will NOT affect the test result unless they make a fault whilst doing it.

If a candidate is following traffic signs and cannot see a sign then the examiner will give them directions until they pick up the next sign.

Pass mark and faults
The pass mark for the driving test is no more than 15 driver faults and 0 serious or dangerous faults. There are 3 different types of fault:

- A dangerous fault is one where there is actual danger to the driver, the examiner, the public or property. If the examiner takes verbal or physical control, this is recorded as a dangerous fault.
- A serious fault is a fault that is potentially dangerous.
- A driving fault is a fault that isn't potentially dangerous, but if you keep making the same fault then it could become a serious one.

If a candidate makes a fault during the driving test it may not affect the test result if it is neither a serious nor a dangerous one. It is good advice to advise your pupils to ignore the examiner's marking sheet whilst the test is in progress as it is very easy to become distracted from their driving by trying to see whether the examiner is marking on the sheet, and this may well lead to further faults occurring.

Test result
If your pupil passes their test the examiner will:

- Advise the pupil what faults they have made during the test (if any).
- Give the pupil a pass certificate.
- Ask the pupil if they want their full licence to be sent to them automatically. If this is the case, then they should give the examiner their provisional licence.

Should your pupil wish to apply for their licence themselves, then they need to do so within 2 years of passing their test and at the following website: www.gov.uk/apply-for-your-full-driving-licence

Successful candidates can start to drive straight away as they have passed their test. If their full licence has not arrived within 3 weeks then they need to contact the DVLA at:

www.gov.uk/contact-the-dvla/y/driving-licences-and-applications

If your pupil does not pass the test the examiner will tell them the faults they have made; they can book a new test so long as they select a date that is at least 10 working days ahead.

Appeal your driving test

There is a right of appeal to the test result if your pupil feels that the examiner didn't follow the regulations when carrying out the driving test. The result of the test will not be changed, but they may get a free re-test if the appeal is upheld. Appeals in England and Wales will be to a Magistrate's Court within 6 months of the disputed test. Appeals in Scotland are to a Sheriff's Court within 21 days of the disputed test. Link for appeals: www.gov.uk/find-court-tribunal

Cancelled tests

If a test is cancelled for any reason, including bad weather (icy roads, fog, high winds, flooding) then the DVSA will:

- Automatically book the next available test date for your pupil.
- Send your pupil details of the new test within 3 working days.

Your pupil can change the date of the test should the date given not be suitable. If the DVSA cancel a test at short notice candidates can apply for out of pocket expenses on the following link:
    www.gov.uk/government/publications/application-for-out-of-pocket-expenses

Driving test result explained

Your pupil will be driving on a variety of roads, with the exception of motorways, so that they are tested under various conditions and they will be required to drive in a safe, competent manner on all of them. The examiner's main thought is, "Can this candidate be allowed to drive on their own after this test?"

The marking sheet used for the test is the examiner's DL25 document seen on the following pages.

As previously stated, there are 3 types of fault:

- Dangerous – faults that involve actual danger to the driver, the examiner, the public or property. An example of this would be causing other road users to have to take avoiding action when you are changing lane.
- Serious – these are faults that are potentially dangerous rather than causing actual danger. An example of this would be, when

Driving Test Report

DL25A

0408 T

I declare that:

- the use of the test vehicle for the purposes of the test is fully covered by a valid policy of insurance which satisfies the requirements of the relevant legislation.
- I normally live/have lived in the UK for at least 185 days in the last 12 months (except taxi/private hire). See note 30.

✗ _____

Candidate

S ☐ D/C ☐

Application Ref. ☐☐☐ ☐☐☐ ☐☐☐ ☐☐

Date ☐☐ ☐☐ ☐☐ D D M M Y Y   Time ☐☐ ☐☐ H H M M   Dr./No. ☐☐☐☐☐

DTC Code / Authority ☐☐☐☐☐☐   Reg. No. ☐☐☐☐☐☐

Examiner: Staff / Ref. No. ☐☐☐☐☐☐

	Auto	Ext
Cat. Type ☐☐☐☐	☐	☐

1 ☐ 2 ☐ 3 ☐ 4 ☐ 5 ☐ 6 ☐ 7 ☐ 8 ☐ 9 ☐ 0 ☐ V ☐

Instructor Reg ☐☐☐☐☐

Instructor Cert ☐☐☐☐☐☐☐   Sup ☐   ADI ☐   Int ☐   Other ☐   C ☐

	Total	S	D
1a Eyesight		☐	
1b H/Code / Safety		☐	☐
2 Controlled Stop		☐	☐
3 Reverse / Left Reverse with trailer — control		☐	☐
observation		☐	☐
4 Reverse/ Right — control		☐	☐
observation		☐	☐
5 Reverse Park — control		☐	☐
R ☐ C ☐ — obs.		☐	☐
6 Turn in road — control		☐	☐
observation		☐	☐
7 Vehicle checks		☐	
8 Forward park / — control		☐	☐
Taxi manoeuvre — observation		☐	☐
9 Taxi wheelchair		☐	
10 Uncouple / recouple		☐	☐
11 Precautions		☐	☐
12 Control — accelerator			
clutch			
gears			
footbrake			
parking brake / MC front brake			
steering			
balance M/C			
PCV door exercise		☐	☐

	Total	S	D
13 Move off — safety		☐	☐
control		☐	☐
14 Use of mirrors- M/C rear obs — signalling		☐	☐
change direction		☐	☐
change speed		☐	☐
15 Signals — necessary		☐	☐
correctly		☐	☐
timed		☐	☐
16 Clearance / obstructions		☐	☐
17 Response to signs / signals — traffic signs		☐	☐
road markings		☐	☐
traffic lights		☐	☐
traffic controllers		☐	☐
other road users		☐	☐
18 Use of speed		☐	☐
19 Following distance		☐	☐
20 Progress — appropriate speed		☐	☐
undue hesitation		☐	☐
21 Junctions — approach speed		☐	☐
observation		☐	☐
turning right		☐	☐
turning left		☐	☐
cutting corners		☐	☐
22 Judgement — overtaking		☐	☐
meeting		☐	☐
crossing		☐	☐

	Total	S	D
23 Positioning — normal driving		☐	☐
lane discipline		☐	☐
24 Pedestrian crossings		☐	☐
25 Position / normal stops		☐	☐
26 Awareness / planning		☐	☐
27 Ancillary controls		☐	☐
28 Spare 1		☐	☐
29 Spare 2		☐	☐
30 Spare 3		☐	☐
31 Spare 4		☐	☐
32 Spare 5		☐	☐

33 Wheelchair   Pass ☐   Fail ☐

Pass	Fail	None	Total Faults	Route No.
☐	☐	☐	☐☐	☐☐

ETA ☐   V ☐   P ☐   D255 ☐

Survey ☐   A ☐   B ☐   C ☐   D ☐
E ☐   F ☐   G ☐   H ☐

Eco Safe driving   Control ☐
Planning ☐

Debrief ☐   Activity Code ☐☐

I acknowledge receipt of
Pass Certificate Number: Licence rec'd
☐☐☐☐☐☐☐☐   Yes ✗

Wheelchair Cert. No: COA ✗
☐☐☐☐☐☐☐☐
No ✗

There has been no change to my health: see note 29 overleaf.

✗ _____

DVSA – An executive agency of the Department for Transport

Form Ref. DL25 D0018000-00

Driving Test Report

DL25B
0113 T

I declare that:

- the use of the test vehicle for the purposes of the test is fully covered by a valid policy of insurance which satisfies the requirements of the relevant legislation.

- I normally live/have lived in the UK for at least 185 days in the last 12 months (except taxi/private hire). See note 30.

X _____

Candidate

S ☐ D/C ☐

Application Ref. ☐☐☐ ☐☐☐ ☐☐☐ ☐☐

Date (D)(D)(M)(M)(Y)(Y) Time (H)(H)(M)(M) Dr./No. ☐☐☐☐☐

DTC Code / Authority ☐☐☐☐☐ Reg. No. ☐☐☐☐☐

Examiner: Staff / Ref. No. ☐☐☐☐☐

Cat. Type ☐☐☐ Auto ☐ Ext ☐

1 ☐ 2 ☐ 3 ☐ 4 ☐ 5 ☐ 6 ☐ 7 ☐ 8 ☐ 9 ☐ 0 ☐ V ☐

Instructor Reg ☐☐☐☐☐☐ Instructor Cert ☐☐☐☐☐☐ Sup ☐ ADI ☐ Int ☐ Other ☐ C ☐

	Total	S	D
1a Eyesight			☐
1b H/Code / Safety		☐	☐
2 Controlled Stop		☐	☐
3 Reverse / Left Reverse with trailer — control		☐	☐
— observation		☐	☐
4 Reverse/ Right — control		☐	☐
— observation		☐	☐
5 Reverse Park — obs.		☐	☐
R ☐ C ☐			
6 Turn in road — control		☐	☐
— observation		☐	☐
7 Vehicle checks		☐	☐
8 Forward park / Taxi manoeuvre — control		☐	☐
— observation		☐	☐
9 Taxi wheelchair			☐
10 Uncouple / recouple		☐	☐
11 Precautions		☐	☐
12 Control — accelerator		☐	☐
— clutch		☐	☐
— gears		☐	☐
— footbrake		☐	☐
— parking brake / MC front brake		☐	☐
— steering		☐	☐
— balance M/C		☐	☐
— PCV door exercise		☐	☐

	Total	S	D
13 Move off — safety		☐	☐
— control		☐	☐
14 Use of mirrors- M/C rear obs — signalling		☐	☐
— change direction		☐	☐
— change speed		☐	☐
15 Signals — necessary		☐	☐
— correctly		☐	☐
— timed		☐	☐
16 Clearance / obstructions		☐	☐
17 Response to signs / signals — traffic signs		☐	☐
— road markings		☐	☐
— traffic lights		☐	☐
— traffic controllers		☐	☐
— other road users		☐	☐
18 Use of speed		☐	☐
19 Following distance		☐	☐
20 Progress — appropriate speed		☐	☐
— undue hesitation		☐	☐
21 Junctions — approach speed		☐	☐
— observation		☐	☐
— turning right		☐	☐
— turning left		☐	☐
— cutting corners		☐	☐
22 Judgement — overtaking		☐	☐
— meeting		☐	☐
— crossing		☐	☐

	Total	S	D
23 Positioning — normal driving		☐	☐
— lane discipline		☐	☐
24 Pedestrian crossings		☐	☐
25 Position / normal stops		☐	☐
26 Awareness / planning		☐	☐
27 Ancillary controls		☐	☐
28 Spare 1		☐	☐
29 Spare 2		☐	☐
30 Spare 3		☐	☐
31 Spare 4		☐	☐
32 Spare 5		☐	☐
33 Wheelchair	Pass ☐	Fail ☐	

Pass	Fail	None	Total Faults	Route No.
☐	☐	☐	☐☐	☐☐

ETA ☐ V ☐ P ☐ D255 ☐

Survey ☐ A ☐ B ☐ C ☐ D ☐ E ☐ F ☐ G ☐ H ☐

Eco Safe driving ☐ Control ☐ Planning ☐

Debrief ☐ Activity Code ☐☐☐

I acknowledge receipt of Pass Certificate Number: ☐☐☐☐☐☐☐ Licence rec'd Yes ☒

Wheelchair Cert. No: ☐☐☐☐☐☐☐ COA ☒

There has been no change to my health: see note 29 overleaf. No ☒

X _____

© Crown Copyright 12/2017

DVSA – An executive agency of the Department for Transport

Form Ref. DL25 D0018000-00

Weather conditions *(please ✓ appropriate box[es])*

1. Bright / dry roads
2. Bright / wet roads
3. Raining throughout test
4. Showers
5. Foggy / misty

6. Dull / wet roads
7. Dull / dry roads
8. Snowing
9. Icy
10. Windy

11. Other

If you tick this box, provide an accurate description of the weather conditions.

DL25B
0113T

Vehicle details

LGV Length Height Artic Rigid
PCV Width MAM Draw bar Automatic

Brief description of candidate

Id

Remarks

Oral explanation comments

Examiner's signature

Disability Tests

Description of any fitted adaptations

The Learner Driver Test

Driving Test Report
DL25C
0113T

I declare that:
- the use of the test vehicle for the purposes of the test is fully covered by a valid policy of insurance which satisfies the requirements of the relevant legislation.
- I normally live/have lived in the UK for at least 185 days in the last 12 months (except taxi/private hire). See note 30.

X _____

Candidate

S ☐ D/C ☐

Application Ref. ☐☐☐ ☐☐☐ ☐☐☐ ☐☐
Date (D D M M Y Y) Time (H H M M) Dr./No. ☐☐☐☐☐☐
DTC Code / Authority ☐☐☐☐☐ Reg. No. ☐☐☐☐☐☐

Examiner:

Cat. Type ☐☐☐☐ Auto ☐ Ext ☐
1☐ 2☐ 3☐ 4☐ 5☐ 6☐ 7☐ 8☐ 9☐ 0☐
Instructor Reg ☐☐☐☐☐☐☐ Instructor Cert ☐☐☐☐☐☐☐ Sup ☐ ADI ☐ Int ☐ Other ☐

	Total S D
1a Eyesight	☐
1b H/Code / Safety	☐ ☐☐
2 Controlled Stop	☐☐ ☐☐
3 Reverse / Left Reverse with trailer — control	☐☐ ☐☐
observation	☐☐ ☐☐
4 Reverse/ Right — control	☐☐ ☐☐
observation	☐☐ ☐☐
5 Reverse Park — control	☐☐ ☐☐
R ☐ C ☐ obs.	☐☐ ☐☐
6 Turn in road — control	☐☐ ☐☐
observation	☐☐ ☐☐
7 Vehicle checks	☐ ☐☐
8 Forward park / Taxi manoeuvre — control	☐☐ ☐☐
observation	☐☐ ☐☐
9 Taxi wheelchair	☐
10 Uncouple / recouple	☐☐ ☐☐
11 Precautions	☐ ☐☐
12 Control — accelerator	☐ ☐☐
clutch	☐ ☐☐
gears	☐ ☐☐
footbrake	☐ ☐☐
parking brake / MC front brake	☐ ☐☐
steering	☐ ☐☐
balance M/C	☐ ☐☐
PCV door exercise	☐ ☐☐

	Total S D
13 Move off — safety	☐ ☐☐
control	☐ ☐☐
14 Use of mirrors- M/C rear obs — signalling	☐ ☐☐
change direction	☐ ☐☐
change speed	☐ ☐☐
15 Signals — necessary	☐ ☐☐
correctly	☐ ☐☐
timed	☐ ☐☐
16 Clearance / obstructions	☐ ☐☐
17 Response to signs / signals — traffic signs	☐ ☐☐
road markings	☐ ☐☐
traffic lights	☐ ☐☐
traffic controllers	☐ ☐☐
other road users	☐ ☐☐
18 Use of speed	☐ ☐☐
19 Following distance	☐ ☐☐
20 Progress — appropriate speed	☐ ☐☐
undue hesitation	☐ ☐☐
21 Junctions — approach speed	☐ ☐☐
observation	☐ ☐☐
turning right	☐ ☐☐
turning left	☐ ☐☐
cutting corners	☐ ☐☐
22 Judgement — overtaking	☐ ☐☐
meeting	☐ ☐☐
crossing	☐ ☐☐

	Total S D
23 Positioning — normal driving	☐ ☐☐
lane discipline	☐ ☐☐
24 Pedestrian crossings	☐ ☐☐
25 Position / normal stops	☐ ☐☐
26 Awareness / planning	☐ ☐☐
27 Ancillary controls	☐ ☐☐
28 Spare 1	☐ ☐☐
29 Spare 2	☐ ☐☐
30 Spare 3	☐ ☐☐
31 Spare 4	☐ ☐☐
32 Spare 5	☐ ☐☐
33 Wheelchair	Pass ☐ Fail ☐

Pass ☐ Fail ☐ None ☐ Total Faults ☐☐

ETA ☐ V ☐ P ☐ D255 ☐

Eco Safe driving — Control ☐ Planning ☐

Debrief ☐

I acknowledge receipt of Pass Certificate Number: ☐☐☐☐☐☐☐ Licence rec'd Yes ☒
Wheelchair Cert. No: ☐☐☐☐☐☐☐ COA ☒ No ☒

There has been no change to my health: see note 29 overleaf.

X _____

© Crown Copyright 12/2017   DVSA – An executive agency of the Department for Transport   Form Ref. DL25 D0018000-00 turning right on a roundabout failing to observe and check for vehicles on the nearside of the vehicle when exiting the roundabout.

- Driving – these are faults that are not potentially dangerous but are worthy of note. If a driver fault is recorded, then this is because the standard of driving has fallen below what is expected on the test. If a driver fault is repeated then it could become a serious fault. An example of this would be adequate clearance to parked vehicles.

Examiner's marking sheet

Eyesight

At the start of the test candidates will have to read a number plate from a distance of:

- 20 metres for vehicles with a new-style number plate.
- 20.5 metres for vehicles with an old-style number plate.

If your pupil fails the eyesight test then they will fail their driving test.

Controlled stop

During the test candidates may be asked to show that they are able to stop their vehicle in good time and under full control as if in an emergency situation. Coach your pupils to remember that weather conditions such as wet or ice can result in the car taking longer to stop safely. This way they are prepared for whatever weather conditions greet them on the day of the test. Your pupil will be required to react promptly, transferring from accelerator to brake, braking firmly, and progressively applying the maximum force to stop the car safely in the shortest distance. Mirror work is not a priority as it delays reaction times. Ensure that the clutch is applied AFTER the brake. Keep both hands on the wheel to keep the car straight and absorb the driver's forward movement.

The most effective way to deal with an emergency stop is not to have one in the first place, so coaching your pupils to avoid one is recommended so that when they are driving they need to:

- Be especially aware, creating a 'safety bubble' around the vehicle. At least 2 seconds, front and back in dry conditions, and 1 metre to both sides of the car.
- If the above gaps are not available then adjust speed to compensate.
- Drive at a speed that they know they can stop in safely.

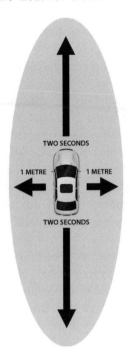

- Anticipation skills will allow the driver to plan ahead to deal with hazards in good time.
- Good observation skills allow for knowing what is around at all times.
- Drive in a style that is considerate to other road users, working in sympathy with the car and driving in a manner that is always safe.

Calculation system for stopping distances in feet

Mph	Thinking + braking =	Overall stopping distance=	mph x ?
20	20 + 20 =	40 =	20 x 2
30	30 + 45 =	75 =	30 x 2½
40	40 + 80 =	120 =	40 x 3
50	50 + 125 =	175 =	50 x 3½
60	60 + 180 =	240 =	60 x 4
70	70 + 245 =	315 =	70 x 4½

Manoeuvres

During the driving test candidates will be asked to perform 1 manoeuvre (boxes 4, 5, and 8 on the marking sheet). The maoeuvre will be selected from the following:

- Reverse park into a bay at the test centre (Box 5) **OR** a parallel park in the road.

- Drive forward into a parking bay, reverse out to the left or right (Box 8).
- Pull up on the right and reverse back (Box 4).

Whilst carrying out the manoeuvre, your pupil must show that their observation skills are excellent. This will require being fully aware of all other road users and taking action according to what they see. This will include giving priority where necessary. Their car control must also be to a good standard whereby they are able to control the vehicle at slow speed in all circumstances. Their accuracy must be demonstrated to a high level on any manoeuvre they are asked to complete, and the following points are of note regarding accuracy:

- *Reverse in a bay at the test centre at the start of the test* (this only applies at test centres where parking bays are available): Candidates will be asked to drive out of the bay either to the left or right and then straighten their wheels to prevent reversing back in on the same lock. They must finish inside the bay, although they are not normally penalised for crossing lines when entering the bay.
- *Parking on the road (parallel park)*: This needs to be completed within about 2 car lengths of the stationary vehicle. Candidates are expected to complete the manoeuvre reasonably close to the kerb and parallel.
- *Driving forward into a parking bay*: This exercise is designed to check that the candidate can manoeuvre the vehicle in a restricted space. Car control, observation and accuracy must be of a very high level. They will be able to choose a convenient bay, and should park within the bay. They would not normally be penalised for crossing lines when entering the bay. When the manoeuvre is completed, the examiner will consider whether the vehicle could reasonably be left in that position. The candidate will then be asked to reverse out of the bay either to the left or the right. **NB** a good point to note is having the windows down when reversing as this may well help the pupil to identify other vehicles or pedestrians before they actually see them.
- *Pulling up on the right*: On a suitable road, candidates will be asked to pull up on the right at a safe place; they will then secure the car, at which point they will be asked to reverse for about 2 car lengths. They will be asked to drive off when they are ready. The purpose of this exercise is to assess your pupil's ability to move

safely across the path of oncoming traffic, to reverse and to move off again safely. Once again car control, observation and accuracy of the vehicle must be excellent.

Precautions (Box 11)

This section covers the cockpit drill; making sure that the car is secure, the candidate's seat is adjusted correctly allowing them to reach all the controls with ease. If the vehicle is not set up correctly then this will affect the driver's ability to control the car accuracy and to be able to take effective observation.

Controls (Box 12)

Driving guides say that the controls should be used smoothly and at the correct time. Vehicle sympathy should be the word. Candidates should always be in the correct gear, at the correct speed and in the correct road position; they should be safe at all times. Candidates will be required to move off on a gradient under full control and also be able to use the controls precisely at slow speed for manoeuvres. The clutch and gears should be used smoothly. Under most driving situations the brakes, not the gearbox, should be used to slow the vehicle. The gearbox may be used on downhill descents to allow engine braking to reduce speed.

Brakes

As with other controls, the footbrake should be used smoothly. Brake progressively to reduce speed. The use of the brakes and brake lights are important in controlling following vehicles. In situations where candidates are being followed at a distance that is less than safe, then early, light, progressive use of the footbrake, with the brake lights showing, will allow your pupils to deal safely with this situation. When using the footbrake candidates should be aware of the braking distances at various speeds. The figures are based on average reaction times and braking. Braking will vary from vehicle to vehicle and will be affected by:

- Weight of the vehicle (including passengers).
- Weather conditions (micro-climate).
- Road surface conditions.
- Maintenance of the vehicle's brakes.
- Tyres (tread depth, pressures, manufacturer).
- Driver's reaction times.

The following table shows how far a vehicle will travel in 1 second at various speeds.

Mph	Distance covered (m)
1	0.45
5	2.23
10	4.47
20	8.94
30	13.41
40	17.88
50	22.35
60	26.82
70	31.29

The handbrake should be used:

- When a pause develops into a wait.
- When parked.
- When the vehicle is stationary on a gradient.

When applying the handbrake in a queue of traffic, keep the brake lights on by use of the footbrake until the vehicle behind has come to a stop. This will help reduce the risk of a rear impact.

Steering

Candidates will be assessed on their ability to steer smoothly and under control. The examiner will look at ability to control the vehicle and will not be looking at a certain method of steering. Therefore, it is not essential to hold the steering wheel at 'ten to two' although this position does have its advantages:

- It keeps the steering balanced.
- It allows the driver to turn the wheel immediately in either direction.

In order to be able to steer to a good standard candidates should be in the correct seating position. To check this, when they extend their arms straight their wrists should rest on the top of the steering wheel, sliding their hands to the 'ten to two' (and preferred position) their elbows will then become slightly bent. This is the correct seating position to attain the preferred steering position too.

The following section is intended to give a general overview of what is being looked for by the examiner on your pupils' test. Familiarising yourself with these requirements will assist you in ensuring that you have coached your pupils to the standard required for safe driving for life and as a consequence, be able to pass their driving test. The section follows the order of the examiner's marking sheet (as shown on pages 264–267) for ease of reference.

Move off (Box 13)

Here, the examiner will be looking to make sure that your pupil can move away smoothly and safely from rest. This will include, where possible, moving away on reasonably steep gradients both uphill and downhill, and will also be required to move off at an angle once they have pulled up behind a vehicle. The move off is expected to be performed smoothly, without rolling backwards or forwards. Observation skills must be effective and all-round. Candidates should also consider the use of a signal.

Use of mirrors (Box 14)

During the test pupils will be marked on their effective use of mirrors. Here, there is no set formula but as a driver pupils should be aware at all times of what is happening around their vehicle. They will be marked down if they fail to make effective use of mirrors before signaling, making a change of direction or before changing speed. Candidates are expected to act effectively and correctly to what they see and where mirrors do not provide sufficient information. They must take effective rear observation where appropriate, such as a blind spot check when moving off or manoeuvering.

Signals (Box 15)

This area covers how candidates communicate with other road users. In its basic form, this covers signal faults such as omitting a necessary signal, failing to cancel a signal, not signalling as per the Highway Code, signalling either too early or too late. Other signals would include the horn, flashing of headlights, brake lights, hazard warning lights, road position, arm signals and the speed of the vehicles. When driving, it is important that pupils sign clearly and in good time to let other road users know what they intend to do.

Flashing headlights should only be used to let other road users know that you are there. Headlights should NOT be used to convey any other message (Highway Code Rule 110). Similarly, the horn should only be used to warn other road users of your presence whilst the vehicle is moving. The horn should not be used aggressively. Examples of correct use of flashing headlights or the horn could be:

- If a vehicle is reversing out of a driveway and hasn't seen your vehicle.
- On approaching a tight, blind bend.

The horn must not be used whilst stationary on the road and also when driving in a built-up area between 11.30pm and 07.00am unless another road user is posing a danger to you.

Signalling can come in more subtle forms where, for example, changes in speed and/or road position will have an effect on other road users. The progress of a car approaching a junction would clearly indicate to other road users waiting to emerge that the car is not turning if it does not slow down. However, a car that slows unnecessarily may give the false impression to a pedestrian waiting to cross, or a driver waiting to emerge.

Signals should be used to inform pedestrians of driver intentions, and often eye contact with the pedestrian will confirm that they have been seen by the driver and reassure them. It is important, however, that drivers do not beckon pedestrians to cross the road since they do not know what the actions of other road users will be and could therefore be putting the pedestrian in danger.

Clearance/Obstructions (Box 16)
When driving, candidates need to give enough space to pass parked vehicles and other obstructions with a safe gap. Anticipation and planning of the road ahead will allow your pupil to be able to deal with changing situations such as a car door opening or a pedestrian stepping out between parked cars. If the available gap reduces, your pupil should be prepared to slow down to accommodate the changing situation; this may include having to stop.

Response to signs/signals (Box 17)
This section of the marking sheet will look at the candidate's ability to react correctly to all traffic signs, road markings, traffic lights and pedestrian crossings. As your pupil will already have passed their theory test their theory knowledge should be at a very good level and a good understanding of the Highway Code and *Know Your Traffic Signs* is required and, indeed, assumed to be in place by this stage of the process.

During the test, candidates will come across many signs, some of which may be time-sensitive such as bus lanes. Drivers need to be aware of the time at which they encounter such signs and should not rely on other motorists' actions, as frequently other road users misunderstand these types of signs.

Coach your pupils to pay particular attention to box junctions and 'keep clear' markings when in heavy traffic conditions as these are often difficult to see when the roads are busy. Having said this, an understanding of why box junctions and 'keep clear' markings are in place should allow a good driver to anticipate them and therefore react to them appropriately.

At a 'Stop' sign candidates must STOP at the transverse line, especially if the road is clear. It is the law, and will result in a serious fault during the test if they do not do so. Candidates should wait at the stop sign until it is possible to proceed safely without inconveniencing other road users.

Candidates are expected to respond correctly to signals given by a police officer, traffic warden, or other persons authorised to direct traffic. They should also be observant for signals given by other road users and take appropriate action based on what they see.

Use of speed (Box 18)

The way that your pupil drives on test day will be dependent upon traffic and weather conditions as well as road signs and speed limits. It is important to remember that, at all times, they should be able to stop within the distance they can see to be clear, and drive within the speed limit for the road. When travelling on higher speed roads their observations will need to be further down the road in order for them to have sufficient time to plan. They will need to scan for distance, then middle distance, then near distance. The controls of the vehicle should be used smoothly and in sympathy with the vehicle.

Following distance (Box 19)

This means keeping a safe distance to the vehicle in front. Candidates must be able to stop well within the distance they can see to be clear. They should leave extra distance in wet or slippery conditions. Should a vehicle be following your pupil too close behind, then they will need to adjust their driving to deal with the safety aspects of their driving and that of the car following. They will need to increase the distance to the vehicle in front of them in order to create a safe gap that allows more time to deal with hazards and allow the following driver more time to respond. In order to do this, coach your pupil to:

- Check mirrors and study/profile the following driver.
- Slow down gradually by either coming off the gas or gently braking.

- Plan and deal early with any issues ahead of them.
- Brake gently when dealing with hazards.

It is important that your pupil manages the situation with the other driver rather than being managed by them. Managing other road users is an essential skill and one that comes with good coaching and plenty of practise.

Following distance will also include leaving enough distance to the vehicle in front when in a queue. Coach your pupil to ensure that, if there is an issue with the vehicles in front of their vehicle, they have a safe escape route. Instructors often refer to 'tyres and tarmac' as a form of everyday saying that they seem to think all drivers will know. By all means use this as a reference point to help transfer information, but please explain the intent behind it rather than simply stating it!

Maintaining progress (Box 20)

During the test (and in general driving), candidates need to show that they can drive at a realistic speed that is appropriate to the road and weather conditions. This means that all hazards should be approached in a safe manner. Your pupil's approach speed needs to be controlled without being over-cautious and they need to ensure that they do not slow or stop other motorists unnecessarily.

When stopped, in order to avoid undue hesitation, candidates should always be ready to move off safely. They should be prepared to move away from junctions as soon as it safe and appropriate to do so.

In order to maintain progress in a safe and controlled manner candidates will need to plan well ahead, looking and scanning in plenty of time in far, middle and near distance in order to always put themselves in a situation where they can identify or anticipate hazards in a safe manner without unnecessarily slowing. And of course your pupils need to be aware of speed limits, being in correct gear and at the correct speed at all times.

Candidates should be aware of micro climates (i.e. local weather conditions) as well as studying the traffic conditions. They need to be aware of the actions of other road users as, for example, they may need to give way at a meeting situation even where they have priority.

Being aware of what is behind at all times is also expected by effective use of mirrors, as well as the taking of appropriate action where necessary. Whilst maintaining a business-like drive, your pupils will be expected to drive in a courteous manner throughout keeping themselves, their vehicle and its occupants, and all other road users safe at all times.

Junctions including roundabouts (Box 21)

Junctions, by nature, are where roads meet. It is essential that candidates deal with these hazards safely as these are high risk areas, particularly where they have to cross the path of traffic. Coach your pupils on the MSPSL routine (Mirrors-Signal-Position-Speed-Look) as they will need to be fully aware of what is around *them,* *their* approach speed and *their* road position. They will also be required to demonstrate that they are able to safely judge the speed and distance of oncoming vehicles, and be very aware of the actions of other road users, remembering that it is often more difficult to identify cyclists and motorbikes.

Speed on approach at junctions and roundabouts must be correct in order to allow candidates to deal with these hazards safely; this will include the correct and safe observation of other road users as well as the ability to move into and away from the junctions without undue hesitation. The positioning of the vehicle must be correct at all junctions.

Judgement (Box 22)

In this section candidates will be assessed on their judgement skills throughout the test. Judgement is therefore a continuous process, and your pupils will need to show sound judgement when overtaking and meeting or crossing the path of other road users. These things should only be done when it is safe and legal to do so. Candidates will need to ensure that their intentions are clear and that they understand the intentions of other road users. Your pupil will need to constantly assess hazards and make decisions as to what action they are going to take in order to deal with them. Assessing the risk of each situation will enable them to make safe decisions, and as the risk may change and develop as they approach, their risk assessment must be a continuous process. Your pupils will need to prioritise the risk and make sound decisions on the actions they will take.

Positioning (Box 23)

Candidates will be expected to position their car safely at all times. This will depend on a number of factors such as the direction being taken, the road layout, road signs and markings and the presence of parked vehicles.

Your pupils will need to make sure that if they change position, for example a lane change, that it is done in good time and gradually, making sure that their position allows sufficient space around the vehicle. A 'safety bubble' would allow at least a doors-width to either side of the vehicle and, in dry conditions, a minimum of a 2 second gap front and rear. Maintaining this type of position will allow pupils to deal with any unplanned event; if this not possible, they should know to adjust their speed to suit the reduced gap. Their normal driving position would be expected to be well to the left of the road.

Pedestrian crossing (Box 24)

Pedestrian crossings come in various forms: zebra, toucan, puffin, pelican, equestrian, and school crossing. It is important that candidates are able to identify the different types and be further able to take the correct action required when dealing with them. On approaching a crossing your pupils need to be fully aware of what is around them and in particular the position and speed of any following vehicles. They should monitor their own speed on approach so as to be able to stop safely if they need to. They will need to show their intention early to other road users by use of brake lights if they need to stop. First pressure braking will illuminate the brake lights without any significant reduction in speed. This will warn following traffic before second pressure braking reduces speed more significantly to eventually stopping. Pay particular attention where your pupil's view of a crossing is partly hidden by a queue or parked vehicles, and coach them in this discipline. They should allow more time for elderly or infirm pedestrians using crossings as these people will require more time to cross the road.

Position/normal stops (Box 25)

When asked to do so, candidates will need to choose a safe, legal and convenient place to stop close to the edge of the road. They must not block the road or create a hazard. If they find that they have stopped in an inconvenient place then they should take full, effective all-round observation and move the car to a more convenient location. Coach your pupils so that they know where to stop without causing inconvenience or danger to other users.

Awareness and planning (Box 26)

This section is looking at how your pupil observes other road users and how aware they are of developing situations and potential ones. They will be required to plan well ahead in order to give themselves time to judge and take action on what they see. They have to be aware of the actions of other road users too, thus allowing them to predict how their actions impact on others and react in good time. Coach your pupils to take particular care to be aware of and plan for the actions of more vulnerable groups of road users such as pedestrians, cyclists, motorcyclists and horse riders.

Ancillary controls (Box 27)

The ancillary controls section covers the safe use of the vehicle's controls such as demisters, heating controls, indicators, windscreen washers and wipers, cruise control, windows and any other relevant switches. Candidates will need to demonstrate that they can use these secondary controls safely whilst on the move (see: Show me, tell me questions on page 260).

Learner driver test summary

Duration of test	40 minutes (approx.)
	70 minutes (approx.) (extended test)
Independent driving	20 minutes (approx.)
Cost of test	£62 weekdays (as of Sept 2018)
	£75 evenings, weekends, bank holidays
Pass mark	15 driver faults maximum
	Zero serious or dangerous
Up-to-date fees	www.gov.uk/driving-test-cost
DVSA customer support	0300 200 1122 (Mon–Fri 8am–4pm)
Book Part 3 test	www.gov.uk/book-driving-test
Take to test	UK driving licence
	Theory test certificate
Eyesight check	20 metres new-style plates
	20.5 metres old-style plates

APPENDICES

1. (ADI) Code of practice

The Driver and Vehicle Standards Agency (DVSA) and the driver training industry place great emphasis on professional standards and business ethics.

This industry code of practice has been agreed between the National Association Strategic Partnership (NASP) and the DVSA.

It is a framework within which all instructors should operate. These professional bodies expect their members to adhere to the code of practice. The current in an NASP member groups are:

- Approved Driving Instructors National Joint Council (ADI NJC)
- Driving instructors Association (DIA)
- The Motor Schools Association of Great Britain (MSA GB)

If you are an approved driving instructor who agrees to follow the code, then you can:

- Upgrade your ADI registration to show that you follow the code (www.gov.uk/update-approved-driving-instructor-registration).
- Use the 'ADI code of practice I've signed up' logo on your website or literature.

Personal Conduct

Driver trainers will be professional, comply with the law, keep clients safe and treat them with respect.

The instructor agrees to:

- At all times behave in a professional manner towards clients in line with the standards in the national standard for driver and rider training.
- At all times comply with legislative requirements including:
  o The protection of personal freedoms, the prevention of discrimination based on age, disability, gender, race, religion or sexual orientation.
  o Not using mobile devices like phones when driving or supervising client's driving and only when parked in a safe and legal place.
  o Demonstrating a high standard of driving and instructional ability of upholding safety standards including showing consideration for other road users, particularly pedestrians, cyclists, motorcyclists and horse riders.
  o Consumer, workplace and data protection regulations, the handling, storing use of dissemination of video and audio recordings made in or around their tuition vehicle.
- Avoid inappropriate physical contact with clients.
- Avoid the use of inappropriate language to clients.
- Not initiate inappropriate discussions about their own personal relationships and take care to avoid becoming involved in a client's personal affairs or discussions about a client's personal relationships and unless safeguarding concerns are raised.
- Avoid circumstances and situations which are or could be perceived to be of an inappropriate nature.
- Respect client confidentiality whilst understanding the actions to take if a client reveals concerns about their private lives.
- Treat clients with respect and consideration and support them to achieve their learning outcomes in the national standards for driving cars and light vans (Category B) as efficiently and effectively as possible.
- Ensure that their knowledge and skills on all matters relating to the provision of driver training comply with the current practice and legislative requirements.
- Use social network sites responsibly and professionally:
  o Insuring the client's personal information is not compromised.
  o Insuring when using social media for marketing purposes the what is written is compliance with privacy and data protection legislation pertaining to digital communications the laws regarding spam, copyright and other online issues.

o Treating of the uses of social media including clients colleagues and their views with respect.
o Be careful not to defame the reputation of colleague's DVSA driving examiners or the ADI register.

Business dealings

Driver trainers all account for monies paid to them record client's progress, advice clients when to apply for a driving tests and guide them fairly through the learning process.

The instructor agrees to:

- Safeguard and account for any monies paid in advance by the client in respect for driving lessons, test fees or any other purpose and made the details available to the client on request.
- On or before the first lesson make clients aware of both this code of practice and their terms of business which should include the following:
  o Legal identity of the school or the instructor with full postal address and telephone numbers of which the instructor or their representative can be contacted.
  o The current price and duration of lessons.
  o The current price and conditions for use of a driving school car for the practical driving test.
  o The terms which apply to cancellation of lessons by either party.
  o The terms under which a refund of lesson fees may be made.
  o The procedure for making a complaint.
- Check a client's entitlement to drive the vehicle and the ability to read a number plate at the statutory distance on the first lesson and regularly during their training.
- Make a record of a client's progress, which will include the number of lessons provided and ensure that the client is aware of their progress and future training requirements to achieve their driving goals.
- Discuss with and advise a client when to apply for their driving tests taking account of DVSA cancellation rules local waiting times and the instructors forecast of a client's potential for achieving the driving test past standard.
- Not cancel or rearrange a driving test without the client's knowledge and agreement, in the event of the instructor deciding to withhold the use of the school car for the driving

test sufficient notice should be given to the clients to avoid loss of the DVSA test fee.

- Ensure that when presenting a client for practical driving test:
  - o The client has all the necessary documentation to enable the client to take the test.
  - o The vehicle complies with all aspects of motoring law displays the instructor certificate or licensed correctly and is fitted with an extra interior rear-view mirror and correctly positioned L or optional D plates in Wales.
  - o Accompany the client on their practical driving test and listen to the debrief when requested to do so by the client.

Advertising

Driver trainers will take care to advertise and promote their business in a clear and fair manner.

The instructor agrees that:

- The advertising of driving tuition should be clear, fair and not misleading.
- Any claims made in advertising should be capable of verification and comply with the current CAP Advertising Codes (www.cap.org.uk/Advertising-Codes.aspx).
- Advertising the refers to pass rates should not be open to misinterpretation and the basis on which the calculation is prepared should be made clear.

Conciliation

Driver trainers will deal promptly with any complaints received and aim for a speedy resolution of any grievances.

The instructor agrees that:

- Complaints by clients should be made in the first instance to the driving instructor, driving school or contractor following the training provider's complaints procedure.
- If having completed the procedure the client has been unable to reach an agreement or settle a dispute further guidance may be sought.
  - o If a client believes that their instructor is not providing a satisfactory business service they can contact their local Citizens Advice Bureau for guidance.
  - o If clients are unhappy with instructor's professional service they can contact the ADI registrar by emailing adireg@dvsa.gov.uk.

2. *Mock theory test answers*

Mock Test: 100 Questions

The pass mark is an overall score of at least 85/100 and a minimum of 80% (or 20 out of 25) in each of the 4 bands.

1. You are on a motorway. There are red lights flashing above every lane. You MUST:
   d) Stop and wait.

2. You must not drive if your breath alcohol level is greater than:
   d) 35 mg/100 ml.

3. People with disabilities are:
   d) Permitted to drive any type of car depending on their disability.

4. Diamond-shaped signs give instructions to:
   c) Tram drivers.

5. On approaching a roundabout you should:
   b) Keep moving if the road is clear.

6. If you are involved in an accident and do not have your insurance certificate with you, you must produce it at a police station within:
   c) 7 days.

7. Reflective studs along the left edge of the road are:
   a) Red.

8. You are entering a roundabout. A cyclist in front of you is signalling to turn right. What should you do?
   d) Allow plenty of room.

9. Your vehicle is parked on the road at night. When must you use your sidelights?
   a) Where the speed limit exceeds 30 mph.

10. Using the gears to slow down should:
    c) Not normally be done.

11. The Highway Code says that well before you turn right you should:
    d) **Use your mirrors to make sure that you know the position and movement of the traffic behind you.**

12. When attending a theory test, candidates must produce:
    c) **A current valid provisional driving licence.**

13. You are driving a goods vehicle not exceeding 7.5 tonnes maximum laden weight. What is the maximum speed limit on a single carriageway?
    a) **50 mph.**

14. A long, heavily laden lorry is taking a long time to overtake you. What should you do?
    b) **Slow down.**

15. 'Red Routes' tell you that:
    d) **Special waiting restrictions apply.**

16. Defensive driving does NOT involve
    b) **Competitive driving.**

17. What is the most common cause of skidding:
    b) **Driver error.**

18. A convex mirror fitted to a car makes vehicle following appear to be:
    c) **Further away than it really is.**

19. In choosing a method of instruction, a trainer should:
    d) **Be prepared to vary the technique to suit the individual trainee.**

20. At night you see a pedestrian wearing reflective clothing and carrying a bright red light. What does this mean?
    b) **You are approaching an organised walk.**

21. You are driving on a motorway in very wet weather. Your tyres begin to lose contact with the road. This is called:
    a) **Aquaplaning.**

22. A trainer's expectations of a trainee's ability can sometimes be too high. This can:
    c) Have a negative effect on the trainee's progress.

23. The main purpose of a trainer giving feedback is to:
    b) Make the trainee aware of how they are progressing.

24. Circular road signs
    c) Give orders.

25. What is the overall stopping distance on a dry road at 70 mph?
    d) 96 m (315 ft).

26. Your vehicle collides with a bridge. You must report it to:
    b) The police.

27. A full driving licence is valid until the driver's:
    b) 70th birthday.

28. You have a collision whilst your car is moving. What is the first thing you should do?
    c) Stop at the scene of the accident.

29. You must not drive if your blood alcohol level is greater than:
    b) 80 mg/100 ml.

30. What is 'client-centred learning'?
    b) Learning based on the abilities, needs and learning style of the pupil.

31. On a driving test a pupil will be required to carry out:
    d) One reversing manoeuvre.

32. Pupils should apply for their theory test:
    c) When they have studied and their driving instructor advises them.

33. 'Red Routes' in major cities have been introduced to:
    b) Help traffic flow.

34. You will use more fuel if your tyres are:
    a) Under-inflated.

35. In a diesel engine which of the following fuels would most improve vehicle emissions?
    c) **Low sulphur diesel.**

36. You may cancel your driving test without losing your fee so long as you give:
    c) **3 complete working days notice.**

37. A pedestrian wanting to cross at a zebra crossing should:
    d) **Put one foot on the crossing.**

38. When coaching a pupil, the pupil should:
    a) **Be encouraged to analyse problems and take responsibility for learning.**

39. During a driving session an instructor observes a driving fault by the trainee. This should be:
    a) **Used as a training opportunity.**

40. A deaf person can drive:
    b) **Any Category B motor vehicle.**

41. Eco-safe driving includes:
    c) **Planning ahead.**

42. Initial assessment would normally be carried out in order to determine:
    b) **The level at which training should begin.**

43. What should you do if you have to use the dual controls?
    b) **Inform the pupil you have used them and ask if they understand why you used them.**

44. Your vehicle has power-assisted steering. It's main purpose is to:
    c) **Reduce driver effort.**

45. In 'question and answer' technique an open question:
    a) **Highlights the pupil's level of understanding.**

46. Before crossing a one-way street, pedestrians should look:
    a) **Both ways.**

47. When booking a theory test, if you have a reading difficulty:
   b) **You can ask to hear the test through headphones.**

48. When travelling at 70 mph how many metres do you travel in one second:
   d) **31.5 metres (104 ft).**

49. Unless a moving vehicle creates a danger, do not sound your horn in a built-up area between:
   c) **11.30pm and 7am.**

50. You have broken down on a 2 way road. What is the shortest distance from your vehicle you should place a warning triangle?
   c) **45 metres (147 ft).**

51. The ADI regulations are part of:
   c) **The Road Traffic Act.**

52. On the driving test, if the examiner uses the dual controls this is marked as:
   c) **A dangerous fault.**

53. A police officer asks to see your documents. You do not have them with you. You may produce them at a police station within:
   c) **7 days.**

54. According to The Official DVSA Guide to Driving, what percentage of pedestrians survive a collision with a car at 40 mph?
   a) **5%.**

55. On a training course, progressive learning should be measured by:
   a) **Having an ongoing assessment.**

56. Driving test routes are designed to:
   d) **Cover a wide variety of road and traffic situations.**

57. If a candidate fails the eyesight check at the start of the driving test (20 m/66 ft or 20.5 m/67 ft older style plates):
   b) **It is marked as a serious fault.**

58. The Highway Code states that where there is an advanced stop line for cyclists:
    b) **Motorists must stop at the first white line reached if the lights are amber or red.**

59. When should you assess a learner driver's progress?
    b) **Continuously, using dialogue and feedback.**

60. The 'learning plateau' sometimes occurs during instructional programmes. This refers to:
    a) **A temporary halt in the learning process.**

61. From 4th June 2018 learner drivers can take motorway lessons when accompanied by:
    d) **An ADI with a car fitted with dual controls.**

62. According to Roadcraft the system of car control follows 4 phases:
    c) **Position, speed, gear, acceleration.**

63. A driving test pass certificate is valid for:
    b) **2 years.**

64. What is the thinking distance at 70 mph?
    d) **21 m (69 ft).**

65. The 'halo effect' is where a trainer:
    a) **Tends to subconsciously ignore minor faults committed by a favoured pupil.**

66. According to Roadcraft you plan your driving in 3 key stages. In what order should these be applied?
    c) **Anticipate, order of importance, decide on action.**

67. The anti-lock braking system (ABS) allows the driver to:
    d) **Continue to steer whilst braking firmly.**

68. If you are receiving Higher Rate Disability Living Allowance you:
    b) **Can start driving at the age of 16.**

69. When coaching, the GROW model (Goal/Reality/Options/Way forward) is used:
    b) **To allow the trainee to goal set and problem solve.**

70. The Highway Code states that you must not reverse more than:
    a) **The distance that is necessary.**

71. A candidate who makes a serious fault on a driving test:
    c) **Will fail their driving test.**

72. Before emerging at a junction a pupil should:
    c) **Look effectively in all directions.**

73. The overall stopping distance at 50 mph is:
    c) **53 m (175 ft).**

74. In 'question and answer technique' a closed question is one which:
    b) **Has only one correct answer.**

75. On a driving test a potentially dangerous incident will be recorded as:
    a) **A serious fault.**

76. A zebra crossing with a central island is:
    b) **2 separate crossings.**

77. What is the braking distance at 70 mph?
    a) **75 m (246 ft).**

78. During a structured session of training you should NOT:
    b) **Rigidly keep to a fixed lesson plan.**

79. According to *Driving: the Essentials Skills*, you should be prepared to make allowances for someone else's mistakes. You should NOT:
    c) **Drive in a spirit of retaliation or competition.**

80. When turning into a minor road you should:
    d) **Give way to pedestrians already crossing when you turn, as they have priority.**

81. When parking downhill you should:
    c) **Turn the steering wheel to the left and leave the vehicle in reverse gear.**

82. Which of the following is most likely to cause a burst tyre when driving?
    d) **Running at constant high speed.**

83. In a skid what should you do if the back end of your vehicle skids to the right?
    c) **Steer carefully to the right.**

84. Anyone supervising a learner driver must:
    b) **Be at least 21 and have held a licence for that type of vehicle for at least 3 years.**

85. When following traffic in dry conditions you should leave a gap of at least:
    a) **2 seconds.**

86. When turning right at a box junction and you have to wait for oncoming vehicles, you should:
    c) **Wait in the yellow box if your exit is clear.**

87. On motorways the earliest information sign of a junction is usually located:
    c) **One mile in advance.**

88. At a puffin crossing what colour follows the green signal?
    a) **Steady amber.**

89. A white stick with a red band is used by:
    b) **Someone who is deaf and blind.**

90. For an instructor to accompany a pupil during the test then:
    d) **The candidate must ask the examiner.**

91. As a professional driver you should:
    b) **Plan routes to avoid busy times and congestion.**

92. You service your own vehicles. How should you dispose of old engine oil?
    a) **Take it to a local authority site.**

93. Before turning left you should have a final look into which mirror?
    a) **Left-hand mirror.**

94. To help a trainee attain a good standard of driving the amount of verbal instruction should be:
    c) **Reduced as their competence increases.**

95. Anti-lock brakes reduce the chance of a skid occurring, particularly when:
    a) **Braking in an emergency.**

96. At a pelican crossing what does the flashing green man mean for pedestrians?
    b) **Do not start to cross.**

97. According to the law the minimum tread on tyres should be:
    d) **1.6 mm.**

98. The main cause of brake fade is:
    a) **The brakes overheating.**

99. Freezing conditions will affect the distance it takes to come to a stop. You should expect stopping distances to increase by up to:
    c) **10 times.**

100. A theory pass certificate is valid for:
    c) **24 months.**

3. Instructor guidance notes
The information in this appendix is designed to help you get started.

As a new driving instructor, the following will help you get started in your new career.

Things you will need

- DVSA licence – This needs to be displayed in the windscreen.
- Diary/pupil record – For your records.
- Rear-view mirror – These can be sourced from most autocentres or supermarkets.
- Lesson presenter – Available from your sponsoring driving school, or readily available to purchase online.
- Business cards – again available from your sponsoring driving school, or readily available to purchase online.
- Pupil handbooks – These are provided by your sponsoring school.
- Highway Code/traffic signs books.
- Pens/pencils/dry wipe markers/notebook.

Things you may find useful

- Pupil handouts – These can be sourced from a number of online suppliers.
- Mock test reports.
- Folders – To keep papers neat.
- Air fresheners.
- Mints.
- Wipes – For the steering wheel etc.
- Duster/cloth.
- Glass cleaner.
- Storage box – To keep everything together.

Contacting customers for the first time

A good first impression is essential to booking your first lesson with a new pupil. Below are a few tips to help you secure that booking.

Call them as soon as you can.

Once you have received their details, it is important to contact them as soon as you are able, if you leave it too long they may find another school.

Find a quiet place.

Find a place where you are not likely to be interrupted by anything or anyone. Spinning washing machines, barking dogs, vacuum cleaners and screaming children are just a few examples of everyday things that could spoil that first impression. You need to sound professional.

Be prepared.

Have your diary to hand and make sure that you have a pen and something on which you can take notes. It may be helpful to you if you have a pre-prepared form on which you can record all the information you need. These are available online.

Introduction.

Ask for the pupil by name… "Can I speak to [their name] please?" or "is that [their name]?" introduce yourself… "Hello, my name is *[your name]* from *[your]* Driving School, I understand you would like to organise some driving lessons."

Previous experience.

A good question at this point would be... "Have you done any driving before?" if the answer is yes, follow up with, "tell me about your previous experience." if the answer is no you could ask "what about motorbikes/pedal cycles?" take notes so that you can refer to them before the first lesson. At this point it is also a good idea to find out if they already have their provisional licence and if they have started studying for the theory test.

Availability.

"When were you hoping to book your first lesson?" it is a good idea to find out their availability for every day of the week and note this down.

Book 2 hours.

Once you know their availability, offer them a 2 hour slot and give them more than one option. For example; "I have 12pm–2pm available on Tuesday or 3pm–5pm on Thursday, which one would suit you best?" Explain that you will need to assess what they can and can't do, so the lesson will need to be 2 hours in duration. Also explain any discounts that you may want to offer for block bookings.

Confirm details.

Confirm their pick up address and contact details and find out the best place to park when you pick them up for the lesson. After concluding the call send a confirmation text.

To conclude.

Be professional, be prepared, and be friendly and open and honest. If their first question is about lesson prices, tell them. Don't try to defer until later in the conversation, because you will appear evasive. Explain your hourly rate, and any discounts you offer.

The first lesson with a new customer

Being new to driving tuition, picking up a customer for their first lesson can be a little daunting, below are a few pointers to help the lesson run smoothly. It can also help to remember that they will probably be more nervous than you.

Be prepared.

In your first conversation with the pupil you will have established their previous experience, or lack thereof, so spend a little time planning for the roads you can use local to the pupil and the subjects you are likely to be covering, but have a backup plan. A pupil may tell you that they have no experience, but in reality they have lots. For example, people who have perhaps driven illegally are not always going to confess over the phone.

Turn up on time.
Wherever possible, arrive at the agreed time. It goes without saying that arriving late for a lesson would be unprofessional at any time, but on the first lesson you really want to make a good impression. Also, don't arrive early. They may not be ready for you and this will cause them to rush; rushing is a bad start to a lesson, you want them to be as relaxed as possible.

Introduce yourself.
When you arrive, most pupils will be ready and waiting for you, but it may be necessary to go to the door. It may also become a family affair, as parents often want to meet the person who will be teaching their children.

Licence check.
It should go without saying that you need to make sure that it is them in the picture, but you also need to check that they have Category B entitlement. You can check their entitlement in more detail at www.gov.uk/view-driving-licence. No licence, no lesson.

Eyesight check.
As you are no doubt aware, 20 metres from a new-style registration plate. Start from further away and get them to move forward until they can read it. If they need glasses or contact lenses, make a note of this and make sure they wear them on all subsequent lessons. Don't allow anyone to drive with defective eyesight.

It's an audition.
There are lots of other instructors out there if you fail to impress. Give them a great lesson so that they want to come back for more. This, however, should happen on every lesson if you want to keep their custom.

Get them to book their theory test.
If they have not already booked their theory test, write down all the information they will need and advise them to book it for 2–3 weeks from now. This sets their first major goal for them and proves that you are not just there to take their money. Also, advise them about study resources.

Forward book.
Before the lesson ends, book their next lesson and the next, and the next. The way to sell forward booking is simple. Tell them that your diary fills very quickly and you want to make sure that they have a secure lesson slot. Write these in their handbook so that they can't forget. At this point, inform them of the cancellation period.

Sell 2 hours.
The DVSA published average number of lessons to test is 45 hours. Doing 1 hour per week would take them almost a year.

To conclude.
Be professional, be enthusiastic and be the instructor that they want to come back to.

Personal appearance/conduct

Personal appearance.
It is not necessary to wear a business suit to a lesson, but you should present yourself in a professional manner. Smart/casual is acceptable. You may find that you spend long hours in the car, so it is important that your own personal hygiene is of a high standard. Keep things like deodorant, mints and wipes handy in your car.

Personal conduct.
As a professional driving instructor it is important that your personal conduct is beyond reproach and that you remain professional at all times. Below are a few pointers that should help you to avoid any pitfalls.

- Avoid physical contact. In any enclosed space, any form of physical contact can be seen as inappropriate and can cause offence. Even a pat on the shoulder that is intended to be reassuring can be misinterpreted. Protect yourself from potential misunderstandings.
- Respect personal space. It can be tempting when explaining controls to point out the control in question. If this would take your hand into their personal space, keep to your own side of the car and explain without pointing. Even reaching to retrieve something from the back seat can make some people uncomfortable. If you need to reach into the back, warn them first. For example; "excuse me, I'm just going to reach for my diary/book." If you need to take control of the steering, try to use the top of the wheel.

- Don't cause offence. We all like to make our lessons enjoyable and fun and maybe tell the odd joke. This is all good, but avoid anything that could be seen as inappropriate and cause offence: religion, sex, politics etc.
- Keep your counsel. Don't discuss other customers with your pupil, they will assume that you will also talk about them when they are not there. You may also find yourself teaching people who are friends or know each other. If they ask about their friend's driving just reply "sorry, I can't discuss anyone else's progress, it would be unprofessional." Don't get drawn into it. Also, most of your customers will not want their test dates known, so keep these confidential.

Handling money and keeping accounts

As this is largely a cash business you may find yourself handling cash frequently. Here are a few things to consider.

Security.
For your own safety, don't carry large amounts of cash, deposit it regularly. Also, when you are teaching keep your doors locked and any cash out of sight.

Responsibility.
Quite often pupils will pay you for a block of lessons, it is important that you keep a record of this and all subsequent lessons taken from that block. It is advisable to get the pupil to sign for each lesson they take from the block, this protects you in case they dispute how many lessons they have taken. Keep these records yourself so that they don't get lost. You can design your own pupil record or search online resources. It is advisable to put any money from block bookings to one side and only take what you have already earned. If a pupil has to cancel their lessons for whatever reason, they may ask for a refund of any credit not yet used. If the money has already been spent this could put you in a very awkward situation.

HMRC.
You are responsible for paying tax and national insurance on your net earnings. Keep all your receipts for anything that is a legitimate business expense and keep accurate records of your income. You will need to inform HMRC that you are self-employed.

Payments.
Ask for payment at the beginning of the lesson. Some customers will tell you that they need to drive to a cash machine, if you don't find this out

until the end of the lesson you may find yourself running late for your next appointment. Occasionally, a customer will ask if they can pay by cheque. If this happens it is advisable to request that any payment by cheque is made 7 days before the lesson takes place, again this protects your income.

Car care
Keep it clean.
Wherever possible, keep your car clean. Understandably, weather conditions can prevent you from keeping the outside clean, if this is the case keep your windows and lights as clean as possible and the interior clean and tidy. Your car is your transport, your classroom and your office, it is vital that you keep it clean and smelling fresh. Unfortunately, not all your customers will come to their lesson clean and fresh. Keep air fresheners etc. in your car just in case. It may also be worth considering using washable seat covers.

POWDER checks.
Your car is a very important tool of your trade, it is therefore essential that you maintain it properly. The acronym POWDER can help with this, it stands for...
Petrol/Diesel, Oil, Water, Damage, Electrics and Rubber.

Petrol/diesel. Try to make sure that you have enough fuel to complete the current lesson. If you do need to refuel during a lesson, make it part of the lesson. Get the pupil to operate the pump, under your guidance, but keep this to a minimum. Never let the fuel run too low as this can cause serious problems with your car.

Oil. This includes engine oil, brake fluid and steering fluid where appropriate. Letting these run low can be very detrimental to your vehicle and could also be dangerous. Check them at least once each week.

Water. This includes coolant and washer fluid. As above check them at least once each week. It is also worth noting that driving with an empty washer reservoir can result in a fine and penalty points.

Damage. Check your car for damage each day and report it as soon as possible.

Electrics. This includes lights, indicators, instrument panel etc. as well as heaters and fans. Check these daily.

Rubber. Check the general condition of your tyres and wiper blades daily and check your tyre tread depth at least once each week. At this point it is important also to check that your brakes are working.

Service intervals. Take note of any service prompts and arrange your service in good time. If you don't adhere to service intervals it can invalidate the vehicle warranty and result in you being charged for repairs.

So... keeping your car in good condition and maintaining it properly should keep you on the road and earning money. Car problems often result in cancelled lessons and upset customers.

Preparing a customer for test.
Are they ready?
It is important to ensure that any candidate you present for test is ready to drive on the roads. It is a good idea to ask yourself if you would trust them to drive your family around. If you take pupils to test who are not ready, the examiners will see this and will probably start to feel uneasy about testing your customers. However, if you consistently take good drivers who are ready, the examiners are likely to be much more relaxed.

Don't be pressured.
Quite often a pupil will have pressure put on them to pass quickly by parents or employers who are funding their lessons. Make them aware from the outset that you do not take anyone to test who is not ready.

Effective mock testing.
Mock tests are a very important tool for preparing your pupils for test. A mock test has many benefits including:

1. It allows you to see how they will cope with the pressure.
2. It shows the pupil what it will feel like to be tested.
3. It shows the pupil what the examiners are looking for.
4. It highlights any areas of weakness that still need work. A series of 2 or 3 mock tests with remedial work in between is usually the most effective.

A mock test should be as close to the real thing as possible. It should include as many different road types as possible. It should include a reverse manoeuvre, an emergency stop where practical, an independent/sat nav drive and should last around 35 /40 minutes. Try to ensure that your mock test routes don't interfere with actual tests being conducted.

On the day.
It is usual to collect your pupil 1 hour before the start of the test, however this can vary due to geography. The hour before the test should only be a warm up drive, a chance for them to relax. Nothing should need working on at this stage. Don't practice manoeuvres as if these go wrong during the warm up, panic will start in your pupil's mind.

As soon as they get in the car, make sure that they have their documents (licence/theory test certificate) and if they normally wear glasses or contact lenses for driving, make sure they are wearing them.

Arrive at the test centre no earlier than 10 minutes before the start of the test. Any earlier than this and you are likely to get in the way of the previous tests coming back. You and your pupil should take a seat in the waiting area and wait for the examiner to call their name. Try to keep them relaxed by talking about things unrelated to driving.

Where possible and with the consent of your pupil it is a good idea to sit in and observe the test so that you can also see what the examiner is looking for and how they mark errors.

Generating new business.
As driving instructors, when we are good at what we do, we lose our customers when they pass their test. Your driving school (if you are with one) will help you to fill your diary and keep it full, you can generate new customers using lots of different methods. Below are a few suggestions.

It is important to note at this point that if you are a Potential Driving Instructor, the DVSA in the section of 'Get a trainee driving instructor licence' states: "Make sure that your advertising doesn't make it seem like you are a fully qualified instructor".

Social media.
Create yourself a Facebook profile if you don't already have one. Let all your friends know that you are offering lessons and in what areas, then ask your friends to share this with their friends. A network can build very quickly. Each time you start to teach a new customer, ask them if you can connect with them on Facebook, then encourage them to share your advertising posts with all their friends.

Most towns and cities have sites for people to sell things, these are usually connected to Facebook they have names like "items for sale in…" Post on as many of these as you can in the area you are working.

Business cards and leaflets.
The best places to put your marketing materials are usually free. Try local shops, takeaways, sandwich shops etc; places frequented by large

amounts of people or where people have to wait. Outside colleges and universities are good places to hand out leaflets.

Park your car.

When you are between lessons, park your car where it will be visible to lots of people; supermarket car park, near the entrance to local college etc. and make sure that it is clean! Leave business cards under windscreen wipers or tucked in to the outside of your windows.

Recommendations.

One of the best ways to generate new business is through recommendations. If you are professional, good at what you do and friendly, people will want to recommend you to their friends. You can also use incentives to help with this by offering a free lesson to your pupils if they refer their friends to you.

Remember that this is your business. The more you can do to promote yourself, the more successful you will be.

Useful numbers.

Make a list of useful numbers such as, your driving school, breakdown services, windscreen replacement services etc.

4. Driving licence categories

In this section we will be looking at particular vehicles and drivers entitlement to drive for that category of vehicle.

View driving licence categories online at www.gov.uk/view-driving-licence.

Mopeds

Category AM

You can drive two-wheeled or three-wheeled vehicles with a maximum design speed of over 25 km per hour (15.5 mph), but not more than 45 km/h (28 mph).

This category also includes like quad bikes with:

- Unladen mass of not more than 350 kg (not including the batteries if it's an electrical vehicle).
- Maximum design speed of over 25 km/hr or 15.5 mph but not more than 45 km/h or 28 mph.

Category P

You can drive two-wheeled vehicles with a maximum design speed of over 45 km/h (28 mph), but not more than 50 km/h (31 mph).

Its engine size must not be more than 50cc if powered by an internal combustion engine.

Category Q
You can drive two-wheeled vehicles with:

- An engine size not more than 50cc if powered by an internal combustion engine.
- A maximum design speed of not more than 25 km/h (15.5 mph).

Motorcycles
Category A1
You can drive light motorbikes with:

- An engine size up to 125cc.
- A power output of up to 11 kw.
- A power to weight ratio not more than 0.1 kw kg.

This category also includes a motor tricycles with a power output up to 15 kw.

Category A2
You can drive motorbikes with a:

- Power output up to 35 kw.
- Power to weight ratio not more than 0.2 kw kg.

You can also drive motorbikes in Category A1.

Category A
You can drive:

- Motorbikes with a power output more than 35 kw or a power to weight ratio more than 0.2 kw kg.
- Motor tricycles with a power output more than 15 kw.
- You can also drive motorbikes in categories A1 and A2.

Light vehicles and quad bikes
Category B1
You can drive motor vehicles with 4 wheels up to 400 kg unladen or 550 kg if they're designed to carry goods

Cars

Category B if you passed your test before 1st January 1997

You're usually allowed to drive a vehicle and trailer combined up to 8,250 kg maximum authorised mass MAM.

View your driving licence information to check (www.gov.uk/view-driving-licence).

You are also allowed to drive a minibus with a trailer over 750 kg MAM.

Category B if you passed your test on or after 1st January 1997

You can drive vehicles up to 3500 kg MAM with up to 8 passenger seats with a trailer up to 750 kg.

You could also tow heavier trailers if the total MAM of the vehicle and the trailer isn't more than 3500 kg.

You can drive motor tricycles with a power output higher than 15 kw if you're over 21 years old

Physically disabled drivers with provisional Category B entitlement will also have provisional entitlement to ride Category A1 or a motor tricycles.

Able bodied drivers can no longer ride motor tricycles with a provisional Category B licence.

Category B Auto

You can drive a Category B vehicle but only an automatic one.

Category B E

You can drive a vehicle with a MAM of 3,500 kg with a trailer.

The size of the trailer depends on the BE 'valid from' date on your licence if the date is:

- Before 19th January 2013 you can do any size trailer.
- On or after 19th January 2013 you can tow a trailer with an MAM of up to 3500 kg.

Medium-sized vehicles

Category C1

You can drive vehicles between 3,500 and 7,500 kg MAM (with a trailer up to 750 kg).

Category C1E

You can drive C1 category vehicles with a trailer over 750 kg.

The combined MAM of both cannot exceed 12,000 kg.

Large vehicles
Category C
You can drive vehicles over 3500 kg with a trailer up to 750 kg MAM.

Category C E
You can drive Category C vehicles with a trailer over 750 kg.

Minibuses
Category D1
You can drive vehicles with:

- No more than 16 passenger seats.
- A maximum length of 8 metres.
- The trailer up to 750 kg.

Category D1E
You can drive D1 category vehicles with a trailer over 750 kg MAM.
The combined MAM of both cannot exceed 12,000 kg.

Buses
Category D
You can drive any bus with more than 8 passenger seats with a trailer up to 750 kg MAM.

Category DE
You can drive Category D vehicles with a trailer over 750 kg.

Other categories

- Category F – Agricultural tractor.
- Category G – Road roller.
- Category H – Tracked vehicles.
- Category K – Mowing machine or pedestrian controlled vehicle.
- Category L – Electrically propelled vehicles.
- Category M – Trolley vehicles.
- Category N – Exempt from Duty.

5. Driving licence codes

Code	Meaning
01	Eyesight correction (glasses or contact lenses)
02	Hearing/communication aid

10	Modified transmission
15	Modified clutch
20	Modified brake system
25	Modified accelerator system
30	Combined braking and accelerator systems (for licences issued before 8/11/16)
31	Pedal adaptations and pedal safeguards
32	Combined service brake and accelerator system
33	Combined service brake, accelerator and steering systems
35	Modified control layouts
40	Modified steering
42	Modified rear-view mirror(s)
43	Modified driving seat
44	Modifications to motorbikes
44(1)	Single operated brake
44(2)	Adapted front wheel brake
44(3)	Adapted rear wheel brake
44(4)	Adapted accelerator
44(5)	(adjusted) Manual transmission and manual clutch
44(6)	(adjusted) Rear-view mirror(s)
44(7)	(adjusted) Commands (direction indicators, braking lights etc.)
44(8)	Seat height allowing the driver, in sitting position, to have 2 feet on he surface at the same time and balance the motorcycle during stopping and standing
44(11)	Adapted foot rest
44(12)	Adapted hand grip
45	Motorbikes only with sidecar
46	Tricycles only (for licences issued)
70	Exchange of licence
71	Duplicate of licence
78	Restricted to vehicles with automatic transmission
79	Restricted to vehicles in conformity with specifications stated in brackets on your licence
79(2)	Restricted to Category AM vehicles of the 3 wheel or light quadricycle type
79(3)	Restricted to tricycles
96	Allowed to drive a vehicle and trailer where the trailer weighs at least 750 kg and the combined weight of the vehicle and trailer is between 3500 kg and 4250 kg
97	Not allowed to drive Category C1 vehicles which are required to have a tachograph fitted

101	Not for hire or reward (this is not to make a profit)
102	Drawbar trailers only
103	Subject to certificate of competence
105	Vehicle not more than 5.5 metres long
106	Restricted to vehicles with automatic transmission
107	Not more than 8,250 kg
108	Subject to minimum age requirements
110	Limited to transporting persons with restricted mobility
111	Limited to 16 passenger seats
113	Limited to 16 passenger seats except for automatics
114	With any special controls required for safe driving
115	Organ donor
118	Start date is for earliest entitlement
119	Weight limit for vehicle does not apply
121	Restricted to conditions specified in the Secretary of State's notice
122	Valid on successful completion: Basic Moped Training Course 125 tricycles only (for licences issued before 29/6/14)

6. Endorsements and penalty points

Each endorsement has a code and penalty points applicable to that code dependent upon the severity of the offence. Penalty points are scaled from 1–11. The more serious the offence, the higher the points value.

Offence codes and penalty points must stay on your driving record for between 4 and 11 years, dependent on the offence.

Accident offences

These stay on a driving record for 4 years.

Code	Offence	Penalty points
AC10	Failing to stop after an accident	5–10
AC20	Failure to give particulars or report an accident within 24 hrs	5–10
AC30	Undefined accident codes	4–9

Disqualified driver

Codes BA10 and BA30 stay on record for 4 years:

Code	Offence	Penalty points
BA10	Driving whilst disqualified	6
BA30	Attempting to drive whilst disqualified	6

Codes BA 40 and BA 60 must stay on a driving records for 4 years from conviction date:

Code	Offence	Penalty points
BA40	Causing death by driving whilst disqualified	3–11
BA60	Causing serious injury by driving whilst disqualified	3–11

Careless driving

Codes CD10 to CD30 must stay on a driving record for 4 years from the date of the offence:

Code	Offence	Penalty points
CD10	Driving without due care and attention	3–9
CD20	Driving without reasonable consideration for other road users	3–9
CD30	Driving without care and attention or without reasonable consideration for other road users	3–9

Codes CD40 to CD70 must stay on a driving record for 11 years from the date of conviction:

Code	Offence	Penalty points
CD40	Causing death through careless driving when unfit through drink	3–11
CD50	Causing death by careless driving when unfit through drugs	3–11
CD60	Causing death by careless driving with alcohol levels above the limit	3–11
CD70	Causing death by careless driving then failing to supply a specimen for analysis	3–11

Codes CD80 and CD90 must stay on a driving record for 4 years from the date of conviction:

Code	Offence	Penalty points
CD80	Causing death by careless or inconsiderate driving	3–11
CD90	Causing death by driving unlicenced, disqualified or uninsured	3–11

Construction and use offences

These codes must stay on a driving record for 4 years from the date of the offence:

Code	Offence	Penalty points
CU10	Using a vehicle with defective brakes	3
CU20	Causing or likely to cause danger by reason of use of unsuitable vehicle, or using a vehicle with parts or accessories (excluding brakes, steering or tyres) in a dangerous condition	3
CU30	Using a vehicle with defectives tyre(s)	3
CU40	Using a vehicle with defective steering	3
CU50	Causing or likely to cause danger by reason of load or passengers	3
CU80	Breach of requirements as to control of the vehicle, such as using a mobile phone	3–6

Reckless/dangerous driving

These codes must stay on a driving record for 4 years from the date of conviction:

Code	Offence	Penalty points
DD10	causing serious injury by dangerous driving	3–11
DD40	Dangerous driving	3–11
DD60	Manslaughter or culpable homicide whilst driving a vehicle	3–11
DD80	Causing death by dangerous driving	3–11
DD90	Furious driving	3–9

Drink

Codes DR10 to DR61 must stay on a driving record for 11 years from the date of conviction:

Code	Offence	Penalty points
DR10	Driving or attempting to drive with alcohol above the limit	3–11
DR20	Driving or attempting to drive while unfit through drink	3–11
DR30	Driving or attempting to drive then failing to supply a specimen for analysis	3–11
DR31	Driving or attempting to drive then refusing to give permission for analysis of blood a blood sample that was taken without consent due to incapacity	3–11

DR61   Refusing to give permission for analysis of a
        blood sample that was taken without
        consentdue to incapacity in circumstances
        other than driving or attempting to drive   10

Codes DR40 to DR70 must stay on a driving record for 4 years from
the date of the offence or 4 years from the date of conviction, where a
disqualification is imposed:

Code	Offence	Penalty points
DR40	In charge of a vehicle while alcohol level is above the limit	10
DR50	In charge of a vehicle while unfit through drink	10
DR60	Failure to provide a specimen for analysis in circumstances other than driving or attempting to drive	10
DR70	Failing to provide specimen for breath test	4

Drugs

These codes must stay on a driving record for 11 years from the date of
conviction:

Code	Offence	Penalty points
DG10	Driving or attempting to drive with drug levels above the specified limit	3–11
DG60	Causing death by careless driving with drug levels above the limit	3–11
DR80	Driving or attempting to drive when unfit through drugs	3–11

Codes DG40 and DR90 must stay on a driving record for 4 years
from the date of the offence of 4 years from date of conviction where a
disqualification is imposed:

Code	Offence	Penalty points
DG40	In charge of a vehicle while drug level is above specified limit	10
DR90	In charge of a vehicle when unfit through drugs	10

Insurance offences

Code IN10 must stay on a driving record for 4 years from the date of
the offence:

Code	Offence	Penalty points
IN10	Using a vehicle uninsured against third party risks	6–8

Licence offences

Code	Offence	Penalty points
LC20	Driving otherwise than in accordance with a licence	3–6
LC30	Driving after making a false declaration about fitness when applying for a licence	3–6
LC40	Driving a vehicle having failed to notify of a disability	3–6
LC50	Driving after a licence has been cancelled (revoked) or refused on medical grounds	3–6

Miscellaneous offences

These codes must stay on a driving record for 4 years from the date of the offence:

Code	Offence	Penalty points
MS10	Leaving a vehicle in a dangerous position	3
MS20	Unlawful pillion riding	3
MS30	Play street offence	2
MS50	Motor racing on a highway	3–11
MS60	Offences not covered by other codes (including offences relating to breach of requirements as to control of vehicle)	3
MS70	Driving with uncorrected defective eyesight	3
MS80	Refusing to submit to an eye test	3
MS90	Failure to give information as to the identity of a driver etc.	6

Motorway offences

Code MW10 must stay on a driving record for 4 years from the date of offence:

Code	Offence	Penalty points
MW10	Contravention of special road regulations (excluding speed limits)	3

Pedestrian crossings

These codes must stay on a driving record for 4 years from the date of the offence:

Code	Offence	Penalty points
PC10	Undefined contravention of pedestrian crossing regulations	3

PC20	Contravention of pedestrian crossing regulations with a moving vehicle	3
PC30	Contravention of pedestrian crossing regulations with a stationary vehicle	3

Speed limits

These codes must stay on a driving record for 4 years from the date of the offence:

Code	Offence	Penalty points
SP10	Exceeding goods vehicle speed limit	3–6
SP20	Exceeding speed limit for type of vehicle (excluding goods or passenger vehicles)	3–6
SP30	Exceeding statutory speed limit on a public road	3–6
SP40	Exceeding passenger vehicle speed limit	3–6
SP50	Exceeding speed limit on a motorway	3–6

Traffic directions and signs

These codes must stay on a driving record for 4 years from the date of the offence:

Code	Offence	Penalty points
TS10	Failing to comply with traffic light signals	3
TS20	Failing to comply with double white lines	3
TS30	Failing to comply with a 'stop' sign	3
TS40	Failing to comply with directions of a constable/warden	3
TS50	Failing to comply with traffic signs (excluding 'stop' signs, traffic lights or double white lines)	3
TS60	Failing to comply with a school crossing patrol sign	3
TS70	Undefined failure to comply with a direction sign	3

Special code

Code TT99 must stay on a driving record for 4 years from the date of conviction; it shows disqualification under 'totting-up' i.e. if the total of penalty points reaches 12 points or more within 3 years, the driver can be disqualified.

Theft or unauthorised taking
Code UT50 must stay on a driving record for 4 years from the date of the offence:

Code	Offence	Penalty points
UT50	Aggravated taking of a vehicle	3–11

Mutual recognition codes
An 'MR' code is allocated on a driving record if a driver is disqualified whilst driving in Northern Ireland or the Isle of Man. The disqualification period will be valid in GB and will stay on a driving record for 4 years from the date of conviction:

Code	Offence
MR09	Reckless or dangerous driving (whether or not resulting in death, injury or a serious risk)
MR19	Wilful failure to carry out the obligation placed on a driver after being in a road accident (hit and run)
MR29	Driving a vehicle whilst under the influence of alcohol or other substances affecting or diminishing the mental and physical abilities of the driver
MR39	Driving a vehicle faster than the permitted speed
MR49	Driving a vehicle while disqualified
MR59	Other conduct constituting an offence for which a driving qualification has been imposed by the State of Offence

Aiding, abetting, counselling or procuring offences
For these offences, the codes are similar, but with the 0 on the code changed to a 2, e.g. code LC20 (driving otherwise than in accordance with a licence) becomes LC22 on the driving record if the driver has helped someone to commit this offence.

Causing or permitting offences
For these offences the 0 on the code is changed to 4, e.g. LC20 would become LC24 where a driver has caused or permitted someone to commit this offence.

Inciting offences
For these offences the 0 on the code is changed to 6, e.g. DD40 (dangerous driving) would become DD46 where a driver has incited someone to commit this offence.

NORTHERN IRELAND

The process of becoming a driving instructor in Northern Ireland is very similar to the rest of Great Britain. However there are differences, and these will be covered in this chapter.

The governing body in Northern Ireland overseeing driving instructors is NIdirect government services and is run by the Driver and Vehicle Agency (DVA).

The basic layout of the qualifying process is the same as it is in Great Britain involving parts 1, 2 and 3. Part 1 is the theory test, part 2 is a test of practical driving ability and part 3 is a test of teaching ability.

When you first apply an enhanced security check will be carried out by Access NI (ANI). Once completed, DVA will send you your eligibility number which you will need to book a theory test.

Access NI criminal record checks for people living or working in Northern Ireland. An individual can apply online for a basic check. You need an NI Direct account to apply online a basic check application cost £26.

When you create your NI Direct account you receive a confirmation email immediately. Once you activate your account you can log-on and apply for a basic check. For this you need the following:

- Your home addresses for the last 5 years.
- Insurance number.
- Three different types of ID. One must be photographic.
- A valid debit or credit card.

You must send proof of identity to Access NI within 14 days.

You could apply for an Access NI check at the following website: www.nidirect.gov.uk

The process of becoming an ADI

You must pass all three tests within a 2 year period of passing your initial theory test. All three tests must be passed in order. If you fail any of the tests three times you must wait 2 years from the date you first sat your theory test before you can begin the process again.

As well as passing all three tests and having a satisfactory ANI check you must also:

- Currently hold a full Northern Ireland, UK, or EU car driving licence.
- Have held a licence or a foreign licence for a total of 4 years out of the past 6 years before the date of your application.
- Not have been disqualified from driving for any part of the 4 years before the date of your application.

You can apply for all three tests online at ni.gov.uk or you can also send a fee and an application form to the following address:

Business Support Unit
Driver and Vehicle Agency
Balmoral Road
Malone lower
Belfast
BT12 6QL

Telephone: 028 9054 7933

Tests and test fees

The part one test in Northern Ireland is carried out in a very similar way to how it's carried out in Great Britain with the important exception that you're only allowed three attempts at this test in Northern Ireland. In Great Britain you're allowed to take this test as many times as you wish in order to pass.

Therefore if you fail the third attempt in Northern Ireland, you'll have to wait 2 years from when you failed your first theory test before reapplying.

The following test fees apply in Northern Ireland:

- Part 1 written test: £64
- Part 2 test of driving ability: £130
- Part 3 test of instructional ability: £138
- trainee licence for you: £120
- registration and renewal: £240

Trainee licence
Use the above Business Support Unit address to apply for a trainee badge or alternatively, apply online.

You are allowed up to two trainee badges, each of which lasts for a period of six months. If required, the application for the second badge must be made before the first one expires. When on a trainee licence, 25% of your lessons as a PDI need to be supervised by your ADI trainer. There is no requirement for additional training.

Part 3 test
The Part 3 test is conducted the same as the rest of the UK, except the test result is posted out to candidates following the test. Should candidates wish for a debriefing session, then this should be booked with the examiner once the test result is received.

INDEX